LAND OF THE DACOTAHS

Awarded a University of Minnesota Fellowship in Regional Writing

LAND
OF THE
DACOTAHS

by **BRUCE NELSON**

UNIVERSITY OF MINNESOTA PRESS • MINNEAPOLIS
LONDON • GEOFFREY CUMBERLEGE • OXFORD UNIVERSITY PRESS

To

MAJOR QUINTUS NELSON, U.S.M.C.

KILLED IN ACTION, PALAU ISLANDS, APRIL 1945

TABLE OF CONTENTS

LIST OF ILLUSTRATIONS

〜〜〜〜〜〜〜〜〜〜〜〜〜〜〜〜〜〜〜〜〜〜〜〜〜〜

LIST OF ILLUSTRATIONS

LAND OF THE DACOTAHS

Chapter 1

THE BIG MUDDY

∿∿∿

The bones of Hernando de Soto had moldered for a hundred and thirty years in the Mississippi's bed when the first white men set eyes on the river called Missouri. Then it was that Marquette and Jolliet, stroking their birch canoes down the tranquil bosom of the Father of Waters, came suddenly upon the mouth of a mighty unknown river. Athwart their course swept a surging yellow torrent, bearing on its swollen crest the fearsome debris of three thousand miles of savage career—twisted snags, uprooted trees, careening logs. Their fragile canoes bucked in the tawny flood as the voyageurs paddled desperately to keep afloat. Father Marquette may well have crossed himself and invoked the saints, for he wrote later, "I never saw anything more frightful."

The priest's phrase was an apt one. They had come upon the Missouri in floodtime, where it hurls its brown weight into the Mississippi above St. Louis and transforms the peaceful Father of Waters into a raging, levee-smashing monster. For the first time in history men of an alien race looked on the turbid Missouri, the Smoky Water of the red man, longest and unruliest of all the streams that course the American continent.

The voyageurs escaped unhurt. Digging their paddles deep into the sinewy current of the swiftening Mississippi, they pressed southward on their illusive quest—a route to the Western Ocean.

IT WAS 1673 and the electric spirit of discovery was in the air. To the northern outposts of Montreal and Quebec the pathfinder Radisson had brought word of an unknown stream which the red men called *Misi Sipi*, Great River. From the Indians, too, the French traders had heard tales of the Shining Mountains which lay to the west, by a great salt sea that rose and fell. And among these adventurous Frenchmen was one who thought deeply. Was it not possible that this unknown river, *Misi Sipi*, emptied into the Western Ocean? It was La Salle, his imagination fired by the

3

thought of a route to fabled Cathay, who conceived the idea of seeking out and exploring the mysterious river of the West.

But a series of misfortunes postponed his quest, and it was Marquette and Jolliet who first led their followers westward to the banks of the Mississippi and launched their birch canoes into the unknown. Paddling southward down the lonely, forest-girt Mississippi, past the turbulent Missouri, past the mouth of the broad Ohio, they came at last to the Arkansas. Here the voyageurs decided to proceed no farther. Satisfied that the Mississippi emptied into the Gulf of Mexico instead of the Western Sea, they turned back toward Montreal with the news of their discovery.

For La Salle was reserved the honor of completing the work they had begun. It was 1681 before he was able to finish his preparations; then, choosing a shorter route than that of Marquette and Jolliet, he followed the Kankakee and Illinois rivers from the Great Lakes down to the Mississippi. Sweltering in tropic heat, tortured by clouds of voracious mosquitoes, facing death daily at the hands of hostile savages, La Salle and his little company of thirty followers pressed southward toward their goal.

Had Marquette and Jolliet guessed correctly? If so, their quest for a route to the Western Ocean was a tragic will-o'-the-wisp; if not, they were on the threshold of a discovery that had beguiled men since the days of Christopher Columbus—a gateway to the riches of the Indies.

Their question was not long unanswered. A few brief weeks after leaving the mouth of the Arkansas, the voyageurs saw before them, not the crashing breakers of the Western Ocean, but the blue, lapping wavelets of the Mexican Gulf.

La Salle, his bright dream shattered, little realized the immensity of the feat he achieved when he raised the flag of France over the Mississippi's mouth and took possession of the territory for his royal master: the most high, mighty, invincible, and victorious prince, Louis the Great, by the Grace of God, King of France and of Navarre, fourteenth of that name.

Says Francis Parkman: "On that day the realm of France received on parchment a stupendous accession. The fertile plains of Texas; the vast basin of the Mississippi, from its frozen northern springs to the sultry borders of the Gulf; from the woody ranges of the Alleghanies to the bare peaks of the Rocky Mountains—a region of savannas and forests, sun-cracked deserts and grassy prairies, watered by a thousand rivers, ranged by a thousand war-like tribes, passed beneath the scepter of the Sultan of Versailles; and all by virtue of a feeble human voice, inaudible at half a mile."

Included in this vast domain was the land of the great Sioux nation, the fierce Dacotahs, whose Seven Council Fires were to burn bright in American history in ensuing centuries, until the flame of their glory was quenched at last in the waters of the Little Big Horn.

When Longfellow sang of the "Land of the Dacotahs," the Sioux had already pressed westward onto the rolling plains of the Upper Missouri Valley, which they were to dominate for a hundred years. Before that, they had lived in the forests of Minnesota and Wisconsin. Before that, they had come out of the south from the Lower Mississippi and the valley of the broad Ohio.

And before that . . .

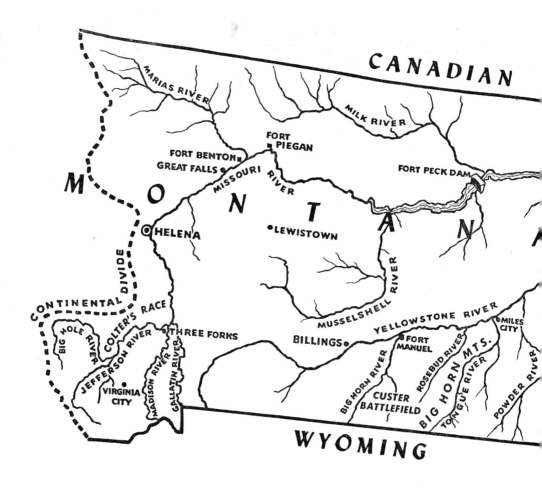

LAND OF THE DACOTAHS

Chapter 2

THE SEVEN COUNCIL FIRES

vvvvvvvvvvvvvvvvvvvvvvvvvvvvvvvvvvvvvvvvvvvvvvvvvvvvvvvvvvvvvvv

Away beyond the dawn of history, in the morning of mankind, the First American came out of the west across the strait that was to be known as Bering, looked upon the land, and saw that it was good.

That was perhaps twenty-five thousand years ago. The hairy mammoth, the giant bison, and the huge ground sloth that grew tall as an elephant still were roaming the American plains. Fossil remains of those ancient beasts, mingled with artifacts of Stone Age hunters, have been found in scattered portions of the United States.

Gradually, probably in small successive waves, the first Americans crossed from the Asian mainland and spread south and east until both southern and northern portions of the continent were occupied by a thinly spread population. A new land, rich in game and temperate of climate compared to the icy wastes of Siberia, it must have seemed a veritable paradise to these Stone Age discoverers, who scientists believe were the founders of the numerous Algonquian race, which still peoples eastern America and scattered portions of the West.

Then, when the Algonquians had made their way over the great empty land, a second Asian influx poured across Bering Strait and grappled with the first discoverers. This second wave, made up of the people we know today as Eskimos, fought long and bloody wars with the Algonquians over the whole length and breadth of Canada, yet in the end were only partially successful in driving the Algonquians before them.

And in the time of Jesus of Nazareth came the third and most savage thrust of all. From the slopes of the Himalayas across the narrow straits swept the Athapascans, fierce, warlike, intractable. They attacked Algonquians and Eskimos alike for hundreds of years, exterminating or intermarrying with lesser tribes until they had become the most widely scattered stock in America. The savage Navahos and Apaches were of this race, whose depredations ceased only when they had at last been absorbed by the peoples they had conquered.

From these three greatest of the Asian invasions, then, and from countless lesser ones, have come the hundreds of American Indian tribes, with the sixty linguistic stocks and hundreds of dialectic variations which we know today.

THERE have been men in the valley of the Upper Missouri for centuries. How long, it is impossible to determine, for there has been little archeological research performed in the northern plains. Nearby Minnesota has yielded a skeleton that may be as much as ten thousand years old, but of the Upper Missouri Valley we know only that more than a thousand years ago the Flint Men were scooping out their pits in quest of the flaky stone that tipped their spears and arrows. Of their mode of life we know nothing; it may or may not have been these early men who built the mounds that are of enormous antiquity. It may be, but again we do not know, that they were the forebears of the great Siouan stock which even today embraces most of the Indian tribes found in the entire Missouri Valley.

Ethnologists are able to place the Missouri Valley tribes in their proper relationship by determining that they belong, for the most part, to a common linguistic stock. Yet their relationship is so lost in the mist of time that such related Siouan peoples as the Crows, the Mandans, and the Hidatsas—groups which had split from the parent stem—fought long and bitterly with their brothers. To the ethnologist these are Siouan peoples, but to history, and perhaps to themselves, only those of the Dacotah nation are known as Sioux. They had no knowledge that they were fighting men of their own race when they attacked the Mandans or drove the Crows westward from the Big Horn country.

They were a valiant race, these Sioux of the Dacotah family, of the Seven Council Fires: the Mdewakantons, the Sacred Water People; the Sissetons, the Marsh-Dwellers; the Wahpekutes, Shooters Among the Leaves; the Yanktons, the End-Village Folk; the Wahpetons, Dwellers Among the Leaves; the Yanktonais, the

LAND OF THE DACOTAHS

Little End-Village People; and the roving Tetons, Dwellers on the Prairie.

It was the Chippewas of the Wisconsin forests who named the Sioux. *Nadowe-is-iw,* they called them, meaning serpents or enemies. Jean Nicolet, one of the first French explorers to visit the Chippewas' country, brought back word of their fierce neighbors, and in Paul Le Jeune's *Relation* of 1640 the first written mention of the Dacotahs appears in the corrupted French form of *Nadowessioux,* which was later shortened to Sioux.

Their own name for themselves meant something quite different. *Dacotah* means friends or allies—a name which the Chippewas, who suffered greatly at their hands, quite naturally found inappropriate. When the Chippewas, who lived to the east of the Sioux, first met white men and acquired guns, they turned upon their ancient foes and drove them westward through Wisconsin and Minnesota out onto the rolling grasslands of the Upper Missouri Valley.

Siouan hunting parties, striking westward before the Chippewas in search of new lands, came upon the earth lodges of the Arikaras along the Missouri River and discovered the horses which were to lend them wings and give them domination of the northern plains.

That was in the middle of the eighteenth century. In 1804, fifty years later, Lewis and Clark found them already ranging west of the Missouri, superbly mounted, the newborn scourge of the prairies, their name feared by all the tribes of the upper river valley.

Their war and hunting parties penetrated the Black Hills country and the plains of northern Dakota; in Montana they ranged over the valleys of the Powder, the Tongue, the Big Horn, and the Yellowstone; in Wyoming they wandered as far south as the north fork of the Platte. Not the forests of Minnesota, of which Longfellow sang, but the valley of the Upper Missouri was the real land of the Dacotahs. The sister states of North and South Dakota take their names from the ancient name of the Sioux; and it was in Montana, in 1876, that the last battle of the Sioux Nation finally broke the Dacotahs' power on the banks of the Greasy Grass—which white men call the Little Big Horn.

10

"A MAN who bestrides a horse," wrote Washington Irving, "must be essentially different from the man who cowers in a canoe." And this was true of the Sioux. The canoemen who had come out of the dark northern forests onto the rolling sea of the northern grasslands were transformed in a few short decades into a virile, proud, and warlike race that bore little resemblance to the people who had fled, fearful and hunted, before the Chippewas.

But it was not only the new-found sense of power that comes to men who bestride horses which altered them. It was the land itself.

One who has not himself seen the northern plains can have no accurate conception of their nature. They have been called a desert; yet, while there are patches of arid land here and there, there are millions of acres of grassy prairies, innumerable creeks and rivers, and heavy growths of timber. They have been called a flat and monotonous prairie, but there are badlands of tortured and twisted beauty, buttes and bluffs and hills and valleys, and gently rolling plains that rise and fall like ocean swells as far as the eye can reach. And in the Black Hills this "flat" land possesses the highest elevation between the Rockies and the Atlantic seaboard: Harney Peak.

The plains have been called treeless, but there are great forests, and all the creek and river valleys are lined with lofty cottonwoods and thick with low-hanging willows. They have been called cold, yet the thermometer sometimes rises in midsummer to 120 degrees; and they have been called hot, although winter temperatures occasionally drop to 40 degrees below zero or lower. They have been called barren, these plains that once supported such a wealth of wild game and profusion of natural vegetation; and this, too, is partly true, for in the 1930's the prairies lay parched and lifeless, but in the 1940's they produced such a wealth of grain and livestock that their wheat crops alone were measured in the hundreds of millions of bushels and lay spoiling on the ground for lack of storage and transportation facilities.

It is a land of savage extremes, this land of the Dacotahs, of bitter cold and intense heat. Yet in spring there are balmy air and soft winds and the revivifying green of prairie grass and flowers, and in fall, when summer's heat has dwindled, the flaming

11

gold and scarlet of wooded hill slopes. But in winter, when the whistling winds knife southward from Saskatchewan and Manitoba, the air is filled with stinging pellets and the blanketed earth lies cold and rigid as iron. The clear bright days of summer turn suddenly black with the purple menacing clouds of the prairie hailstorm, and hot summer nights erupt into flashing thunderstorms of incredible awesomeness and beauty: every lowering cloud hurls its lances of flame earthward and the thunderous artillery of the skies is continuous and deafening. There are times of drought and protracted heat, when the land lies prostrate and gasping, the prairie roses droop and die, and the very native grasses wither; and there are times of fearful flood and disaster, when the glutted rivers spread destruction over the level bottomlands.

It is a land of superb sunsets and magnificent distances, of limitless arch of sky. On its eastern border the broad yellow curve of the Missouri sweeps sharply southward toward the sea; to the west the jagged peaks of the Rockies thrust themselves up boldly, like a great sinew in the shoulder of a sprawling continent. And between river and mountain range is the vast running sweep of the plains country: prairie and hill and lake and forested valley.

And always there is the wind . . .

WHEN the Sioux first came into the land that was later to be known as the Dust Bowl, no settler's plow had sunk its blade into the earth's natural cover. Thirty millions of buffalo fed on the prairie grasses that stretched away in the sunlight to the far horizons; innumerable bands of antelope, elk, and deer bounded over the plains; wild fowl and game existed in such numbers as to seem incredible today, were it not that their plentitude is established by written records of the first explorers.

Alexander Henry reported that he once rode for an entire day in a vain effort to find the outer edge of a vast herd of buffalo in northern Dakota. On another occasion, after one of the roaring prairie fires had devastated a great tract of country, he wrote pityingly of the "incredible number" of dead, dying, blind, lame, and singed and roasted buffalo. Colonel Dodge has related how he stood on Pawnee Rock and looked out for ten miles in every direction upon a herd of the great, shaggy wild oxen that covered the prairie like a black blanket.

It was Pte, the buffalo, who provided the Sioux of the northern plains with all the necessaries of existence. Flesh for immediate cooking, dried meat and fat for pemmican and other foods were only the obvious uses to which the bison was put. Heavy robes, made from the buffalo's thick hide, were the Indian's winter covering and his bed; in summer, the hides, tanned and with the hair removed, served him as a sheet or light blanket and made leggings, hunting shirts, moccasins, and women's apparel. His tipis were made of dressed cowhide; light, airy, warm, and comfortable, they were perhaps the most efficient movable houses ever invented. The hide of a tough old bull, stretched over a light frame of green willows, made the famous bullboat with which the Indian transported his family, goods, and gear across the rivers; while the thick hide that guarded Pte's neck was shrunken into a circular shield that could turn the sharpest lance or arrow.

Trunks and boxes to contain the Indians' smaller possessions were made from the raw hide of the buffalo, with the hair shaved off; sledge runners for their dog-drawn sleds were made from the rib bones; hoes and axes were made from the shoulder blades; tools for dressing hides came from the ribs and cannon bones. The hoofs of the bison, boiled, made a glue for feathering their arrows and cementing their arrowheads; the hair of the animal furnished them with soft cushions and padding for their saddles; Pte's long black beard served as an ornament for their clothing, shields, or quivers. Bone for needles and sinew for thread and bowstrings also came from the buffalo's bulky body, while the long horns, peeled and polished, made ornaments, spoons, and ladles. The green hide of the animal was sometimes used as a receptacle in which to boil meat, and the lining of the paunch served as an efficient water bucket. The skin of the buffalo's hind leg, cut off between the hock and the pastern, made a tough boot or moccasin; long brushes to keep off flies and other troublesome insects were made from the tail; and saddlecloths, knife sheaths, quivers, bow cases, gun covers, and scores of other miscellaneous articles,

13

all indispensable to the prairie red man, came from the bison's massive framework.

Small wonder that Pte was honored above all other animals by the Sioux, for he bore in his huge body virtually everything necessary to the Indians' peripatetic existence. With the mysterious affinity which they felt with all animals, they might call the eagle Brother; but for Pte alone was reserved the title of Uncle—a word of respect roughly comparable in English to Father, for Grandfather is the Great Mystery Himself! Small wonder that the nomads of the plains made Pte a part of their religious life, holding buffalo dances in his honor—a plea which Pte never failed to answer by appearing before his nephews, for they danced until the buffalo came.

Along the timbered river bottoms where there were wood, water, and shelter, or perhaps out on the open prairie in summer, the tipi villages of the Sioux began to cover the plains country, once they had acquired the horse and begun to follow the migrations of the buffalo herds which formed their main subsistence. The breeding season of the bison was in summer, from June until early September, and as spring came each year to the prairies the males and females—separated during the winter months—mingled in vast seething herds for the mating season.

The roaring and bellowing of the bulls, the clicking and battering of horns and skulls and forefeet as they battled with each other in the fury of rut time, made the prairies echo with a noise as of thunder. Their savage stampings and the wild, rank ox-reek of their shaggy bodies made their presence known tens of miles away, where Siouan buffalo hunters saddled and bridled in haste to slay the meat supply that would sustain them through the long winter months when the bison had drifted southward and the land lay blanketed in snow. For with the coming of September, in The-Time-When-the-Wild-Plums-Ripen, the buffalo ceased their bellowings of lust and their gargantuan couplings, the herds separated once again into groups of males and females, and a few weeks later began their long annual migration southward, to be seen no more in large numbers on the northern plains until the following spring.

Stupid, slow, and clumsy as were these great beasts, it was nevertheless no simple feat to bring one to earth from the back of a racing pony by means of a hurled lance or a hastily aimed flint-tipped hunting arrow. Nothing could stand before the terrible stampede of a buffalo herd: a driving, compact mass of horned might that crushed everything in its path. The individual bull stood five to six feet high at the hump of his shoulders and measured ten to twelve feet from nose to tail tip: two thousand pounds of ill-tempered, shaggy-coated, dim-sighted fury that might turn in an instant and disembowel horse and rider with a single lunge and toss of his foot-long horns.

Even the Siouan hunters, cunningest of the buffalo-hunting peoples, preferred to employ strategem where possible in pitting their strength against Pte, the bison. There were Indian bowmen who could drive a hunting arrow clear through the bulky body of a buffalo bull, but the more common and more effective methods were to drive the animals over a steep precipice where hundreds of them would be killed or disabled, and to construct huge pens into which they might be driven and dispatched at leisure.

In late fall, when the summer's hunting and foraging were ended and the horse-drawn travois had been laden with great bags and blocks of pemmican and other foodstuffs, the village sought some timbered river bend for a winter camp.

It was a colorful pageant: pack horses, heaped high with camp duffel; old men, women, and children, some mounted, others afoot; mounted warriors with gay-pennoned lances and marching police to keep order along the moving column; great herds of horses strung out for miles along the procession, with the shrill barks of hundreds of yapping curs adding to the din and confusion. All moved slowly across the rolling plain toward the spot selected for winter quarters. At night, in the pitched camps, there was visiting and dancing and jollity and wooing; the blue, bitter smoke of campfires and the savory smell of buffalo meat rose from the cooking pots; and they were merry at the end of the march, for it was a good life.

As the dark of evening deepened, some famed teller of tales or elderly tribal sage would gather the young people of the village about him and instruct them in the ancient ways of their people or in the Siouan legends that had been handed down from generation to generation. With the wonderful memory of the unlettered, these tribal storytellers were able to pass on legends whose form and content remained virtually unchanged as they passed from the lips of father to son and from son to grandson through the years. Geography, history, domestic science, natural history, manual arts, civil government, and the arts of warfare and the chase were ably taught among the Siouan peoples. Not by the rote of the classroom, it is true, but by the force of living speech and practical example.

And there was always a tale of the olden time to climax the evening's instruction. Perhaps it was a story of the Iktomi, the tiny spider-men, whose tapping hammers can be heard on still nights from the distant hilltops, where they are busily shaping flint arrowheads and heaping them in piles for their friends the Indians to find. Or it might be a tale of Wasiya, the Giant of the North, whose icy breath brings winter to the plains; or of the mysterious monster that lives beneath the waters of the Missouri and breaks up the ice with fearful crashing and booming sounds in the spring.

And there was the famed tale of the Thunderbirds, who lived in the hollows of the sky between heaven and earth, and the flashing of whose fierce yellow eyes made the lightnings. The beating of their great wings in the sky brought rain, and thunder came from the sound of their eggs as they hatched.

In the long ago the Thunderbirds tired of living in the sky and begged of the Great Mystery that they might go down and live among men upon the earth. The Great Mystery gave them their wish, saying that they should become like unto no men who had ever before been seen upon the earth. It befell as the Great Mystery had promised: they became giants such as the world had never known, men who could step from the Missouri River to the Atlantic Ocean in a single stride. Where they scooped up handfuls of earth in sport, the Great Lakes were formed, and the earth they cast aside made mountains. One of them dug a ditch from

16

the Minnesota forests to the Gulf of Mexico and so created the Father of Waters.

But at last the Thunderbird-Men grew old and died and went back to their places in the gulfs between the stars, where they still live. And on stormy nights you can see the lightnings that flash from their eyes and hear the muffled beating of their mighty wings.

"THERE are many humorous things in the world," wrote Mark Twain, "among them the white man's notion that he is less savage than the other savages." The great historian Francis Parkman did not agree with him. Parkman, who visited the prairie Sioux in their wild and untamed state, was a frank admirer of their courage, honor, independence, courtesy, integrity, and generally superior qualities. But he could not bring himself to admit them to the select society of Back Bay, for their manners were not those of Boston Brahmins. They spoke of legs instead of limbs, and they ate without forks; hence they were manifestly savages and patently inferior to the rum-running, blackbirding New Englanders of Parkman's Boston.

It is true that in certain respects the Sioux were quite as savage as their white contemporaries. Their sexual lives were as free and uncomplicated as those of the courtiers and courtesans of their fellow Frenchman, Louis XIV. They did not bathe any more frequently than did the Pilgrim Fathers, and like Mary, Queen of Scots, they blew their noses with their fingers.

But in other civilized refinements they were far behind the white man. They had not progressed far enough up the cultural scale, for example, to have learned to beat their children. Instead of absolute rulers who imposed upon them the advanced doctrine of the divine right of kings, they had democratic parliaments where women voted on all important questions on an equal footing with men.

They had no tiny upper class, lapped in luxury, while the mass of the nation starved; land and food were shared communally, and the theory of ownership in fee simple was unknown to their simple minds. They had a government of law, sternly enforced,

17

instead of the European fashion of kingly whim or caprice; for they lived a life of nomadism, "that most deep and biting social discipline," as Lawrence of Arabia has aptly termed it.

An Indian with a public-be-damned attitude who engaged in the "free enterprise" of attacking a herd of buffalo alone in the hope of glutting his personal larder, would have been tried and promptly executed. Under the stringent laws of the hunt, the chase was made communally and the kill divided equally among all the people of the tribe. They had a system of inheritance taxation which was considerably more effective than any yet devised by their white successors: the dead man's property was divided among the whole tribe, his own family and children faring no better than the rest.

The red men were nevertheless far from perfect. They behaved, in fact, remarkably like human beings. Some were as stupid as George III, some as greedy and syphilitic as Louis XIV, some as evil and lecherous as Pope Alexander VI, some as lazy as George Washington, some as great and gifted as Pericles or Marcus Aurelius, and some as cruel and perverted as the Marquis de Sade. In short, save for their superior social and economic institutions, they were discouragingly like white men. Today, now that those institutions have been destroyed, you can scarcely tell the difference.

Except for their names. Howard Fast, in his memorable novel *The Last Frontier*, has suggested that of all names, Indian names are the silliest. A skeptic might suggest that an Indian named Slow is not much sillier than a white man named Fast; that Rain-in-the-Face is not necessarily a more mirth-provoking title than Praise God Barebones; that Corn Stalk, Red Top, and Strike-the-Ree are not per se more humorous than Roosevelt (Rose Field), Schwartzkopf (Black Head), and Eisenhower (Iron-Striker); and that Shake Tomahawk is no more ridiculous than that mighty name which has come ringing down the English centuries—the magic name of Shake Spear.

No, Mr. Fast's argument is not well founded. Time and custom have dulled our ears to our own ridiculous names, while they have not had the same effect upon the unfamiliar names of the red man—some of which, to our English-trained ears, are truly startling. H. L. Mencken has reported an Indian chieftain with the astounding name of Unable-to-Fornicate. Fingernails-Off, Callous-Leg, Stretches-Himself, and Rattling-Tail are names not uncommonly found on modern reservations. And among the Miniconjou Sioux of the last century there survived a warrior with the picturesque and restless name of Pacing-Hermaphrodite.

The Indian was not orthodox—and God knows he was not modest—in the naming of his children. But his system of nomenclature was both simple and practical. The famous Chief Gall, for example, was so named because his mother one day found him nibbling at the gall (Siouan: *pizi*) of a dead animal. Had it been the entrails of the same animal—a not unlikely occurrence, for they were considered a delicacy—she would have called him simply Guts, and no Indian would have thought twice about it. The great warrior Crazy Horse received his name when a wild pony dashed through the village at the time of his birth.

Ignorant or illiterate translators have contributed greatly to the ambiguity and crudity of most Indian names. The famous warrior Afraid-of-Soldier is a conspicuous example. Their-Soldiers-Fear-Him is what his name means literally, but this excellent fighting man has gone down in history under the ignominious name the translator attached to him.

Where it was once the custom to exaggerate the beauty and poetry of Indian names, it has now become fashionable to deny that such beauty and poetry ever existed—an error of no lesser proportions than the original conception. The homely name of Big Road might be offered as an example of the ugliness of Indian names, but the translator is again at fault; the name would be more accurately rendered as Broad Trail, a not ungraceful combination.

Virtually all the well-known Indian names were translated originally by semiliterate frontiersmen who understood the Indian tongues imperfectly and their own but little better. Minnewaukan, Sacred Water, the white men called Devils Lake, which is scarcely an improvement on the literal meaning. But there are names of remarkable beauty or picturesqueness which survive despite the translators and debunkers: Flying Cloud, Red Bird, Black Moon, Crow King, Red Cloud, and White Fawn.

The white man, unfortunately, has not been able to learn that Indian and white names do not blend well. Since the advent of the missionary with his Bible and the representative of business with his mail-order catalogue, the romance has all gone out of Indian nomenclature. Such biblical-Siouan characters as Levi Stretches-Himself, Joseph Comes-Flying, and Mary Takes-a-Wrinkle now adorn the reservations. And in Montana there is a brave who, combining the ancient traditions of his people with the modern credo of service, bears the proud name of Montgomery Ward Two Bellies.

THE historian is enthralled, at first, to learn that the Sioux possessed an annual historical record known as the Winter Count, the work of a tribal artist in which the outstanding event of the year was recorded in pictographs. The Winter Count, extending back more than two centuries, might have proved an invaluable record had the aborigines possessed any sense of historical values as we know them. But their sense of history was trivial, to say the least, and it is all too seldom that an event of more than passing interest emerges from the faded colors painted on the ancient buffalo hides.

In the year 1796, for example, so the crude pictures tell us, a game of hoop-and-sticks was in progress among a number of young men of the Miniconjou Sioux. Penis, a young brave of evil temper, attacked two of his fellow players with his stick, and when the scuffle was over, Penis lay dead on the ground. The surviving young men, who were apparently of a practical turn, decided to make use of his corpse, and since the game of hoop-and-sticks requires a log for a backstop against which to roll the hoop, they dragged the dead body into place and proceeded with their game.

The elders of the tribe, meeting that winter in solemn council to select the year's outstanding event for recording by the tribal artist, voted that this scarcely world-shaking occurrence deserved to be recorded for posterity, and named Penis their Man of the Year. And so it is that the year 1796, in the annals of the Miniconjou Sioux, is known with classic simplicity as The-Year-When-the-Hoop-Rolled-against-Penis.

CONTRARY to the Fenimore Cooper conception that Indians were stoics and grimly humorless, they possessed a highly developed sense of the ludicrous. They were indefatigable gossips and veritable Babbitts when it came to joining the innumerable societies, both secret and otherwise, which made up the fabric of Indian social life. The notion of the Silent Red Man perhaps had its inception in the fact that they were both shy and dignified in the presence of whites; the notion that they were humorless perhaps grew out of the fact that they did their laughing at the white man in private.

When they forgot themselves, however, they could whoop with laughter after the manner of children. An early steamboat captain has described the antics of a group of Indians he watched as they tried to climb a stairway for the first time in their lives. To us whose feet are staircase-trained from infancy this may not seem a difficult task, but these mature warriors, splendid athletes and trained to feats of arms from childhood, became tangled up in their own feet and came tumbling down headlong when they tried to imitate the white men who ran up and down the steep steps. The steamboat captain who witnessed the scene wrote that it went on for a considerable time, to the accompaniment of whoops of laughter, as one after another of them came bouncing downstairs moccasins over scalp-lock. In their absorption they had completely forgotten that they had an audience, and their vaunted stoicism and dignity vanished in an instant.

Their wit was by no means crude. Of the white man's inexplicable ways they said, with a chuckle, "The white man looks at his watch to see if it's time to be hungry." One ancient chieftain of the Sioux who was invited to Washington as a guest of the government in the middle of the last century, was taken to New York, where he made a speech in his own tongue from the platform of historic Cooper Union. It was perhaps as well that only the interpreter understood him at the time, for he began his address with these words: "My brothers, before the white man came to my country I was thin and scrawny. Today I am fat and bloated as you see me. That is because I have been stuffed so full of lies. . . ."

The Indian was no stoic in his social relationships, either. Suicide was not uncommon among them, in cases where they were disappointed in love. And the family was a far closer knit unit among the Sioux than among their white brothers. All the early missionaries commented on the strong bonds of affection between parents and children—a thing these good men were inclined to deplore, for it made it difficult to take the children away and place them in mission schools where they might learn the white man's teachings.

The ancient religion of the Sioux has completely disappeared today. In his native state, however, it is probable that his faith was a more or less utilitarian one which he did not allow to interfere too greatly with his personal desires—much as the white man keeps his religion for use on Sundays and conveniently forgets about it the rest of the time. To his many spirits, good and evil, the Indian gave anthropomorphic existence. The good were respected, the evil propitiated. An Indian who, as he believed, was merely being practical in making an offering to an evil spirit which was frustrating him, was quite naturally branded as an idolater by the early missionaries.

The fault lay in the point of view of the missionary, rather than in the heart of the Indian; for these symbolic gestures were a part of his physical religion alone and had nothing whatever to do with his higher conception of an all-powerful supernatural force which pervaded all nature and all living things and shaped the destinies of mankind.

THE law of property among the Indians, founded as it was on a communal basis, with no provision for the private ownership of land, was one of the many causes of the frequent clashes between white man and red. No man or family could own land outright; it was allocated or appropriated according to the needs of each— and held only so long as good use was made of it. Thus the land belonged to no man or tribe to sell or give away, and the mis-

Rain-in-the-Face. He fought against Custer on the Greasy Grass.

Red Tomahawk. He fired the bullet that killed Sitting Bull.

The sun dance of the Sioux

A sod shanty, often the early settler's first home in the grasslands

Army scouts examining the body of a scalped plainsman

A typical homesteader's cabin, inside and out, during a
later wave of settlement, 1907

In the days of the diggings. Four gold-seekers in the Black Hills in 1875, and "Last Chance Gulch," Helena, Montana, in the 1870's.

Vigilante justice. Hangman's Tree, Helena, Montana, 1870.

The Marquis de Mores,
Badlands emperor

Theodore Roosevelt, the four-
eyed dude from New York

Pte the buffalo. The last of thirty millions.

One of the deepest gashes on the continent. A twist in the canyon of the Big Horn River in Montana.

The romance of the red man still lingers

Modern Sioux at Standing Rock

understandings that arose from the two opposing views of property often brought warfare in their wake.

The fault lay principally with some of the early white settlers who sought to foster the idea of chiefs or kings after the European fashion. This made possible the acquisition of the Indians' lands by a means which would later appear valid in a white man's court; the signature of the chief, or king, would be sufficient. Indian chiefs, in reality, possessed no power save that which they might exert through the force of their own characters and wisdom. They were elected, usually, for their wise heads, but their followers were not bound to abide by their sage counsel.

White men, knowing this fact well, were nevertheless quite willing to bribe minor chieftains to cede lands which they did not own, merely for the sake of having a document that would appear to be a proper transfer. Once the transfer was made, the military stood ready to enforce it, and the Indian had no recourse save to fight. And in war he was fully as honorable a foe as his white brother.

Much absurd fiction has been written of the red man's savage customs and barbarous tortures. The customs of scalping and torturing prisoners appear to have existed among the Iroquois of eastern America before the coming of the whites, but it was the white man who spread them far and wide. English and French offered bounties to the Indians for each other's scalps. Among the tribes of the Upper Missouri prisoners were seldom tortured, although the dead bodies of fallen enemies were usually scalped or, in certain tribes, slit from hip to knee with a hunting knife that they might be disgraced in the Land of the Ghosts.

Crime of any sort was rare among the Sioux. Murder for gain was virtually unknown among them. The pangs of hunger drove none of them to theft, for the door of every lodge was open to whoever would enter, and any person could help himself to food from the great kettles which stood always full and bubbling. But there were few who had need to practice this method of securing food, for the only personal property recognized by the Sioux—and all they needed for successful living—could be had by the meanest man: a horse, a weapon, and a lodge. And the horse, which was most important, could always be acquired by stealth from some enemy pasture.

Horse-stealing was considered eminently respectable by all the plains tribes; hence *stealing* is scarcely the proper word. The position of an Indian who was able to steal horses from an enemy was precisely that of a present-day businessman who is adept at stealing customers from a rival firm: he would be honored and promoted. But white men, applying their own standards of moral conduct to the Indian, called him a thief when he stole their horses.

Had the Indian understood that the white man considered him a thief, he would have been quick to resent the slur, for thieves were given short shrift among his people, and he would not for a moment have considered stealing from a member of his own tribe or nation. As is always the case with separate cultures, red man and white looked at each other across vast gulfs of mutual miscomprehension.

THE variety and abundance of the Indians' harvest, it may be conjectured, made certain that the women would not lack homework, but the popular belief that they were abused drudges, suffering lives of slavery and maltreatment under their lazy and improvident husbands, is far from a true one. The manufacture of household implements, as well as the strenuous duties of the chase and protection of the tribe from attack, fell to the men. Tribal taboos against men's performing women's work were strong, just as they are today among white persons, and the province of the Indian woman was the home and garden.

The belief that Indian men were lazy is largely an outgrowth of the fact that few white men—literate ones at any rate—saw the Indian in his native state, before his way of life had vanished and his ancient occupations disappeared. With the destruction of the buffalo, the fencing in of the lands, and the reduction of the Indians to reservation status, they found themselves suddenly bereft of the work they had done since time immemorial.

While the women's work—the home and garden—remained, the men loafed about with little or nothing to do, for they were unable to adapt themselves quickly to the white man's ways. But it was not always so; they had dignity and pride of achievement once, and so did their womankind.

The Indian husband had little authority over the person of his wife; she could leave him at will if he mistreated her. Their marriages were much the same as are found in modern society. Tribal councils, in which the women participated, were held to determine all important courses of action; in other words, Indian women had the vote at least two centuries before their white sisters.

So THE great Sioux Nation, numbering more than fifty thousand people, lived in harmonious concord with nature and their wild environment all along the rich valley of the Upper Missouri. For three quarters of a century after they had become subjects of Louis XIV they made their slow way westward from the Minnesota forests into a land where no white man had ever set foot. They hunted the buffalo, prayed to their tribal gods, and danced their tribal dances as they had done for generations, paying little heed to the fact that they had legally become Frenchmen.

But trouble was brewing for them in the east. In Quebec and Montreal men still dreamed of a route to the wealth of the Orient. And in 1731, at about the time when the Sioux were trading with the Arikaras for their first horses, another Frenchman, Pierre Gaultier de Varennes, Sieur de la Vérendrye, set out from Montreal in search of the Western Ocean. His route lay to the west, toward the Shining Mountains that rose by a great salt sea.

Chapter 3

THE SHINING MOUNTAINS

∿∿

Pierre Gaultier de Varennes, Sieur de la Vérendrye, was no ordinary adventurer. Bold, resourceful, a man of action, he had, too, the far look of the dreamer. Born near Three Rivers, Quebec, in 1685, he became a cadet in the French army at the age of twelve. A soldier of France at fourteen, he served in the campaigns of New England and Newfoundland and later in Europe, where, at the battle of Malplaquet, he was left on the field for dead with nine wounds in his body. He was but twenty-seven when he returned to Canada, eager to begin a career of discovery. The Indians' tales of the Western Sea that lay beyond the Shining Mountains caught at his imagination. They spoke, too, of a westward-flowing river which emptied into that sea; and La Vérendrye came at last to a decision: He would seek out those mountains whose peaks were eternally sheathed in shining snow and search for the westward-flowing river. Perhaps where La Salle had failed, he would succeed.

But La Vérendrye was a poor man and the canny French merchants at Montreal were hesitant to advance money to such a visionary. They were interested in profits, not in the illusive dreams of a young adventurer, and La Vérendrye was approaching middle age before he was able to persuade the Montreal fur traders to back him in his quest.

Their reasons were good, if selfish. Russia was moving in the Pacific and so were the Spaniards in the South and West; if France was to keep her Western empire she must act. Fearful of losing their trade to foreign rivals, the merchants grudgingly consented, and La Vérendrye began preparing his expedition.

It was on the afternoon of June 8, 1731, when the explorer and his fifty followers marched out of the frontier stockade where the great Canadian city of Montreal now stands. La Vérendrye's three eldest sons, Jean, Pierre, and François, accompanied the expedition as his lieutenants; Sieur de la Jemeraye, a young nephew of the explorer's, was second in command. A fourth son, Louis, was to join the party later. The rest of the company was a colorful aggregation of soldiers, voyageurs, woodsmen, and Indian guides and interpreters. Of their quest they knew only that it lay toward the setting sun.

Launching their canoes at St. Anne's, the voyageurs paddled westward toward the Great Lakes, the chansons of the boatmen pealing out strangely in the virgin wilderness, as they stroked the heavy thirty-foot canoes against the Ottawa's swift current or bore them on husky shoulders over short portages.

It was as well, perhaps, that they were unaware what lay before them. For seven long years La Vérendrye and his little party drove their slow way westward along the border waters between Canada and the present United States. The men were often mutinous, irked to the edge of endurance by the hardships and delays of the journey. The tight-fisted Montreal backers again and again refused to forward the necessary supplies until their investments had been balanced by profits in furs. Rations ran short and the expedition suffered through the bitter northern winters on a diet of boiled roots and strips of leather cut from their moccasins. More than once exploration was halted, while some of the party returned to Montreal to beg for the supplies they needed; twice La Vérendrye himself had to make the long journey eastward to plead his case with the grudging merchants.

Then tragedy struck. La Jemeraye fell ill and died during the winter of 1734, and a few months later, as La Vérendrye waited in the terrible isolation of his wilderness fort for the supplies he had sent his son Jean to bring back, a wandering band of friendly Indians brought him the news of Jean's death. On a tiny island in Lake of the Woods the Indians had found Jean and his nineteen followers dead and mutilated. Not a man had escaped. The Frenchmen's heads had been piled in a heap on the ground and the naked bodies bore the gruesome marks of a Sioux war party's vengeance.

But La Vérendrye's vision was undimmed. It drew him onward, ever westward, and a string of wilderness forts sprang up to mark the party's slow progress toward the Shining Mountains: Fort

LAND OF THE DACOTAHS

Pierre on Rainy Lake, near the present site of International Falls, Minnesota; Fort St. Charles on Lake of the Woods, near the present Warroad; Fort Maurepas on Lake Winnipeg. Each of these was in turn a new base of operations, where they stored their supplies and cached the furs they gathered.

THE winter of 1737–38 was a profitable one, and when the ice broke in the spring La Vérendrye was able to take back fourteen canoeloads of valuable furs to Montreal. His backers were appeased, and the expedition was saved for the time being. September 1738 saw La Vérendrye once more at Fort Maurepas. Again he set his face westward.

Launching their canoes on the bosom of the Red River of the North, La Vérendrye and his men set out for the forks of the Assiniboine. Ever west and southward the voyageurs stroked their craft, past the site of the present city of Winnipeg and onward through lush, rolling grasslands that swept in undulating infinity toward the horizon.

Of the Shining Mountains the explorers could discern no sign; nor of the Western Ocean that, so their Indian guides told them, lay somewhere beyond the vast expanse of virgin prairie. For the first time in history white men looked on the illimitable reaches of the Canadian Northwest, but their sensations were of disappointment, rather than the elation of discoverers. La Vérendrye established Fort Rouge where Winnipeg stands today, then turned again toward the southwest.

His Assiniboin guides had told him of a tribe called the Mandans who knew the whereabouts of the Western Ocean. Wearily La Vérendrye began building another fort on the Assiniboine River as a base of supplies for his next attempt to reach the Western Sea. When the new fort, called La Reine, was completed it was already late summer, but La Vérendrye, perhaps sensing the culmination of his search, set out immediately in quest of the Mandans.

His route followed the Souris River country through the fringe of the Siouan land, but with more than six hundred friendly Assiniboins accompanying the party he had little fear of attack. In the chilly month of November the adventurers became the first white men to set foot in what is now the state of North Dakota. Laden with gear and camp duffel, the big party moved slowly through a rolling prairie country dotted with herds of antelope and shaggy buffalo. For four weeks they made their way southward, and the bitter cold of December was upon them when they came at last to one of the stockaded villages of the Mandans.

The grave chieftains of the tribe, bearing the pipe of peace, came forward to greet the first white men to enter their domain. La Vérendrye unfurled the flag of France while his followers fired a commemorative volley, and the party entered the village in ceremonial fashion. The explorer looked about him in surprise. Here was no encampment of skin or bark tipis inhabited by nomadic hunting peoples. Instead, hundreds of acres of tilled fields stretched away across the level bottom lands in every direction. The village, numbering several hundred inhabitants, was a heavily palisaded fort, surrounded by a moat after the European medieval fashion.

Scanning their fortifications with the practiced eye of the professional soldier, La Vérendrye noted in his journal that their defenses were virtually impregnable and denoted a high degree of ingenuity.

"M. de Lammarque and I took a walk to examine the extent of their fortifications," he wrote. "I gave orders to count the cabins and we found that there were about one hundred and thirty. All the streets, squares, and cabins are uniform in appearance. Often our Frenchmen would lose their way in going about. . . . The ramparts are smooth and wide; the palisade is supported on cross-pieces mortised into posts fifteen feet apart with a lining. . . . As to the bastions, there are four of them at each curtain well flanked. The fort is built on an elevation in mid-prairie with a ditch over fifteen feet deep and from fifteen to eighteen feet wide. . . . If all their forts are similar you may say they are impregnable to savages. Their fortification, indeed, has nothing savage about it."

Then, taking note of an enigma which was to puzzle later explorers and present-day historians, he added: "This tribe is of mixed blood, white and black. The women are rather handsome, particularly the light-colored ones; they have an abundance of fair hair." This fact could scarcely have been due to any admixture of white blood, for La Vérendrye's party were the first white persons the Mandans had ever seen. That it was a fact, however, is attested by later explorers—Lewis and Clark, Catlin, Maximilian—who remarked on the same phenomenon.

While the elder explorer rested with his friendly hosts, his son led a small party to another nearby Mandan village. A day's journey brought them to the banks of a frozen yellow river that coursed out of the west and bent southward. To their already long list of exploratory honors the Vérendrye family now added that of discoverers of the Upper Missouri.

LA VÉRENDRYE's journal said little about the unusual Mandans and their way of life, except to describe their fortifications and note, with surprise, that they served him more than twenty dishes of corn, squashes, beans, pumpkins, and other produce of their fields. From later explorers, however, we have information in abundance concerning the remarkable tribe, and it is not difficult to visualize the scene that must have met the Frenchmen's eyes when they entered the Mandan villages.

The lodges which La Vérendrye inaccurately called "cabins" were actually constructed of earth and were shaped precisely like the snow igloos of the Eskimos. But there the similarity ends, for the lodges of the Mandans were huge structures measuring from forty to ninety feet in diameter at the base and supported from the inside by heavy pillars of cottonwood. Warm in winter and cool in summer, they were admirably adapted to the climate of the northern plains. The houses were arranged in orderly fashion facing the center of the village, where stood a large barrel-like structure symbolizing the Big Canoe of the First Man.

The story of the flood, which is found not only in Christian mythology but among races all over the earth, was a part of the Mandans' religious belief. It was the First Man who, when the waters rose and covered the earth, built a great canoe, or ark, and crowded his people into it. Even as Noah's floating menagerie came to rest on distant Ararat, so did the First Man's storm-tossed canoe, filled to the gunwales with drenched Mandans, find haven at last on a lofty hill near the Cannonball River in North Dakota. This hill, like Noah's, still exists to confound skeptics.

The Mandans were not a numerous people and consequently did not range far in search of game for fear of the Sioux. Since their principal subsistence came from agriculture they preferred to remain close to their stockaded towns. Perhaps because they engaged less in warfare than most plains tribes, they were markedly more friendly to strangers, particularly so toward the whites.

They were a dignified and courageous race, too, as befits the first people to be created in the world. For so they believed themselves to be. The Great Mystery made Mandans before he made any other people, and in the days when the world was young they lived inside the earth's surface, where they existed by raising vines, among other things. One auspicious day a particularly tough vine forced its way through the earth's crust and several of the tribe climbed the vine and came out into the sunlight upon a land that was rich and smiling. Others followed. But at last an extremely fat woman, in attempting to ascend, broke the vine, and the rest of the Mandans live beneath the earth's surface to this day.

There is grim irony in this simple tale, at that. In the years that followed, the white man came with his diseases and his whiskey, and it is doubtful that there is a single pure Mandan alive today. Once more they are all underground.

With this amiable and interesting people La Vérendrye and his party spent several days attempting to obtain the information he sought, but the Mandans could tell him little of the Western Sea. Other tribes to the west had told them of the Shining Mountains and of a white-skinned people who dressed in metal and lived by a great salt sea. But they were not a roving people and knew nothing of these things for themselves.

His hopes dashed again, La Vérendrye left two men behind to learn the Mandan language and began the long journey back to Fort La Reine. Raging blizzards lashed the shivering band of explorers as they fought their way northward. La Vérendrye himself was stricken with a serious illness, but by the middle of February they had sighted the walls of Fort La Reine. The explorer noted in his journal: "I have never been so wretched from illness and fatigue in all my life as on this journey." At the fort he was notified that his creditors had seized all his properties and goods to liquidate his indebtedness. Leaving his sons to carry on the work to which he had given a decade of his life, the weary, ill old soldier returned to face his creditors in Montreal. He never returned to the Northwest.

For two more years of heartbreaking search his sons ranged south and westward from their tiny wilderness forts, seeking to learn the whereabouts of the Western Sea or the Shining Mountains. They found and explored another unknown river, the Saskatchewan; then once more they turned southward toward the stockaded villages of the friendly Mandans.

Following the route they had taken two years before, François and Louis arrived without incident at the Mandan lodges, but they found little encouragement. The Sioux were too dangerous. None of the Mandans wished to attempt to guide them in the long and hazardous journey from the Missouri to the Western Sea. They would, however, guide them to another tribe to the west which might escort them farther.

This time the brothers traveled southwestward, making their way along the Little Missouri Valley toward the Black Hills. Below the Yellowstone River their guides led them through portions of what are now the states of Wyoming and Montana; and at the end of five weeks of grueling travel they had seen no sign of human life. A few more days passed swiftly by and the Mandan guides recognized smoke signals on the distant horizon. It was a party of Crow Indians, who welcomed the two young Frenchmen and their followers and furnished them with guides to continue the journey westward. From tribe to tribe, ever westward, the brothers were passed along until, on the first day of the New Year, 1743, they stood in the shadow of the Rockies. Before them rose the jagged outline of the Big Horns, the Shining Mountains!

The brothers, the fulfillment of their dream at last in sight, urged their guides to conduct them over the mountains to the shores of the Western Sea, but the Indians refused. It was perhaps as well, for the Vérendryes had no conception of the vast distance that still separated them from the Western Ocean.

The icy grip of winter was upon them. The brothers, forced to turn back, accompanied the returning braves eastward to the banks of the Missouri in what is now the state of South Dakota; and on March 30, 1743, they buried on a bluff above the frozen river a lead plaque inscribed with their names, the date, and the arms and inscription of the King of France, covering the spot with a protective pyramid of stones. Wrote young La Vérendrye in his journal: "I told the Indians, who had no knowledge of the plaque I had placed in the ground, that I was setting up these stones in memory of our coming to the country."

Back at Fort La Reine bad news awaited them from Montreal. Their thirteen-year quest had come to an end with its final objective almost within grasp. The elder La Vérendrye's enemies, jealous of his success in the fur trade, had now effectively conspired to keep him and his sons out of the Northwest. The old explorer was replaced by another commander—who in his inexperience ruined the carefully built fur trade, antagonized the Indians, and destroyed the work of a decade and a half of patient toil. Within a few months half the far-flung outposts were abandoned and France had thrown away an empire.

In 1749 Pierre Gaultier de Varennes, Sieur de la Vérendrye, died in Montreal, an embittered and broken old man.

Together with his sons and his nephew, he had opened the Canadian Northwest, discovered the Saskatchewan, Assiniboine, Red, and Upper Missouri rivers, been responsible for the discovery of the Rocky Mountains and the present area of North and South Dakota, Wyoming, and Montana, and given to France the beginnings of a fur trade that might later have enabled her successfully to keep her hold on Canada. In return, he had not even the thanks of an ungrateful government.

In 1913 a group of school children playing on the bluffs above the Missouri near Fort Pierre, South Dakota, unearthed a heavy, earth-encrusted object. It was the lead plaque of the Vérendryes, buried a hundred and seventy years earlier in the earth of the valley they had been the first to explore.

Chapter 4

HALF HORSE AND HALF ALLIGATOR

In the half century that followed the explorations of the Véren-dryes, the valley of the Upper Missouri saw few white men. From St. Louis in the south a thin trickle of hardy French trappers began to penetrate the river upstream toward the Mandan villages, while to the north English traders followed slowly in the path of the Vérendrye party.

In 1775 a Frenchman named Pierre Dorion came into what is now the state of South Dakota and married a woman of the Yankton Sioux. He was the first white settler of the upper river valley. Dorion was followed in the 90's by Jean Baptiste Trudeau, who constructed the first building on the Upper Missouri—a trading post which was to become the famed Pawnee House. Others followed quickly in Trudeau's footsteps and the fur trade of the American Northwest was born—a trade that was to grow to tremendous proportions, flourish for a few brief decades, and then vanish as swiftly as it had come.

Canoes, bateaux, keelboats, and pirogues, manned by as lusty a set of scoundrels as ever swindled a savage anywhere, made their floundering way upstream to unlock the wealth of a continent. In a rollicking passage that might have come from the pen of Rabelais himself, Mark Twain has given us a memorable glimpse of these early river titans:

"In time this commerce increased until it gave employment to hordes of rough and hardy men; rude, uneducated, brave, suffering terrific hardships with sailor-like stoicism; heavy drinkers, coarse frolickers in moral sties like the Natchez-under-the-Hill of that day, heavy fighters, reckless fellows, every one, elephantinely jolly, foul-witted, profane, prodigal of their money, bankrupt at the end of every trip, fond of barbaric finery, prodigious braggarts; yet, in the main, honest, trustworthy, faithful to promises and duty, and often picturesquely magnanimous."

Such a one was Mike Fink. To separate fact from legend in the life of this most famous of the keelboatmen is no simple task. Countless river tales have grown up around his name until his stature in American folklore more nearly approaches that of Paul Bunyan than of an actual living man. Yet, out of the mass of intermingled truth and fancy, there emerges now and then an authentic glimpse which indicates that his fame is not entirely without foundation in fact.

Mike was no low-browed and brutish gorilla of a man. A description of him in the *Western Monthly* states that "his weight was about 180 pounds; height about five feet, nine inches; broad, round of face, pleasant features, brown skin, tanned by sun and rain; blue, but very expressive eyes, inclined to gray; broad, white teeth, and square, brawny form, well proportioned; and every muscle of his arms, thighs and legs was fully developed, indicating the greatest strength and activity. His person, taken altogether was a model for a Hercules, except as to size."

Mike's pleasant appearance and apparent good nature, however, were belied by his activities when in liquor—which was a good share of the time. When two or more of these rugged keelboat crews met ashore at some trading post like the Pawnee House, the consumption of alcoholic spirits and the resultant carnage were appalling. Whether or not they drank the liquor which was customarily purveyed to the Indians in exchange for furs is a debatable question. If they did, their antics are perhaps explicable on that ground. Here is the recipe:

> 1 quart of alcohol
> 1 pound of rank, black chewing tobacco
> 1 handful red peppers
> 1 bottle Jamaica Ginger
> 1 quart black molasses
> Water from the Missouri River *ad libitum*

Mix well until all the strength is drawn from the tobacco and peppers.

And serve with a shovel, probably. At any rate, after a few tin cups full of this or some similarly lethal concoction, Mike was ready for action. Mounting the nearest stump—or table, or bar, or whatever was convenient—he would roar out his challenge to all comers.

43

"Whoo-oop! I'm half horse and half alligator—a mite touched with snapping turtle. I'm a wild Missouri roarer and I'm chock full of fight! I can jump higher, hit harder, spit farther, move sideways quicker and drink more tanglefoot whiskey than any son-of-a-bitch on the Missouri River! Whoo-oop! Any gentleman here like to try me out?"

Generally the offer was taken up before the speaker had time to finish it, and, as the awe-stricken Indians who witnessed these battles later attested, "It was as the coming together of two buffalo bulls in summer!" Kneeing, nose-biting, and eye-gouging were the gentler aspects of these gargantuan brawls. Often, too, merely for sport, they engaged in head-butting contests that left the vanquished human billy goat stretched unconscious on the ground with a broken neck.

There are countless tales of Fink's somewhat distorted sense of humor; in *Flint's Western Review* appeared a story which is not only in keeping with Mike's known character, but is authenticated by records of the actual court proceedings which followed the incident. Mike noticed one day, in St. Louis, a Negro lad along the wharves who had an oddly shaped foot with a heel that protruded far out behind his ankle. "This unshapely form offended Mike's artistic eye and outraged his sense of symmetry. He determined to correct it. Lifting his rifle at thirty paces he actually shot the heel away, inflicting an ugly wound. The boy dropped to the ground, screaming 'murder!' Mike was indicted in the circuit court of the county, tried and found guilty. His plea in justification of the offense was that he wanted to fix the boy's foot so that he could wear a genteel boot."

It was a year after this incident that Mike set out with Ashley and Henry's expedition to the Upper Missouri. With him were his two boon companions, Carpenter and Talbot, the former a hawk-eyed marksman almost equal to Fink. Together they had originated a pastime with which they entertained their fellows at odd moments: the shooting of tin cups of whiskey off each other's heads at the lethal distance of seventy paces.

At the mouth of the Yellowstone a portion of the expedition constructed a fort, while others of the party scattered throughout the country to begin hunting and trapping operations. As usual, Carpenter, Fink, and Talbot were companions; they spent the winter trapping along the Musselshell River among a village of friendly Indians. And here it was that the stanch friends fell out.

Like most of the trappers and boatmen of the day, they considered it a winter ill-spent without the company of an Indian girl as a temporary wife or companion, and Carpenter and Fink came to blows over the ownership of a pretty half-breed maiden of the tribe. In the person of his friend Carpenter, Mike met his fellow in ferocity and brawn at last; when the battle ended, Mike lay battered into unconsciousness. Carpenter, by right of conquest, took the girl for his wife, and Mike, once he regained his senses, surlily acquiesced. But beneath his mask of feigned friendship he awaited an opportunity for revenge.

It came in the spring, when the three trappers returned to the post at the mouth of the Yellowstone. Fink, after another quarrel with Carpenter, agreed to let bygones be bygones, and suggested that as a sign of their comradeship they should once more "shoot the cup." Carpenter was loath to agree, but at the urging of friends finally accepted Mike's proposal.

"Let's sky a copper," said Mike, "to see who gets first shot."

A coin was accordingly flipped into the air and the right to fire first fell to Mike. Carpenter at once resigned himself to death. He gave his rifle, bullet pouch, powder horn, belt, pistol, and accumulated wages to his friend Talbot. Though the other spectators tried to assure him of Mike's friendly intentions, Carpenter remained unconvinced. But rather than repudiate his word, he filled the whiskey cup, set it on his head, and waited while Mike stepped off the customary seventy paces.

Mike dawdled over loading his rifle and "picking his flint." Several times he lifted the weapon to take aim, then slowly lowered it again.

"Hold your noodle steady, Carpenter," he said with a grin. "Don't spill the whiskey; I'll want some soon."

Then Mike raised the gun and shot Carpenter squarely in the center of the forehead. As Carpenter slumped to the ground, Fink calmly lowered his weapon and carefully blew the smoke out of the barrel. Then, eying the dead body of his best friend, he spoke words that were phrased for history.

"Why, Carpenter," said Mike, in tones of shocked and hurt surprise; "why, Carpenter, you've spilled the whiskey!"

Carpenter's angry comrades surrounded Mike, demanding an explanation. "It was all a mistake," protested Mike. "I took as fine a bead on the black spot on the cup as I ever took at a squirrel's eye. How did it happen?"

Fink's pretense of innocence fooled nobody, of course, but it was a lawless land and there was not a man in the company who cared to accuse Mike eye to eye and charge that he had done the deed purposely. It was accordingly described by all concerned as an "accident."

But little Talbot, to whom Carpenter had bequeathed all his possessions, awaited the time when he could avenge his friend's murder. Mike, Talbot thought, was sooner or later bound to boast of his exploit. Talbot was right. A few months later, during a drunken brawl, Mike bragged of the deed, and little Talbot shot him through the heart with the pistol Carpenter had bequeathed to him.

As Mike had escaped the law, so now did Talbot, for it was felt that his act was only tardy justice. But he was not to survive long. A few months afterward he was drowned while attempting to cross the Teton River—last of the most famous triumvirate in the history of Missouri keelboating.

THE lives of Mike Fink and his fellows were not all murder and drinking bouts and amorous dalliance with complaisant Indian maids. They had work to do, such work as few men have been called upon to do before or since, and the story of their prodigious labors is a fascinating chapter in the history of the Upper Missouri.

Early traffic on the river was in canoes hewn out roughly from entire cottonwood trees; in pirogues, which were merely two canoes fastened together with a board flooring between; and in mackinaw boats, huge craft of fifteen tons' burden and as much as fifty feet in length. Flat-bottomed and unwieldy, the mackinaw boats were used only on downriver trips and then broken up and sold for lumber at the end of the voyage.

The keelboats, though, were the most useful as well as the most picturesque of the early river craft. For a period of more than thirty years they and their villainous crews carried on virtually the entire upper river traffic; then, with the coming of the steamboat, they passed forever from the stage of history. But even in that brief span of a single generation they left an imperishable imprint upon the life and literature of the West.

The keelboat itself was an ingenious craft, constructed, as its name implies, with a keel extending its entire length. It drew two and a half feet of water or less. A hold of three or four feet in depth and a beam of fifteen to eighteen feet were the usual dimensions. It was often as much as seventy feet long, a sturdy and well-made craft that cost two thousand to three thousand dollars. But it was constructed solely for utilitarian purposes and was far from graceful or beautiful. A huge cargo box took up the entire length and breadth of the vessel, save for a dozen feet at either end and a narrow, cleated catwalk along each side.

It was along these two cleated walks that the crews of the keelboats toiled back and forth when other means of propulsion failed and they were forced to resort to poling. Known as the *passe avant*, the walk provided room for eight or ten voyageurs furnished with long sturdy ash poles on either side of the vessel. The poles, made with a round ball at one end which fitted into the shoulder of the voyageur, were operated in unison under the direction of the *patron*, or commander, of the boat. At the *patron's* cry of "Lower the poles," the twenty-odd voyageurs simultaneously thrust their poles into the river bottom, leaned heavily on the balls which nestled against the hollows of their shoulders, and pushing in unison, forced the vessel upstream as they made their way aft along the *passe avant*. When the foremost man had reached the stern of the boat, the *patron* gave the order "Raise the poles," the men dashed back with all possible speed to the bow of the craft, and the process was repeated.

It was man-killing labor, grueling toil of the most painful kind. The men, leaning into their poles and forcing themselves forward by the cleated foothold, were often almost horizontal with the deck and used their free hands to clutch at the cleats ahead of them. Captain Joseph La Barge, an early keelboatman and later a famous steamboat skipper, declared in his old age that men could not then be persuaded to undergo such hardships as he and his fellows had suffered in their youth. The terrible diet of lyed corn and salt pork for day after monotonous day was only a minor hardship; the men were driven fifteen, sixteen, or as many hours a day as they could stand; clouds of mosquitoes stung their faces until their eyes were swollen shut; and the *patron* stood ready with his club to encourage any who mutinied or faltered. For deserters the penalty was often death. If they were caught, that is, before the Sioux found them.

The poling method of propulsion was used only as a last resort and the keelboat was a vessel of infinite resource. The usual means of locomotion was the cordelle, a line a thousand feet in length which was attached to the top of the boat's mast and manned by thirty or forty voyageurs ashore who dragged the vessel upstream by main strength. Another method was to make the line fast to a tree or other anchor, while the men stayed aboard and warped the boat up to the place of anchorage, after which the line was again carried forward, made fast, and the warping process repeated.

Cordelling was strenuous and dangerous work too. The men were in constant danger from caving banks; rattlesnakes and wild beasts lurked in the tangle along the stream's bank; often they were knee-deep in water and muck and soaked to the skin from dawn till dusk as a result of frequent slips and falls in the treacherous footing.

But when the wind stood fair the keelboat hoisted her sail on the thirty-foot mast that rose from the center of the deck and the voyageurs relaxed aboard, amusing themselves with their own peculiar forms of entertainment. As much as seventy-five miles a day were made under sail by early river keelboats driven before the lash of the whistling winds that whip the Missouri Valley. These strange, boxlike craft, carrying a hundred square feet of canvas in the midst of a howling wilderness, must indeed have been awesome sights to the wild beasts and only slightly less wild human beings of the plains.

In that wonderful chapter which Mark Twain wrote for *Huckleberry Finn* (but which never appeared therein), Huck has given us a delightful glimpse of the boatmen at play:

"There was thirteen men there—they was the watch on deck of course. And a mighty rough-looking lot, too. They had a jug, and tin cups, and they kept the jug moving. One man was singing —roaring, you may say; and it wasn't a nice song—for a parlor, anyway. He roared through his nose, and strung out the last word of every line very long. When he was done they all fetched a kind of Injun war-whoop, and then another was sung. . . . It was kind of poor, and when he was going to start on the next verse one of them said it was the tune the old cow died on; and another one said: 'Oh, give us a rest!' And another one told him to take a walk. They made fun of him till he got mad and jumped up and began to cuss the crowd, and said he could lam any thief in the lot.

"They was all about to make a break for him, but the biggest man there jumped up and says:

"'Set whar you are, gentlemen. Leave him to me; he's my meat.'

"Then he jumped up in the air three times, and cracked his heels together every time. He flung off a buckskin coat that was all hung with fringes, and says, 'You lay thar tell the chawin'-up's done;' and flung down his hat, which was all over ribbons, and says, 'You lay thar tell his sufferin's is over.'

"Then he jumped up in the air and cracked his heels together again, and shouted out:

"'Whoo-oop! I'm the old original iron-jawed, brass-mounted, copper-bellied corpse-maker from the wilds of Arkansaw! Look at me! . . . I take nineteen alligators and a bar'l of whiskey for breakfast when I'm in robust health, and a bushel of rattlesnakes and a dead body when I'm ailing. . . . Whoo-oop! Stand back and give me room according to my strength! Blood's my natural drink and the wails of the dying is music to my ear! Cast your eye on me, gentlemen! and lay low and hold your breath, for I'm 'bout to turn myself loose!'

49

". . . When he got through, he jumped up and cracked his heels together three times, and let off a roaring 'Whoo-oop! I'm the bloodiest son of a wildcat that lives!'

"Then the man that had started the row tilted his old slouch hat down over his right eye; then he bent stooping forward, with his back sagged and his south end sticking out far, and his fists a-shoving out and drawing in in front of him, and so went round in a little circle about three times, swelling himself up and breathing hard. Then he straightened, and jumped up and cracked his heels together three times before he lit again (that made them cheer), and he began to shout like this:

"'Whoo-oop! bow your neck and spread, for the kingdom of sorrow's a-coming! Hold me down to the earth, for I feel my powers a-working! Whoo-oop! I'm a child of sin, *don't* let me get a start! Smoked glass here, for all! Don't attempt to look at me with the naked eye, gentlemen! . . . I'm the man with a petrified heart and biler-iron bowels! . . . Whoo-oop! bow your neck and spread, for the Pet Child of Calamity's a-coming!'

". . . Both of them was edging away in different directions, growling and shaking their heads and going on about what they was going to do; but a little black-whiskered chap skips up and says:

"'Come back here, you couple of chicken-livered cowards, and I'll thrash the two of ye!'

"And he done it, too. He snatched them, he jerked them this way and that, he booted them around, he knocked them sprawling faster than they could get up. Why, it warn't two minutes till they begged like dogs—and how the other lot did yell and laugh and clap their hands all the way through, and shout, 'Sail in, Corpse-Maker!' 'Hi! at him again, Child of Calamity!' 'Bully for you, Little Davy!' . . . Little Davy made them own up that they was sneaks and cowards and not fit to eat with a dog or drink with a nigger; then Bob and the Child shook hands with each other, very solemn, and said they had always respected each other and was willing to let bygones be bygones.

". . . They stumped back and had a drink around and went to talking and singing again . . . They sung 'Jolly, Jolly Raftsman's

50

the Life for Me,' with a rousing chorus, and then they got talking about the differences betwixt hogs, and the different kinds of habits; and next about women and their different ways; and next about the best way to put out houses that was afire; and next about what ought to be done with the Injuns; and next about what a king had to do, and how much he got; and next about how to make cats fight; and next about what to do when a man has fits; and next about the differences betwixt clear-water rivers and muddy-water ones. . . .

"The Child of Calamity said . . . there was nutritiousness in the mud, and a man that drunk Mississippi water could grow corn in his stomach if he wanted to. He says:

"'You look at the graveyards; that tells the tale. Trees won't grow worth shucks in a Cincinnati graveyard, but in a Sent Louis graveyard they grow upward of eight hundred foot high. It's all on account of the water the people drunk before they laid up. A Cincinnati corpse don't richen a soil any.'

"Then they talked about how to keep tobacco from getting mouldy, and from that they went into ghosts. . . ."

COLORFUL though the boatmen were, it was only when on the lower rivers that they could engage in such horseplay. On the Upper Missouri there was sterner work and the ever-present danger of hostile Sioux or Blackfeet. No account of the early keelboatmen and hunters—they were often both in one—would be complete without the story of the indestructible Hugh Glass and his epic journey across two hundred miles of savage wilderness after being maimed by a grizzly bear.

Glass was a Pennsylvanian by birth. It is not known when he began his fabulous career as a keelboatman and hunter, but it must have been well before 1800, for he was already an old man when he encountered the grizzly in the early 1820's. He had been wounded in a fight with Arikara Indians only a few months before, but when Major Henry announced that he needed men for an overland expedition into the Upper Missouri Valley, Hugh Glass was one of the first to volunteer.

Despite his years, he was acting as a scout ahead of the main body of the expedition when, according to the *Missouri Intelligencer* of June 18, 1825, "he suddenly came upon a grizzly bear that had lain down in the sand. Before he could set his triggers, or even turn to fly, the bear seized him by the throat and lifted him off the ground. Then flinging him down, the ferocious animal tore off a mouthful of his flesh and gave it to her cubs. Glass now endeavored to escape, but the bear, followed by her cubs, pounced upon him again. She seized him by the shoulder and inflicted dangerous wounds on his hands and arms."

Glass's companion had by now been able to get in a shot at the creature and managed to distract her attention from the fallen hunter by attacking her cubs. When the rest of the expedition arrived on the scene the bear was dead, and Hugh Glass appeared to be in little better case. His body was horribly torn and mangled. One leg was utterly useless. He was unable to stand and, though only semiconscious, was suffering unspeakable agony. There was, of course, no medical aid available, and the old hunter was too badly wounded to be moved. His companions believed it to be only a matter of time until he succumbed to his dreadful injuries.

Major Henry was faced with an unpleasant decision. He dared not halt the entire party in the midst of hostile Indian country to await Glass's death; yet he would not leave the wounded man alone. A reward of eighty dollars offered by Henry brought forward two volunteers who agreed to stay with the dying man and see that his body was properly interred. So certain were they that it was only a matter of a few hours that they spent some time preparing a grave nearby and then sat down to await the end.

But tough old Hugh Glass seemed to have no notion of dying. He lay unconscious for five days, while the two watchmen grew more and more panicky over the prospect of being found by the Indians. At last the faithless pair, certain that Glass was doomed anyway—and justifying their shameful deed on the grounds that the old man had no right to take such an unconscionable time dying—took his rifle and other gear and set out after the main party. Major Henry thought nothing further of the matter when the men reported to him that Glass was dead and buried. They exhibited his rifle and other possessions as evidence of their story, and the old hunter was quickly forgotten.

But far back along the trail Hugh Glass had awakened to consciousness and the realization of his comrades' perfidy. Alone, robbed of his rifle and other possessions, the gallant old fighter set out to cover the terrible two hundred miles to Fort Kiowa, his failing strength buoyed up by a flood of revengeful thoughts. He could not walk. He had tasted no food for five days and he was pitifully weak from loss of blood. Somehow he crept to a nearby stream, quenched his burning thirst, and, on hands and knees, dragging his maimed leg behind him, began The Crawl.

Roots and berries were his only food the first day. Prairie cactus ripped and pierced his naked hands and unprotected knees. The sun was like a flaming torch overhead, and when nightfall came he had covered a scant few hundred yards. But luck was with him. By an almost unbelievable stroke of fortune he came upon the partly eaten carcass of a buffalo that had been left by wolves. He lay here gorging himself on buffalo flesh while strength flowed slowly back into his wasted body. How long he lay he did not remember, but he woke and ate and slept and ate again; and when he was stronger he tore strips of flesh from the animal and carried them with him on the next stages of his journey.

He made better progress for a day or two, but his buffalo meat was soon gone. He had begun to weaken again when fortune smiled on him a second time; he came upon an Indian village site, where he found a sick dog that had been abandoned by its master. Now ensued a macabre and monstrous duel; the starving dog-beast on the one side and the wild-eyed, starving man-beast on the other. Man's cunning triumphed; Hugh, feigning death, was able to entice the creature close to him and slay it, and again he feasted and carried meat with him on the next lap of his terrible odyssey.

As the days lengthened into weeks, his maimed leg began to mend. A convenient tree near a small stream gave the creeping man an idea; a day later he was hobbling upright with the aid of a rude crutch fashioned from a branch. And at last, risen from the dead as truly as any man ever rose, Hugh Glass came to Fort Kiowa.

He did not stop long. Burning with a desire for revenge upon his faithless comrades, he set out upriver with an expedition headed for the Yellowstone. A war party of Arikaras attacked the group and killed every man of the expedition with the exception of Glass, who happened to be hunting some distance away at the time of the attack. He was saved from the pursuing Arikaras—for his crippled condition would not have allowed him to escape—by a party of friendly Mandans, who escorted him to Tilton's Fort. He did not tarry here either. Alone, and still unrecovered from his wounds, he set out overland for Major Henry's post at the mouth of the Big Horn River—a solitary journey of thirty-eight days through hostile Indian country.

At Henry's post he learned that his journey had been in vain; the faithless two were far downriver at Fort Atkinson. With four companions Glass again took up the trail of the traitors. Making their way to the headwaters of the Platte, the five launched out onto the stream in a bullboat bound for the Missouri and Fort Atkinson.

Again a roving Arikara war party fell on the white men, and for a second time Hugh Glass was the sole survivor of an ambush! Unarmed, and so unable to help his companions, he lay hidden in a heap of rocks while the Indians hunted down and killed his comrades within sight and sound of his precarious hiding place. But the old man was undaunted.

"Although I had lost my rifle and all my plunder," he said later, "I felt quite rich when I found my knife and steel in my shot pouch. These little fixens make a man feel right peart when he is three or four hundred miles away from anybody or anywhere —all alone among the painters and the wild varmints."

Alone, Hugh Glass set out a second time for Fort Kiowa, fifteen days' journey away, but this time his trip was less hazardous. It was an easy matter in that season of the year to catch young buffalo calves, and the old frontiersman arrived at the fort fresh and ready to pursue his quest of the men who had deserted him.

HALF HORSE AND HALF ALLIGATOR

A few days later he joined a party of keelboatmen bound downstream and came at last to Fort Atkinson, his remarkable journey of retribution ended. One of the deserters was at the fort, and men who knew the story looked for a quick and tragic ending to the betrayal of Hugh Glass. But here, just as interest mounts to a climax, history is silent on what took place between Glass and the deserter. There was no killing; there was not even a fight; and we are left to ponder what causes prompted Glass to forgo the revenge he had nursed so long.

Perhaps, as Hiram Chittenden, whose monumental tomes on the northwest fur trade and the history of navigation on the Missouri are classics of their kind, suggests, "Glass' sudden relinquishment of his purpose of revenge may have been due to new light obtained from the men who deserted him. It was asking a great deal for those two men to expose themselves to destruction for one whose life they doubtless believed was as good as lost, and whatever may have been the considerations of humanity, it was only heroic indifference to personal safety that could have induced them to stay. They should have stayed, of course, but their failure to do so is not without its justification."

For the next decade old Hugh Glass trapped, traded, and hunted on the Upper Missouri. He was employed at Fort Union and later at Fort Cass, from where he set out in the winter of 1832 to hunt along the Yellowstone. Together with two companions he was crossing the frozen river when a band of his ancient enemies, the Arikaras, plunged at the three men from the underbrush along the river's bank. This time there were no survivors. Not even the indestructible Hugh Glass.

THE wealth of the fur trade had now been made known to the world through the labors of these first of the Upper Missouri boatmen and trappers. Commercially minded men in St. Louis and the East saw that there were fortunes to be made if the business was placed on an efficient and well-organized basis. Unfortunately, in the years when the first keelboatmen were pressing into the upper river valley, the land did not belong to the United States. But with the turn of the century the clash of empires in old Europe evoked climactic changes in the destiny of the land of the Dacotahs.

Napoleon Bonaparte, with greedy eyes fixed on England, sat cooling his heels in the Channel ports, his victorious legions held at bay by the sea power of the British fleet—just as, almost a century and a half later, another and more sinister little corporal was to stand baffled before Britain's gallant armada of the skies.

Despairing of saving his distant possessions, and fearful lest they fall to his rivals, Napoleon tossed into the lap of youthful America all of France's New World continental possessions. "I have given to England," he snarled, "a maritime rival that will sooner or later humble her pride!"

He had given more than that to canny old Tom Jefferson, President of the young republic. To Jefferson it was an old, fond dream come true at last; and we find him writing to his good friend Benjamin Rush, Philadelphia physician and signer of the Declaration of Independence:

"I wish to mention to you in confidence that I have obtained authority from Congress to undertake the long desired object of exploring the Missouri and whatever river, heading with that, leads into the western ocean. About 10 chosen woodsmen, headed by Capt. Lewis, my secretary, will set out immediately and probably accomplish it in two seasons. Capt. Lewis is brave, prudent, habituated to the woods, and familiar with the Indian manner and character. . . . I ask the favor of you to prepare some notes of such particulars as may occur in his journey & which you think should draw his attention and inquiry."

Chapter 5

TO THE WESTERN OCEAN

〰〰〰〰〰〰〰〰〰〰〰〰〰〰〰〰〰〰〰〰〰〰〰〰〰〰〰〰〰〰〰

On the fourteenth day of May, 1804, Captain Meriwether Lewis completed his final preparations for the voyage of discovery. There was no longer need for secrecy, for Louisiana had now been officially transferred to the United States; and the party had spent the winter of 1803–4 at Camp River Dubois, opposite the mouth of the Missouri at St. Louis, awaiting the day when favorable weather would launch their little flotilla upstream on its way to the Western Ocean.

The winter months had been well spent. Guides and adventurous frontiersmen were recruited and enlisted in the Army's service, along with likely soldiers whom Lieutenant William Clark, second in command, selected from the scattered western military posts. Supplies for the long trip were purchased; the boats built and outfitted; a stock of goods and medals loaded for gifts to the Indians —who were now subjects of the Great White Father at Washington as a result of Jefferson's purchase from Napoleon.

Captain Lewis looked with approval on the hardy crew who were to accompany him in his perilous undertaking. William Clark was a lieutenant in the U.S. Artillery and Lewis's closest friend; they had shared campaign hardships together before. Sergeants Charles Floyd, Nathaniel Pryor, and John Ordway and Corporal Richard Warfington were his noncommissioned officers. Enlisted as privates at double pay—ten dollars a month—were men from Ohio, Pennsylvania, Kentucky, New Hampshire, and Vermont; farmers, soldiers, blacksmiths, boatmen, trappers, hunters, and guides, they were a veritable cross section of young America. Lieutenant Clark's huge Negro servant, York, was the final member of the party.

It was four o'clock on the rainy afternoon of May 14 when the little flotilla of three boats—a 55-foot keelboat and two pirogues equipped with oars and sails—stood out from Camp River Dubois on the first lap of the journey. An auspicious beginning was furnished by "a gentle breeze up the Missouri," a motley crowd of St. Louis citizens to see them off, and a keg of liquor which was passed out freely to all hands. A final shout of farewell as the corps manned their oars, and the adventurers moved slowly upstream on their way to the Western Sea.

Captain Lewis evidently found it difficult to take leave of the St. Louis belles at the last moment. At St. Charles, Missouri, where he was to meet his little fleet the next day, there was no sign of the commander; it was only after three days that he finally appeared, arrayed for the wilderness in buckskins, moccasins, and coonskin cap. There was further delay, so that it was the thirty-first of the month before the adventurers began their journey in earnest.

The mighty force of the Missouri, beginning to swell with the early June floods, fought the explorers like a living creature. Great sandbars, hidden snags and sawyers, and mighty logs that came hurtling downstream like missiles aimed at their fragile craft were constant hazards. Whirlpools and perverse crosscurrents spun their boats beneath the constantly caving banks or under the sweeping boughs of the dense forest that grew down to the river's edge.

The magnificent wilderness through which the adventurers were passing excited the party's admiration. Great forests lined the riverbanks. Rolling prairies dotted with wild game stretched away toward the distant horizons. Wrote Lewis in his journal: "Game is very abundant, and seems to increase as we progress, our prospect of starving is therefore consequently small. On the lower portion of the Missouri, from its junction with the Mississippi to the entrance of the Osage river we met with some deer, bear and turkeys."

One day late in June they met a party of hunters coming downstream with two raftloads of hides and tallow. One of the group interested Captain Lewis. He was a half-breed French and Indian trapper named Charbonneau, who had been living with the Mandans and Hidatsas on the Upper Missouri and was familiar with their language and character. Lewis had need of such a man. After a brief parley Charbonneau was hired as guide and interpreter; without a backward glance he left his erstwhile partners and joined the explorers on their long journey northward to the Mandan country.

As the month of June drew to a close, travel became more difficult. The great forests along the riverbanks thinned, giving place to clumps of cottonwood and willow trees. The stream's channel was clogged with island sandbars, heavily matted with undergrowth. The Missouri was in full flood stage now, and the men fought stubbornly to drag the heavy keelboat against the dead brown weight of the river.

The prairies on either hand were black with great herds of bison. Graceful bands of antelope bounded away at the party's approach. Squirrels and wild turkeys abounded in the trees along the river's edge, and red-shouldered blackbirds flashed through the low-hanging willow branches. The corps lived regally on the generous amounts of game the hunters brought in each day.

Following his orders, Captain Lewis made frequent stops among the tattered Indian villages they encountered; Council Bluffs in Iowa is named for one of the parleys which took place near there. The captain urged peace among the tribesmen and distributed flags and medals to show the Great White Father's good will.

Not far from Council Bluffs, Sergeant Floyd fell desperately ill with an ailment which the officers diagnosed as "a Billiouse Chorlick." Treatment was of no avail and the sergeant breathed his last in Captain Lewis's arms. It was the party's first death, almost before the journey was fairly begun. The sergeant's comrades buried his body on a bluff above the river, and called the tributary at whose mouth they camped that night "Floyd's river." Next morning, as the little flotilla stood out into midstream, Floyd's comrades turned back for a last look at the grave of the first American soldier to die west of the Mississippi.

SUMMER months were merging into autumn when the adventurers came at last into the land of the Dacotahs. Near the mouth of the James River they set fire to the prairie as a signal for nearby tribes to come in for trade and council. Setting up a great American flag, the captain awaited the approach of the first Sioux tribesmen.

LAND OF THE DACOTAHS

They were Yanktons, the "people who dwell at the far end," and Captain Lewis was not greatly impressed by their appearance. He addressed the chiefs, however, through his interpreter Drouillard, and in return the grave Siouan elders made speeches of welcome and pleas for aid and gifts.

Two young squaws who fell to quarreling provided an interesting insight into Yankton customs. While they scratched at each other's eyes and pulled hair after the manner of women everywhere, a burly Indian brave armed with a whip appeared suddenly and parted the battlers. Stripping first one and then the other, the Indian threw the girls to the ground and administered a sound whipping. It was explained that this official was a "Peacemaker," elected by the tribe for the purpose of maintaining order—a kind of aboriginal village constable, as it were.

As the adventurers moved upstream into the country of the Arikaras, September brought nights of chilling cold. The brush of autumn painted the forests in brilliant reds and yellows. On a great, willow-fringed island in the river's channel, the party found an Arikara village of more than five hundred warriors, "the best looking, most cleanly, most friendly and industrous Indians," wrote the captain, "I saw anywhere on the voyage."

The friendly Arikaras gave the white men ample supplies of their native foodstuffs: corn, squashes, and beans; and in return the captain presented the Arikara chief with gifts of the white man's civilization: a sunglass for fire-making and presents of salt and sugar. The Arikaras were generous folk in other ways as well. Wrote the captain in his journal:

"These women are handsomer than the Sioux; both of them are, however, disposed to be amorous, and our men found no difficulty in procuring companions for the night by means of the interpreters. These interviews were chiefly clandestine, and were of course to be kept a secret from the husband or relations. The point of honor indeed is completely reversed among the Ricaras; that the wife or sister should submit to a stranger's embraces without the consent of her husband or brother is a cause of great disgrace and offense, especially as for many purposes of civility or gratitude the husband and brother will themselves present to a stranger these females, and be gratified by attentions to them.

"The Sioux had offered us squaws, but we having declined while we remained there, they followed us with offers of females for two days. The Ricaras had been equally accommodating; we had equally withstood their temptation; but such was their desire to oblige us that two very handsome young squaws were set on board this evening, and persecuted us with civilities. The black man York participated largely in these favors; for, instead of inspiring any prejudice, his color seemed to procure him additional advantages from the Indians, who desired to preserve among them some memorial of their wonderful stranger. Among other instances of attention, a Ricara invited him into his house and, presenting his wife to him, retired to the outside of the door; while there one of York's comrades who was looking for him came to the door, but the gallant husband would permit no interruption until a reasonable time had elapsed."

Unlike many of the lower river tribes who had begged the explorers for whiskey, the Arikaras refused all offers of drink. "They were surprised," wrote Lewis, "that their father should present to them a liquor which would make them fools. . . . no man could be their friend who tried to lead them into such follies."

But there was another instance in which the Arikaras displayed a humanity quite incomprehensible to these white men accustomed to the harsh standards of their own civilization and age. Sometime during the month of October, Private John Newman was placed under arrest for "mutinous expressions." Tried by a court-martial of his fellows, he was sentenced to receive seventy-five lashes on his "bear back" and to be henceforth cast out from the party of exploration. This brutal punishment may seem unduly severe, but discipline had to be maintained if the whole journey was not to be jeopardized. Sternly the corps assembled to witness the execution of the court's judgment.

An Arikara chief was among the group which saw the carrying out of the sentence; and it was this "savage" who screamed aloud in sympathy with the suffering Newman and begged that the punishment cease.

LAND OF THE DACOTAHS

As the party moved northward through the heart of the Sioux country in what is now South Dakota, they one day came upon a gigantic skeleton—a massive framework of bones which the adventurers believed to be that of a fish. More than thirty-five feet long, it was unlike any creature they had seen or imagined, and Captain Lewis doubtless recalled the words of Thomas Jefferson, whose active scientific imagination had envisioned the possibility of giant prehistoric monsters still living in the unexplored wilderness they were about to enter. Had Captain Lewis but known it, he was looking upon the fossilized skeleton of one of the great dinosaurs which once roamed the Black Hills country, and whose bones are found there today in almost every exposed hillside.

It was late October and the chilling winds that presaged winter were beginning to sweep down from the north when the corps of discoverers approached the country of the Mandans. Great flocks of geese and ducks, southbound for their winter nesting grounds, darkened the skies and flecked the surface of the river. The captain decided an early winter camp was imperative. The men were ill and exhausted, the boats leaky and poorly mended where great snags had jarred their timbers.

Above the present city of Bismarck, North Dakota, the Mandans swarmed out of their earth lodges to greet the explorers. Big black York created a sensation, as usual. "These Indians were much astonished at my Servant," wrote William Clark; "they never saw a black man before, all flocked around him & examined him from top to toe, he Carried on the joke and made himself more turribal than we wished him to doe."

Captain Lewis, noting with surprise the extensive fields of corn cultivated by the tribe, presented them with an iron mill with which to grind their crops into meal; but iron, apparently, was too valuable a commodity to be wasted for such pacific purposes. Did they not have squaws who could grind the corn by hand with stone pestles? A trader who visited them later, wrote: "I saw the remains of an excellent large corn mill, which the foolish fellows had demolished to barb their arrows; the largest piece of it, which they could not break or work into any weapon, was fixed to a wooden handle and used to pound marrow bones to make grease."

A few miles below where Knife River joins the Missouri, the explorers began construction of their winter quarters. It was already early November, but before the snows of winter fell, twelve stout log cabins, chinked with river mud and equipped with rock chimneys and fireplaces, were completed. The Mandans were amazed at the skill and energy of the white builders, marveling as the buildings took shape before their eyes.

When the winter quarters were finished, the explorers visited the lodges of the friendly Mandans, learning their customs and teaching them the white man's dances and music. York shone again as a ladies' man, while the Frenchman Cruzatte astounded the Indians by dancing on his hands.

Christmas day at Fort Mandan found the adventurers in high spirits. Warning the Indians to stay away because it was a great medicine day for the white men, the party passed the time in drinking innumerable toasts of Christmas cheer, firing volleys, and singing. A special dinner was prepared by the cooks, and as a final celebration these rough, lonely frontiersmen engaged in one of their frequent dances—a wild wilderness "breakdown" that shook the walls of their crude log ballroom. The fact that they were obliged to dance with each other seemed no drawback; more than once during the long journey an old-fashioned breakdown served to revive their flagging spirits and send them back to their labors with renewed energy.

As winter closed in and heavy snowfalls blanketed the prairies, the explorers found hunting difficult; they stayed close to camp during the blinding blizzards, going out only when game stores ran low or the wood supply was depleted. The Mandans, seemingly unaffected by the bitter weather, were constant visitors. Chief Big White, of a nearby village, called one day with a gift for the white men. "He packd about 100 lbs of fine meet on his squar for us," wrote William Clark in his quaint orthography. She apparently "packd" her papoose on her back as well, for he added that they had later given the child some presents.

The captain put the camp blacksmiths to work fashioning iron arrowheads and axes to exchange with the Mandans for food. Blockaded in their snow-heaped cabins, the men repaired gear, while the captain and the lieutenant busied themselves with journals and map making. Lewis superintended the collection of a huge crate of specimens for Thomas Jefferson: stuffed animals, Indian implements, native grains, and other products of the country.

With the breaking of the river ice in early spring, the precious crate was loaded on a raft to be sent back to St. Louis and Washington under the command of Corporal Warfington. Then boats for the continuance of the journey had to be fashioned, since the big keelboat would no longer be useful on the narrowing waterway. The two pirogues were chopped free of the ice and reconditioned.

Spring brought back to the prairies abundance of game. Once again the camp hunters brought in buffalo, deer, and elk. The men's spirits rose with the temperature. But the leaders had a new worry to plague them. Charbonneau's seventeen-year-old Indian wife, Sacajawea, was to accompany the party on the journey to the Western Sea; she had been captured from the Shoshonis, who lived in the Shining Mountains, and her ability to speak the Shoshoni tongue might prove useful. Now, however, she was about to have a child, and Lewis and Clark dreaded the thought of an infant's presence on the hazardous journey into the unknown.

They accepted the situation with good grace, however; and in February William Clark, acting as assistant midwife to young Sacajawea, set down his medical observations for posterity: "It is worthy of remark that this was the first child which this woman had born, and as is common in such cases her labor was tedious and the pain violent. Having the rattles of a snake by me I administered two rings of it broken into small pieces to the woman, and added a small quantity of water. Whether this medicine was truly the cause or not I shall not undertake to determine, but I was informed that she had not taken it more than ten minutes before the child was born." Despite this nauseous nostrum, both Sacajawea and little Baptiste survived the ordeal and were ready to set out with the expedition when favorable weather permitted.

Behind the explorers lay sixteen hundred miles of journeying. Before them, though they were fortunately unaware of it, lay another twenty-five hundred miles of weary traveling, much of it through mountain peaks such as Americans had never before seen. Traders from both north and south had been to the Mandan villages; a few had penetrated to the mouth of the Yellowstone; but from the Yellowstone westward no white man had ever explored the Missouri. With high hearts, nevertheless, the little flotilla set out in early April on what they believed to be the final stage of their route to the Western Ocean.

Wrote Captain Lewis: "This little fleet altho not quite as respectable as those of Columbus or Captain Cook, was still viewed by us with as much pleasure as those deservedly famed adventurers ever beheld theirs, and I dare say with quite as much anxiety for their safety and preservation. I could not but esteem this moment of departure as among the most happy of my life. . . . We were now about to penetrate a country where the foot of civilized man had never trodden; the good or evil it had in store for us was for experiment yet to determine."

Toward the end of the month they came upon the junction of the Yellowstone and the Missouri, near the border of the present states of North Dakota and Montana. As the Missouri muddies the Mississippi, which is moderately clear above St. Louis, so did this swift new river darken the Missouri and give it its characteristic yellowish tinge. Once past the Yellowstone's mouth, the party noted that the Missouri was as clear as any mountain-fed river.

They had come into the fringes of the Badlands country, where high bluffs flanked the river's brim and lonely trees, set stark against the sky, furnished nesting places for giant bald eagles. The huge buffalo wolf, larger by far than his modern counterpart, lurked in the brush-tangled bottoms; but most feared of all was the savage "white bear," the grizzly. Adventures multiplied in this virgin wilderness.

Captain Lewis, hunting buffalo one day along the river's brink, had just succeeded in bringing down one of the big, shaggy beasts when he discovered a bear almost upon him. His rifle was empty. For eighty yards it was a nip-and-tuck race to the riverbank. Lewis, in desperation, ran out waist-deep in the water and turned to face the roaring beast with his spontoon. The bear, however, halted at the water's edge, turned, and disappeared.

A few moments later, as the drenched Virginian emerged from the water, he came suddenly upon a strange brownish animal that he later described as of "the tiger kind." It seemed about to spring at him, but a shot from his reloaded rifle frightened it into its nearby burrow.

Pondering on the nature of this unfamiliar beast, Lewis looked up to see three huge buffalo bulls bearing down on him with lowered heads and thundering hoofs. This danger he escaped by merely standing motionless, and he returned to camp "inclined to believe it all enchantment if the thorns of the prickly pear piercing my feet did not at every moment dispel the illusion." But the day's adventures were not yet over. He found that he had made his bed beneath a tree where a rattlesnake lay coiled.

There were other trials, too, less dangerous to life but nevertheless maddening. Clark recorded in his diary: "One trio of pests still invate and obstruct us on all occasions; these are the mosquitoes, eye knats, and prickly pears, equal to any three curses that ever pour Egypt laibored under except the Mahometant yoke."

Sacajawea and her little Baptiste had become great favorites with the lonely men of the expedition, but on May 14 Sacajawea proved her worth as a resourceful voyager as well.

"A squall of wind struck our sail broadside," wrote William Clark, "and turned the perogue nearly over. . . . The articles which floated out were nearly all caught by the squaw who was in the rear. This accident had like to have cost us dearly; for in this perogue were embarked our papers, instruments, books, medicine, a great proportion of our merchandise, and, in short, almost every article indispensably necessary to further the views and insure the success of the enterprise in which we are now launched to the distance of 2,200 miles."

The loss suffered was little, thanks to Sacajawea's quick-wittedness, and Captain Lewis, in his account of the accident, wrote: "I ascribe [to her] equal fortitude and resolution with any person on board." Janey, as the jovial Clark had nicknamed her, was now a full-fledged member of the corps of discovery.

As the month of May drew to a close, Captain Lewis, scouting ahead of the party, one day glimpsed majestic peaks in the distance. The Rockies! "While I viewed these mountains I felt a secret pleasure in finding myself so near the head of the heretofore conceived boundless Missouri; but when I reflected upon the difficulties which this snowy barrier would most probably throw in my way to the Pacific; and the sufferings and hardships of myself and party in them, it in some measure counterbalanced the joy I had felt."

ALONG in June the explorers came to the long portage around the Great Falls, where the river rushed between rock-walled bends in cascades of tumbling beauty. With a set of clumsy oaken wheels which they had carried all the way from St. Louis for just such an emergency, the men built a crude wagon to transport one of the rowboats and the heavier supplies over the prairies. Each member of the party, Janey included, carried a 100-pound pack. The ingenious York fashioned a sail from an old canvas, which they set up on the creaking wagon to lessen the labor of dragging it over the rough earth.

The long portage through the burning heat of late June took its toll of the weakened adventurers. Spiny cactus cut their moccasined feet until they left bloody footprints on the rock rim above the river. Water was scarce. Lewis, sharing the men's labor, wrote pityingly of their condition: "they are obliged to halt and rest frequently . . . at every halt these poor fellows tumble down and are so much fatigued that many of them are asleep in an instant. . . . some are limping under the soarness of their feet. Others faint and are unable to stand . . . yet no one complains, all go on with cheerfulness."

The long haul done, the adventurers dropped exhausted in their tracks and slept for thirty-six hours without awakening, while their leaders prepared a surprise party. Lewis himself took over the duties of camp chef, barbecued half a buffalo, and prepared his own culinary specialty—suet dumplings. The men, quick to recover their strength and spirits, urged Drouillard to produce his fiddle; and there, in the midst of the wilderness, they had another of their old-fashioned breakdowns. York capered and "carried on turribel"—Clark's standard expression for the big Negro's terpsichorean antics. They felt ready for anything once more.

Fresh boats hollowed out of giant cottonwoods were needed now in the narrowing river, which flowed swift and clear between lofty mountain peaks. Sacajawea told the captain they were nearing the country of the Shoshonis; she was beginning to recognize old landmarks and there were other signs of her people's nearness: smoke signals and discarded clothing which bore the stamp of the Shoshonis' handiwork.

In the thousand miles they had traversed since leaving the country of the Mandans they had seen no human being. Now the captain realized that he must soon find the Indians. The river was narrowing so that portages were almost a daily occurrence. The men's feet were slashed and sore. They must have horses; it would be suicidal to attempt to cross the mountains without them. So with three companions Lewis set out on foot in search of the Shoshonis.

On the second day they sighted a solitary horseman who fled when the captain attempted to signal him. But their hopes rose; at least the Shoshonis were near. Another day's travel brought them to what they thought was the ultimate source of the river, where a tiny cold rivulet spurted from a mountainside. Lewis knelt and drank from this "most distant fountain of the mighty Missouri in search of which we had spent so many toilsome days and restless nights. Thus far I had accomplished one of those great objects on which my mind had been unalterably fixed these many years. Judge then of the pleasure I felt in allaying my thirst with this pure and ice cold water which issues from the base of a low mountain."

When at last a party of mounted Shoshonis swept suddenly into view and their leader returned Lewis's friendly greetings, the captain, recalling it later in his diary, found it something of an anticlimax: "He embraced me very affectionately in their way, which is by putting your left arm over your right shoulder and slapping your back and applying their left cheek to your right and frequently vociferate the word *ah-hie-e* that is, *I am much re-*

joiced . . . we were all caressed and besmeared with their grease and paint till I was heartily tired of the national hug."

At the Shoshoni village Lewis and his men were treated to a friendly banquet, while the captain made known his desire to purchase thirty horses for their journey over the mountains. The Indians had many horses, but they were suspicious of Lewis's request that they accompany him downstream to find the remainder of the white men's party. At the river the Shoshonis' fears increased when the expected expedition did not appear and for a time the four lone white men were in danger.

Then, as the Indians' patience was almost at the breaking point, a scout discovered the approach of Clark and the remainder of the party. Sacajawea, among the first ashore, was brought to act as interpreter. And a scene to tax the credulity of a cinema-addict took place. Sacajawea took one long look at the Shoshoni chief, Cameahwait, and then flew into his arms weeping tears of joy. He was her brother, whom she had not seen since her capture by the Hidatsas five years before!

Indians and whites engaged in a wild celebration. The Shoshonis examined York's black skin with awe and cheered while he danced for them; the tricks performed by Lewis's pet dog excited their wonder; and the gifts of blankets, beads, tobacco, mirrors, and bright uniforms completely won their hearts. If there were horses to be had, the captain would surely get them now!

From Chief Cameahwait, Lewis learned of the great westward-flowing river which he sought. "The chief informs me that he has understood from the Indians who inhabit this river below the Rocky Mountains that it ran a great ways toward the setting sun and lost itself in a great lake of water that was illy tasted, and where the white men lived."

Autumn was near when the expedition completed its horse trading and took leave of the Shoshonis for the assault on the Shining Mountains. An old Shoshoni—whom Clark promptly christened Toby—volunteered to guide the party through the lofty rock-strewn passes, where the slightest misstep often meant sudden death. The first snows were falling in early September, and the men were gaunt and ill from lack of food before the crossing was fairly begun. A lean wolf was the party's only food one day; another day there were only two "pheasants" to feed more than thirty mouths. Dogs and horses provided part of the menu, and one miserable day they ate nothing save roots. The horses, too, grew weak; their only food was leaves and brushwood. Then Toby, the old Shoshoni guide, disappeared, leaving the exhausted adventurers to find their own way through the mighty mountain passes.

Swirling snow choked the trail and the men were staggering from weakness when at last they began the slow descent toward the western slope of the Bitterroots. They had conquered the citadel of the Rockies.

Now that the great barrier had been crossed, Lewis's overdriven body collapsed; he became so ill he was unable to walk. Clark took over the command and wrote worriedly in his diary: "Captain Lewis is very sick. nearly all men sick. all men able to work commence building five canoes." They had come to the banks of the Clearwater, and Clark decided that travel by water would be more practicable for the weakened men. More of the remaining horses were killed to provide food, and when the canoes were completed, the corps shoved off downstream on the swift current of the Clearwater.

The stream's bed, choked with rapids, taxed the strength of the weary men. Portage followed portage as they floated down the Clearwater and into the Snake until they came at last to a thunderous five-mile stretch of foaming white water. It was the last hurdle. They had reached the Columbia.

Now Flathead Indians traded them quantities of fish and young dogs, and the ailing crew began to revive with improved diet and lighter labor. Down the bosom of the mighty Columbia, past great racks of willow branches laden with drying fish, the adventurers floated toward the culmination of their journey.

The tang of salt water was in the air and great fogs came rolling in from the west. On the night of the sixth of November they could hear a distant rumble like the long volleying of thunder. Fog blanketed the river next morning. They paddled on slowly through the white mist until, near noon, the sun dissolved the fog blanket, and before them lay the vast expanse of the Pacific!

The weary explorers burst into a cheer. Clark scribbled in his diary: "Ocian in view! Oh the joy! We are in view of the ocian, that great ocian which we have been so long anxious to see!" Four thousand and two hundred miles of trackless wilderness lay behind them.

First to ascend the Missouri to its source, first Americans to traverse the continent, the expedition raised the flag of the United States on the lonely Pacific shore ahead of any other nation which might have had rival ambitions. Their intrepid journeying had clinched for the infant American nation the future ownership of the Pacific Northwest.

COLD November rains fell as the corps set about felling trees and shaping logs for cabins for winter quarters. Clatsop Indians and other coast tribes came to watch the white men at work, and Captain Lewis was quick to note that other English-speaking men had left their traces among these simple children of the forest. Phrases such as "Heave the lead!" and "Damned rascal!" fell from their innocent lips to verify the fact that British and American sailing vessels had touched here before. One squaw proudly exhibited on her arm a tattoo mark which said simply, "J. Bowman."

Weary days of waiting followed through the rainy winter months. On March 21, eager to return to home and civilization, the party broke camp for the long trip back over the mountains. The route was easier now; the great barrier of the Rockies was crossed with little difficulty; and late summer found them afloat on the yellow current of the Missouri. The voyageurs drove downstream with eager oar blades, and mid-August found them once again in the friendly lodges of the Mandans. The wilderness journey was over. From here on they were traveling charted and familiar waters.

As they journeyed downstream from the Mandan villages to St. Louis, they came one day upon a party of white men bound for the northwest country. News was eagerly exchanged. Yes, Thomas Jefferson was alive and well, they told the captain in response to his volley of questions. Alexander Hamilton had been killed by Aaron Burr in a duel. There was trouble with England on the high seas and talk of war in the capitol at Washington. The men, relishing their first drink of whiskey in more than a year, roared with laughter to learn that the whole nation had given them up for dead.

Six months to the day from the time they had left Fort Clatsop on the Pacific they were back in St. Louis. The journey outward had taken them eighteen months. A hundred and forty years later a captain of the U.S. Army Air Corps could climb into his plane in St. Louis at dawn and be in Portland for lunch.

St. Louis received the adventurers with a tremendous celebration. Papers throughout the nation acclaimed the venture or scoffed at it, according to their political complexions. Many predicted that the region would never be traversed again. But to western men there was no question of the exploration's value. Lewis and Clark had opened the way for the fur traders of St. Louis and the East; they had brought back proof of the riches and resources of the Northwest; and the traders lost no time in moving in to exploit the new-found wealth of the Upper Missouri Valley.

Chapter 6

THE JUG OF EMPIRE

~~~~~~

"Whiskey as applied to the noble savage is a wonderful civilizer. A few years of it reduces him to a subjection more complete than arms, and accomplishes in him a humility which religion can never achieve. Some things men will do for Christ, for country, for wife and children; there is nothing that an Indian will not do for whiskey."

So wrote the historian George Bancroft in the nineteenth century. He was not the first to discover the red man's terrible thirst. The early trappers and traders who made their way into the Upper Missouri Valley soon learned that their most successful approach to any transaction with the natives was the suggestion that they line up at the traders' kegs. Liquor was their most profitable article of barter; often they could make a profit of many thousand per cent if they managed to stupefy the Indians sufficiently. They had other goods in reserve, such as blankets, gunpowder, beads, salt, sugar, and coffee; but too often the unfortunate red man who had come to replenish his stocks of these staples awakened to learn that his furs were gone and only a monumental hangover remained to indicate the price he had been paid for them.

Our United States Army outposts might have warred with the savage plains tribes far longer than they did, had it not been for the demoralizing effects of John Barleycorn upon the Indian populations. It was whiskey and starvation, far more than the generalship of the Indian fighters, that finally humbled and reduced to the confines of reservations the proud and warlike nomads of the northern plains. In some cases forts and trading posts were saved from attack by rolling kegs of liquor out to the besieging red men, who promptly forgot their warlike intentions and departed reeling and hiccoughing whence they had come.

The aboriginal tribes of the Northwest had apparently never known intoxicating liquor until the coming of the white man. Its effect upon them was—and is to this day—terrible to behold. Not possessing the racial immunity that Europeans have acquired through hundreds of generations of guzzling, the Indians reacted to alcohol in ways that at times frightened even the white traders who purveyed it to them.

A parallel case is smallpox, which, when it spread among the Indians, killed them literally by thousands, although the whites suffered from it but moderately.

The extent to which this trade spread and flourished in a few brief years might today seem unbelievable were it not for the unimpeachable proofs contained in the daily journals of the early traders. Alexander Henry, who came into the Dakota country in the 1800's, has left us a voluminous and fascinating record. A few excerpts, selected at random, will perhaps shed some light on the harried life led by an early fur trader among the red men:

April 30: Indians having asked for liquor, and promised to decamp and hunt well all summer, I gave them some. Grande Gueule stabbed Capot Rouge, Le Boeuf stabbed his young wife in the arm, Little Shell almost beat his old mother's brains out with a club, and there was terrible fighting among them.

Feb. 22: Grande Gueule stabbed Perdrix Blanche with a knife in six places; the latter, in fighting with his wife, fell into the fire and was almost roasted, but had strength enough left, notwithstanding his wounds, to bite her nose off. He is very ill, but I don't suppose he will die.

Oct. 30: After the gates were closed, I gave them a quart of rum. They drank very quietly. About two I awoke at the report of a gun in the hall, and William Henry rushed in to tell me that Nawic had shot Duford.

Nov. 2: Gave the Indians liquor after their successful hunt.

Nov. 4: Gave the Indians a nine-gallon keg of liquor on their promise to pay their debts on their return from the hunt.

Feb. 9: Men and women have been drinking a match for three days and three nights, during which it has been drink, fight—drink, fight—drink, and fight again—guns, axes and knives their weapons—very disagreeable.

With that closing phrase of masterly understatement, Henry turned to more agreeable matters and totted up the year's account of what he termed a "very successful winter." In exchange for the nine-gallon kegs of liquor—two gallons of alcohol to seven of water, liberally laced with chewing tobacco and red peppers—the trader's winter had netted him 643 beaver skins, 125 black bear, 23 brown bear, 2 grizzly bear, 83 wolf, 102 red fox, 7 kitt, 178 fisher, 96 otter, 62 martin, and 97 mink. What the Indians had received in exchange, aside from the horrible hangovers peculiar to Amerinds, is not known.

Hiram Chittenden has described the astounding lengths to which the canny traders went in making gulls of their red brethren: "It was the policy of the shrewd trader to first get his victim so intoxicated that he could no longer drive a good bargain. The Indian, becoming more and more greedy for liquor, would yield up all he possessed for an additional cup or two. The voracious trader, not satisfied with selling his liquor at a profit of many thousand per cent, would now cheat in quantity. As he filled the cup, which was standard measure, he would push in his big thumb and diminish its capacity by one-third. Sometimes he would substitute another cup with bottom thickened by running tallow into it until it was one-third full. He would also dilute the liquor until, as the Indian's senses became more and more befogged, he would treat him to water pure and simple."

The trading posts were scenes of the extremest debauchery and violence during those periods when the tribes brought their furs in for barter. They were customarily locked inside the enclosure lest they depart for some rival trading post, furnished with all the liquor they could consume, and permitted to leave only when the trader had secured the last purchasable portion of their possessions. Henry relates that Indian fathers came to him with their ten- and twelve-year-old daughters, whom they offered to trade to him for another dram of liquor.

After a two- or three-day session of drink, trade, and battle within the tiny enclosure of the fort, there were always two or three bodies to be carried away and buried, and the post trader was kept busy treating wounds of all descriptions. An early traveler who witnessed one of these bargain days at Fort Union asserted that he had never heard such sounds as emanated from the drunken Indians who were penned up in the post's outer enclosure. Men, women, and children were all "raving drunk" in the cramped space and pitch darkness; screams and war whoops filled the air; and an occasional scuffle and accompanying shriek of pain told that another redskin had bit the dust—this time by a brother's hand.

It was this civilizing effect of the liquor traffic which Mark Twain doubtless had in mind when he paid his respects to John Barleycorn as a beneficent influence in the world's steady march toward perfection:

"How solemn and beautiful is the thought that the earliest pioneer of civilization, the van-leader of civilization, is never the steamboat, never the railroad, never the newspaper, never the Sabbath-school, never the missionary—but always whiskey! Look history over; you will see. The missionary comes after the whiskey —I mean he arrives after the whiskey has arrived; next comes the poor immigrant, with axe and hoe and rifle; next, the trader; next, the miscellaneous rush; next, the gambler, the desperado, the highwayman, and all their kindred in sin of both sexes; and next, the smart chap who has bought up an old grant that covers all the land; this brings the lawyer tribe; the vigilance committee brings the undertaker. All these interests bring the newspaper; the newspaper starts up politics and a railroad; all hands turn to and build a church and a jail—and behold! civilization is established forever in the land. But whiskey, you see, was the van-leader in this beneficent work. It always is. It was like a foreigner—and excusable in a foreigner—to be ignorant of this great truth, and wander off into astronomy to borrow a symbol. But if he had been conversant with the facts, he would have said: 'Westward the Jug of Empire takes its way.'"

Mark Twain was himself in error when he attributed the astronomical symbol to a foreigner (it was John Quincy Adams who misquoted Bishop Berkeley's famous line and made it "Westward the star of empire takes its way"), but the general truth of the rest of the passage is beyond dispute. Traders bearing liquor into the Indian country were always assured of a hearty welcome from the red man; and the thirty years following the Lewis and Clark expedition saw the whole vast sweep of the Upper Missouri Valley dotted with forts and rendezvous of the great fur companies and the mountain traders.

FORERUNNER and king of them all was the free trapper, who hunted when and where he willed, owed allegiance to no company, and pitted his skill and wits unaided against the wilderness. "In this early race for empire," says Lewis Crawford, "none except fur seekers entered. Their rhythmic paddle blades swished up every stream of the West to its rivulet head; every mountain height and forbidding gorge knew their intrepid feet. Every nationality had a part. These were the true pathfinders, the true explorers, the heralds of empire. Their fur-laden vessels floating down the familiar waters of the Missouri and its tributaries represented the wealth, the adventure, the romance of the Northwest."

Typical of these lone knights of the wilderness was John Colter, a lad from Kentucky who had accompanied Lewis and Clark to the Pacific and back again to the Mandan country, where he chose to turn westward once more and plunge into the unknown fastnesses of the plain and mountain wilderness.

For years this strange and solitary man wandered, sometimes accompanied by a companion or two but more often alone, through all the secret and hidden places of the West. He discovered the headwaters of the Yellowstone River and Yellowstone Lake; the upper waters of Clark's Fort and the Big Horn River; the course of the Shoshone; the Teton and Wind River mountain ranges; Jackson's Hole and Pierre's Hole, famed rendezvous of the trappers; Pryor's Gap, and Union and Teton passes. Somewhere in his lonely journeying he came upon the awesome grandeur of today's Yellowstone Park, with its boiling springs, its riot of weird colors, its mighty geysers; and when he brought the tale back to civilization he was branded the biggest liar in the northwest country.

"Colter's Hell," chuckled the mountain men when they spoke of this fantastic discovery, and winked at each other in appreciation of their comrade's inventive powers. But they lived to eat their words, most of them, for every year the restless free trappers who roamed over the upper river basin found new natural wonders to marvel at.

In the spring of 1807 Colter joined the service of Manuel Lisa of St. Louis, and that fall he helped to construct Fort Lisa—sometimes called Fort Manuel—near the mouth of the Big Horn: the first trading post and the first building to be erected in what is now the state of Montana. The fort, located in the heart of the Crow country, was a source of great displeasure to the Blackfeet, who resented the white men's trading with their hereditary enemies. In 1808, while Colter was leading a band of Flatheads to trade at the post, the Blackfeet attacked the party. A band of Crows came to Colter's aid and the fierce northern tribesmen were beaten off, but not before they had marked Colter's presence among the Indians—and for a quarter of a century the Blackfeet remained hostile toward all white men.

Colter had been badly wounded in the leg during the battle, but immediately upon his recovery he set out for the Three Forks country in company with John Potts, another member of the Lewis and Clark expedition who had returned to trap and trade in the Northwest. They had launched out on the Jefferson River and were stroking their way upstream, each in his own dugout, when a war party of Blackfeet signaled them from the river's edge and beckoned them to come ashore. There was no escape, for a hundred weapons were leveled at them from a few yards' distance; their only chance was to comply with the Indians' orders and hope it would mean nothing worse than robbery.

Colter, not wishing to lose his precious beaver traps, dropped them over the side of his dugout and paddled to the riverbank, where he was seized, disarmed, and stripped of all his clothing. Potts remained in his canoe. Colter called to him, urging him to surrender, but Potts replied that he preferred death to falling into the hands of the Blackfeet. One of the braves, apparently comprehending his answer, fired on the canoe and Potts fell, shot through the hip.

"Are you hurt bad?" Colter called.

"Yes, too bad to get away, but I'll get one of them."

Potts raised his rifle and fired into the Indians, killing a Blackfoot brave, an act of unparalleled rashness considering the white men's position. Every Blackfoot bow and gun was instantly turned on the wounded man and discharged. "He was made a riddle of," said Colter later, in the odd jargon of the mountain man. A dozen of the Blackfeet waded out into the stream and dragged canoe and corpse ashore, where they hacked and dismembered the body before Colter's eyes and flung the gory entrails in his face.

Colter was sure his last hour had come. After a brief council, the Indians seemed to have come to a decision concerning his fate. One of the warriors turned to him and made a sign that he should set out over the prairie. "Go," he said in the Crow tongue, which Colter understood. "Go away."

Colter, expecting a bullet in the back, started away at a walk. The warrior shouted at him to hurry. A backward glance told him the reason. Several of the younger braves were stripping themselves to their breechclouts, tossing off leggings and selecting lances as if for a chase. For some obscure reason they were giving him a chance, however slender, for his life. It was to be a race with death, a contest with his own life as the stake.

Colter wasted no time. It was five miles to Madison Fork; he knew the country as a man knows his own back yard; and he was in splendid physical condition, tough as rawhide and in the prime of his youth and strength. He had a start of perhaps a hundred yards, and fear lent wings to his feet as the first war whoops of the pursuers rang out behind him.

He was badly handicapped by the loss of his moccasins. The spiny prairie cactus ripped his flying feet as he fled before the yelling horde, but he felt no pain at the time; it was only later that he discovered the terrible wounds he had suffered. When he had covered less than three miles of the distance to Madison Fork, he began to weaken. A nasal hemorrhage induced by his violent exertions brought the blood spurting from his nostrils in pumping jets of crimson. Unable to continue, he turned for a hasty glance at the pursuing braves and saw that he had left them far behind— all but one who, far ahead of his fellows, was bearing down on the naked and defenseless man with lifted lance.

Colter called to him in the Crow tongue and asked for mercy, but the Blackfoot raised his spear with both hands to transfix the helpless white man. Perhaps he was overeager, or perhaps Colter found the strength of desperation in the final moment; at any rate the white man clutched the descending lance by the head and broke it in two, while the brave, carried along by the momentum of his assault, fell sprawling on the ground.

Now it was the Indian who held up his empty hands and pleaded for his life. "But Colter," says one of the ancient chroniclers, "was not in a mood to remember the Golden Rule, and pinned his adversary through the body to the earth by one stab with the spearhead."

By now the howling pack was drawing near again, and the white man knew he could expect scant mercy at their hands after killing one of their comrades. Recovering the spearhead from the dead brave's body, he set out again on his desperate race toward Madison Fork, where the river and timber might afford him a chance for safety. The pause had refreshed him and as he raced ahead of the angry braves, he found his second wind; he began to draw away from his pursuers for a second time.

He reached the river well ahead of the foremost of the Indians. As he broke through the willows that fringed the bank, and plunged into the stream, he saw a beaver lodge a few yards away, its top just protruding above the water. A sudden inspiration struck him and, before any of the Blackfeet were in sight, he dived under the surface, found the submerged entrance to the lodge, and forced his way through the door. Inside the domed structure, and above the water level, he stretched himself out on the ledgelike floor which is the beaver's second story and awaited the arrival of his enemies.

He lay holding his breath while the moccasined feet of his pursuers scuffed overhead on the roof of his precarious shelter. Apparently the braves gave no thought to the fact that he might be hidden under their feet. For several hours the exhausted man lay listening to the shouts and noises of his enemies as they splashed through the stream or beat the nearby timber in search of him. By nightfall the cries had died away and ·Colter ventured forth from his inverted foxhole to find the Indians had gone.

But his troubles were far from over. He was naked and almost defenseless; his feet were terribly cut and swollen; and, worst of all, he was trapped in a valley which had only one pass for an outlet. Knowing the Blackfeet, he was certain the pass would be guarded. To escape he must somehow climb the almost perpendicular side of the mountain before him in order to avoid the waiting Blackfeet.

Up the treacherous cliffs which, as one of his friends later wrote, "seemed impassable even to a mountain goat," Colter clambered through the darkness of the night, clinging to rocks, shrubs, and branches of stunted trees. By dawn he had reached the summit safely. He lay hidden through the day, resting from his labors, and that night set out for Fort Lisa two hundred miles away. For eleven days he traveled, pausing only when exhaustion forced him to sleep briefly; his only food was roots, berries, and bark; and when he came at last to the post on the Big Horn, his comrades did not at first recognize him. Only when the gaunt, bearded, and filthy creature spoke to them would they believe it was Colter.

For two more years John Colter roamed and trapped the Upper Missouri country; then, in 1810, he set out alone from the headwaters of the river in a dugout canoe for civilization and home. Thirty days later he was in St. Louis for the first time since his departure with Lewis and Clark six years before. He had covered the three thousand miles at the record rate of one hundred miles a day, aided only by the Missouri's current and his own husky arms.

Colter's end was anticlimactic. After all the hair-raising adventures he had survived, he settled in St. Louis, married, and died three years later of jaundice.

IN THE meantime, back in the upper river country, Colter's comrades and the men who followed in their footsteps were opening the way for the coming of the great fur companies. John Jacob Astor's American Fur Company, which was later to dominate the Upper Missouri, had not yet fastened its grip on the northwest trade; but Manuel Lisa's Missouri Fur Company and its rival, the Rocky Mountain Company, were trading in the Northwest almost before Lewis and Clark's expedition had returned to civilization. Unlike the loose associations of free trappers or traders, the St. Louis companies were organized on an efficient basis, backed by ample capital, and planned their operations with a view to permanence and businesslike administration.

Elaborately fortified and well-stocked fixed posts were built along the upper rivers at strategic locations, and large parties of hunters and trappers in the employ of the companies were sent out to cover the surrounding territories. In the mountains the institution of the rendezvous came into being—a sort of gala annual fur fair in the wilderness that drew Indians and trappers alike from hundreds of miles around.

The personnel of the early companies was largely recruited from among the French Creoles of the Louisiana country or, in some cases, was made up of French-Canadian voyageurs imported from the North to man the heavy keelboats and shoulder the menial tasks of the trade. The native-American keelboatman of the Mike Fink variety was too independent to submit to the drudgery imposed by the companies' *patrons* or *bourgeois* during the peak of the fur combines' activities. He became either a free trapper or a hunter for one of the St. Louis firms.

The jolly French voyageurs were admirably suited for the duties of *engagés* with the companies. They were usually illiterate, profoundly ignorant, devoutly religious, and childishly superstitious. But they were capable of the most cheerful and willing service under conditions of extreme adversity; their chansons and boat songs were never stilled throughout the longest days of toil—days that often began at four o'clock in the morning and lasted until darkness forced a halt in the late evening.

The salary of the *engagés,* the lowest-paid workers in the employ of the fur traders, was only one hundred and fifty dollars a year, and seldom did they collect any of that. It was a deliberate purpose of the companies to keep them perpetually in debt, and they were forced to pay exorbitant prices at the company stores for any extra articles they wished to buy. Signed up for a period of five years as a rule, the voyageurs usually returned to St. Louis empty-handed at the conclusion of their engagements. Often they did not return at all if they had been frugal and had any sizable draft on the company offices. There are well-authenticated cases in which these ignorant and faithful laborers were murdered by hired killers; then the company was not obliged to cash the draft that might have been presented had the *engagé* reached St. Louis. Human life was cheap in the northwest country.

The *bourgeois* in charge of the fixed posts were usually men of marked ability: competent executives and excellent business administrators who might have made their mark in civilization had they chosen to do so. They had complete freedom of action in conducting the company affairs and were a law unto themselves in the isolated outposts, dealing out summary justice as the occasion demanded. They were iron-fisted, too, and needed to be, for they dealt with fierce and untamed native populations as well as with white renegades and semi-outlaws of all descriptions.

Under the peculiar conditions existing in the fur trade there were virtually unlimited opportunities for peculation and double-dealing, and it speaks well for most of these wilderness executives that their employers in New York or St. Louis found little cause for complaint. Occasionally, of course, some wily *bourgeois* would abscond with a year's catch of furs and bankrupt his employers, but offenders were ruthlessly hunted down and punished, and the great majority of *bourgeois* were faithful and diligent servants of the men whose fortunes had been placed in their keeping.

Under the *bourgeois,* and responsible for a great part of the work, were the clerks, engaged at salaries of five hundred dollars a year. They were often young men of promise whom the company was training for the more complex duties of *bourgeois* in some other outpost. Carpenters, blacksmiths, boatbuilders, and other artisans were to be found at all the larger posts, most of which had a *chantier,* or shipyard, where mackinaw boats and other craft were built to float the annual cargoes of peltries downstream. Several dozen trappers and hunters in the company's employ were always a part of any big post's personnel, and the lowly *engagés* completed the roster of the *bourgeois'* employees.

IN TIME the American Fur Company of John Jacob Astor, the immigrant lad who had arrived in America with nothing save his wits

and a consuming ambition, established forts that effectively controlled the entire trade of the region. Fort McKenzie at the mouth
of the Marias River, Fort Cass at the mouth of the Big Horn, Fort
Union at the mouth of the Yellowstone, and Fort Pierre downriver in what is now South Dakota were among the posts of the
Upper Missouri Outfit, as Astor's northwest branch was commonly
called.

Fort Union was by far the most important of them all. It was
in 1828 that Kenneth McKenzie, an employee of the American
Fur Company, sent the keelboat *Otter* upriver from the Mandan
villages to establish a post at the Yellowstone's mouth and secure
the trade of the Assiniboins. Built on a bluff overlooking the river,
it became in time the finest and most famous post in the Northwest. Two hundred and forty feet long and two hundred and twenty
feet wide, it was surrounded by a palisade of heavy logs twenty feet
high and protected by stone blockhouses. Scattered about the
enclosure were barracks for the *engagés,* storehouses, workshops,
stables, a stone powderhouse with a capacity of fifty thousand
pounds, and a reception room where trading with the Indians was
carried on. The house of the *bourgeois,* ruler of this little domain,
was a handsome two-story structure with glass windows, a fireplace,
and other luxuries seldom seen in the wilderness.

Kenneth McKenzie, who presided over Fort Union during its
palmiest years, was not only one of the ablest of the *bourgeois,*
but a personality of considerable interest as well. Known as the
"King of the Upper Missouri," he maintained in the wilderness an
establishment of regal splendor that did not belie his title. He
dressed usually in handsome blue or red uniforms decorated with
gold braid, although for occasions of state he sometimes donned a
medieval suit of armor which he had had especially imported from
Europe. The fame of his banquet table had spread all through the
Northwest, for he served the finest of wines and delicacies; snowy
damasks and silver tableware graced his board; and, like a true
Scotsman, he had a quartet of bagpipers to entertain his guests on
special occasions.

McKenzie was the first trader to open the Blackfoot country in
northern Montana, after the disastrous experiences of Manuel Lisa

and John Colter twenty-five years before. In 1830 the *bourgeois* made the acquaintance of an old trapper named Jacob Berger, who had served for many years with the famous Hudson's Bay Company—the H.B.C., which old mountain men asserted stood for "Here Before Christ." Berger knew the Blackfoot tongue and was personally acquainted with many of their leaders, for the H.B.C. had long traded with the northern Indian tribes and it was partly the company's intrigues against American traders that kept the Blackfeet hostile.

Berger, probably for a handsome consideration, was persuaded to transfer his allegiance to McKenzie, and he set out at once with a small party for the land of the northern tribesmen. For four weeks the white men traveled westward without sighting a human being. Then, near the mouth of the Marias River, they came upon a group of mounted warriors. Berger's companions lost their nerve at this critical moment, but the old plainsman advanced alone, bearing a huge American flag and calling out to the Indians in the Blackfoot tongue. Fortunately, several of the Indians recognized him and the party was escorted to the Blackfoot village where, after a lengthy parley, a number of them agreed to accompany Berger to Fort Union and open trade relations with the Americans.

Given this opportunity, McKenzie completely won the confidence of the Indians, made trade agreements with them, and signed a treaty of peace between the Blackfeet and the Assiniboins which brought peace to the border and assured the American Fur Company of a rich trade in furs.

This notable feat accomplished, McKenzie turned to other methods of increasing the company's dominance of the Northwest. In July 1832 Congress had passed stringent laws intended to keep liquor out of the Indian country; inspectors were placed along the upper river at various points to search all boats engaged in the fur traffic; and McKenzie found himself unable to secure his most important article of trade. Some of his competitors were smuggling it overland, and the British companies were enjoying a considerable advantage as a result of the new regulations.

But McKenzie was a resourceful man. Noting that the law merely prohibited the "introduction" of liquor into the Indian country, he constructed a huge still at Fort Union, and with native corn from the Mandan villages began the manufacture of a product that proved quite as effective as any imported brand. Envisioning an expansion of his activities, he sent men to the Iowa country to buy land, plant corn, and arrange for transport of the grain upriver to his wilderness distillery.

As a result of McKenzie's activities his competitors protested, and the company very nearly lost its license. Congress found it necessary a year later to amend the law so that manufacture as well as importation of liquor was prohibited. The result was what might have been expected. The traders began now to bootleg in earnest.

Fort William, which had been built by the Sublette & Campbell Company to compete with the American Fur Company's Fort Union, apparently had no difficulty in circumventing the new regulations. Charles Larpenteur has described in his journal the scene at the opening of the new post:

"It was not until night that we got ready to trade. It must be remembered that liquor was the principal and most profitable article of trade, although it was strictly prohibited by law, and all boats on the Missouri were thoroughly searched at Fort Leavenworth. Notwithstanding this, Mr. Sublette managed to pass through what was wanted. The liquor trade started at dark, and soon the yelling and singing commenced. The Indians were all locked up in the fort, for fear that some might go to Fort Union, which was about 2½ miles distant. Imagine the noise! Five hundred Indians with their squaws, all drunk as they could be, locked up in that small space! Gauche, the Indian chief, had provided himself with a pint cup, which I know he did not let go during the whole spree, and every now and then he would rush into the store with his cup, and order it filled, and to 'hurry up.' The debauch continued during the entire night and well into the next day, Gauche being a leading figure until the end, when Indians in stupor from drink lay in every direction."

McKenzie's post on the Marias River in the Blackfoot country saved itself from an Indian attack by employing somewhat similar measures. The post, built by James Kipp after Berger had successfully negotiated his agreement with the Blackfeet, aroused the jealousy of rival British traders, who bribed the Blood Indians to attack the fort. Says Hiram Chittenden: "Kipp turned his own weapons of war—the goods of the trader—upon the Indians and poured into them incessant charges of alcohol until the whole band was utterly vanquished and surrendered body and soul to the incomparable trader." Instead of losing his fort and probably his life, Kipp returned to civilization with a great cargo of furs secured from the bemused savages.

While the trading posts dealt principally in robes and furs, they also purchased quantities of buffalo and bear tallow, and shipped such delicacies as buffalo tongues to eastern markets. Made up in the post's fur press into bundles, or "packs," of about one hundred pounds each, the annual cargoes of peltries were shipped south to St. Louis and New Orleans, where they were transshipped to New York and repacked before reaching their eventual destination in the luxury shops of Europe. The best market for otter skins was China, and most of these fine furs found their way there, to be exchanged for Chinese silks and spices.

But it was the beaver, more than any other fur-bearer, that was the foundation for the fur trade of the Northwest. The beaver hat was worn all over the civilized world, and when it went suddenly out of fashion, to be replaced by the silk topper, the trade suffered a crushing blow. Since the complete round of the companies' merchandise from the factories of Europe to the wilderness and back again to Europe occupied some four years, many companies suffered heavy losses when the demand for beaver furs fell off and they were left with large inventories of skins for which they had paid high prices.

The furs were never paid for in cash, but in merchandise, and in order to compete with the English companies, American traders were forced to buy European manufactured goods; American goods were of such inferior quality at that time that the Indians would have none of them.

Prices were naturally high by the time the imported merchandise had been transported from Europe across the sea and finally by keelboat into the heart of the northwest fur country. Scarlet cloth was priced at $6 a yard; fourth-proof rum at $13.50 a gallon; handkerchiefs $1.50 each; gunpowder, $1.50 a pound; three-point blankets, $9 each; buttons, $5 per gross; and lead, indispensable for bullet-making, $1 a pound. Four cheap handkerchiefs, at the trader's price of $1.50 each, would bring in return a fine beaver skin, valued by the companies at $6 but actually worth considerably more.

Despite the huge volume of furs taken at the height of the upper river trade, the business was carried on by comparatively few individuals. It has been estimated that the entire northwest trade was conducted by five or six hundred white men; yet in the winter of 1838–39 Fort Union alone dispatched eight mackinaw boats laden with two hundred and fifty packs of fur each—a pack consisting usually of ten buffalo skins, sixty otter, eighty beaver, a hundred and twenty fox, or six hundred muskrat. In cash the annual value of the upper river trade amounted to less than a million dollars a year, but the sum was a large one considering the few traders involved, and the fact that the furs were obtained at ridiculously low prices made the business a lucrative one.

MANUEL LISA, first of the fur traders to enter the far upper reaches of the valley, was responsible more than any other individual for the later preeminence of American companies in the northwest trade. At the time of his birth in New Orleans in 1772 the territory of Louisiana was under Spanish rule, and when the young man was but eighteen years of age he went north to the tiny settlement of St. Louis to begin his career as a fur trader. A man of shrewd judgment, vigorous nature, and prodigious capacity for labor, he quickly obtained from the Spanish government the exclusive rights to trade with the Osage Indians along the river which bears their name.

When Jefferson acquired Louisiana from Napoleon, Lisa became an enthusiastic and sincere American; before Lewis and Clark had returned from their exploration, Lisa was preparing an expedition to enter the territory in their footsteps; and after establishing Fort Lisa at the mouth of the Big Horn River, he returned to St. Louis and organized the Missouri Fur Company.

William Clark, who was made a general in the United States Army and placed in charge of the Indian territories as a reward for his services in the expedition to the Pacific, recognized Lisa's great abilities at once. When the War of 1812 broke out, Clark appointed Lisa as subagent for all the Indian tribes of the Upper Missouri; and it was largely through the clever trader's work that many of the northern tribes were kept either neutral or on the side of the United States, despite the efforts of British agents to inflame the natives against Americans.

In Lisa's fifteen years of trading in the Northwest he made at least twelve trips up and down the Missouri, a record that could not have meant less than twenty-five thousand miles of arduous river travel. Many of his winters were spent in the frozen north country, where his strenuous activities were the despair of his competitors. More than once they conspired to keep him out of the Indian territory by reporting his allegedly unscrupulous acts to the federal authorities at St. Louis. The reports may well have been partly true, for Lisa doubtless found it necessary to fight fire with fire; but so valuable were his services to his adopted country, and so shrewd was his defense of his actions, that he remained until his death the king of the early traders.

In a letter to General Clark, resigning his commission as subagent after the War of 1812, Lisa proved himself a shrewd advocate in his own defense. His explanation of the attacks against him might well have served as a guidebook on how to get along with Indians:

"I have had some success as a trader; and this gives rise to many reports. 'Manuel must cheat the government, and Manuel must cheat the Indians, otherwise Manuel could not bring down every summer so many boats loaded with rich furs.'

"Good. My accounts with the government will show whether I receive anything out of which to cheat it. A poor five hundred dollars, as sub-agent salary, does not buy the tobacco which I annually give to those who call me father.

"'Cheat the Indians!' The respect and friendship which they

have for me, the security of my possessions in the heart of their country, respond to this charge, and declare with voices louder than the tongues of men that it cannot be true.

" 'But Manuel gets so much rich fur!' Well, I will explain how I get it. First, I put into my operations great activity; I go a great distance, while some are considering whether they will start today or tomorrow. I impose upon myself great privations; ten months in the year I am buried in the forest, at a vast distance from my own house. I appear as the benefactor, and not as the pillager, of the Indians. I carried among them the seed of the large pompion, from which I have seen in their possession the fruit weighing 160 pounds. Also the large bean, the potato, the turnip; and these vegetables now make a comfortable part of their subsistence, and this year I have promised to carry the plough. Besides, my blacksmiths work for them incessantly, charging nothing. I lend them traps, only demanding preference in their trade. My establishments are the refuge of the weak and of the old men no longer able to follow their lodges; and by these means I have acquired the confidence and friendship of these nations, and the consequent choice of their trade.

"These things I have done and I propose to do more. The Aricaras, the Mandans, the Gros Ventres, and the Assiniboines find themselves near the establishment of Lord Selkirk upon the Red River. They can communicate with it in two or three days. The evils of such communication will strike the minds of all persons, and it is for those who can handle the pen to dilate upon them. For me I go to form another establishment to counteract the one in question, and shall labor to draw upon us the esteem of these nations, and to prevent their commerce from passing into the hands of foreigners.

"I regret to have troubled your excellency with this exposition. It is right for you to hear what is said of a public agent, and also to weigh it, and to consider the source from which it comes. In ceasing to be in the employment of the United States, I shall not be less devoted to its interests. I have suffered enough in person and property, under a different government, to know how to appreciate the one under which I now live."

THE JUG OF EMPIRE

WITH the growth of the fur trade and its extension westward into the mountain country, the free trapper and the mountain man played an increasingly important part. Men like Jim Bridger, Jedediah Smith, and Kit Carson were the prototypes of the footloose hunters and trappers who were bound to no company and lived what was perhaps the freest and most untrammeled life known to the world in any age since men first came together in the cave and the squatting place.

Theirs was an occupation and a way of life unique in American history. Their mark is ineradicably established on the western country, not only in the names they gave to the land, but in the Homeric deeds they essayed in its taming. They sought out the mighty mountain passes, the springs, the Indian trails and buffalo paths which were to make feasible the successful passage of the waves of settlers to follow; their hard-won and specialized knowledge made the task of the frontier army far less difficult in the final struggle to wrest the land from its rightful owners.

With the passage of time there grew up among the mountain men and the free trappers a kind of exclusive fraternity of the wilderness, with its own colorful language compounded of French, English, and Spanish, and with a professional slang that was as fascinating as it was baffling to uninitiates.

Expressions that grew out of the practices and customs of their daily toil were usually pithy and terse; they had little use for speech, for their lives were lived in surroundings that made silence a requisite for survival. Like the Indians whose dress and mode of life they copied, they spoke often in sign language; sometimes to avoid attracting the notice of hostile savages, sometimes to avoid alarming the animals they stalked and trapped. Long months of solitude and enforced silence made them taciturn even when in safe surroundings and amiable company, and when they did speak, it was in words direct and to the point.

"Joe, he lost his hair," was their laconic phrase for a friend who had been scalped.

From their practice of staking beaver traps to the bottom of a stream, with a rawhide leading to the surface and tied to a floating twig to mark the spot, came their pithy phrase for "if that's what

91

you mean." "If that's the way your stick floats," said the trappers.

Lurking Indians, ever on the lookout for horses to steal, made it necessary for the trapper to keep his horses tethered and fed on a diet of tree bark, instead of turning them out to graze. "A man'd better count ribs than tracks," was their gruff explanation. If a comrade was killed and left on the prairie, the trappers accepted his fate philosophically. "He was made wolf-meat of," they said, and let it go at that.

Prodigious trenchermen—though they ate without benefit of trenchers—they wasted little time in conversation over their meat. "Toss us another bait," a trapper would call when he wanted a second helping; "this beaver feels like chawin'." Like the nobility of ancient Europe they needed no dining utensils save a sheath knife and their bare hands; and like the savages among whom they lived they included in their menu every kind of food from dried ants to the delicious beaver tail.

The buffalo provided the main items in their diet—because of his omnipresence and relative stupidity, rather than because they preferred his somewhat tough flesh. Elk, antelope, bear, and deer meat were other common items on the wilderness bill of fare. Surprisingly enough, the cat-flavored flesh of the panther—or *painter*, to the trappers—was a favorite, with the meat of fat young dogs running a close second. Since there was always a feast or a famine in the wilds, they soon learned to adopt the Indian custom of fasting for long periods and gorging themselves when meat was plentiful. Snakes, scorpions, rodents, insects, and roots were eaten when necessity demanded, and there were even rare cases of cannibalism, with a slain Indian as the *pièce de résistance*.

When a party of trappers made a kill of buffalo after days of fasting, they flung themselves on the warm carcass with animal-like ferocity. Strips of flesh were hacked off and devoured raw; the skull was split open and the raw brains—a special trapper delicacy—were passed around among the half-famished men. Then, with the first sharp edge taken off their hunger, they proceeded with the butchering of the animal and preparations for a real "buffler feed."

The animal was placed belly down, its four legs extended outward to form a supporting frame, and an incision was made in the hide along the spine. The skin on either side was then flayed loose and spread out as a receptacle for the meat. Such choice bits as the tongue and tenderloins were the trappers' favorite cuts, but the rest of the animal was not allowed to go to waste. From the heavy bones they extracted marrow—trapper's butter, they called it— and the animal's blood was caught in containers. The marrow and blood were later mixed to form a rich soup. The long strips of fat that lay along either side of the buffalo's spine were stripped off, dipped in hot grease, smoked, and hung up to dry. This was the bread of the mountain man; to make a sandwich he had only to place a strip of dried meat between two slices of the smoked "trappers' bread."

Strangest of all the treasure trove found in the bison's huge body were the *boudins*, or small intestines, which the hungry mountain men ripped from the animal and carried with them to their wilderness bivouac. Bloody, and filled with the remainder of the buffalo's last meal, the *boudins* were cut into convenient lengths, wound around sticks, and roasted to the eater's taste over a blazing fire.

The feasting that took place at one of these buffalo barbecues was, according to eyewitnesses, almost impossible to believe. For hours the starved trappers sat devouring such quantities of food that the beholders marveled they did not burst. Delicious baked buffalo tongues, sides of deer and buffalo ribs, buffalo steak and hump, huge lengths of *boudins*, and quantities of blood soup and trappers' bread vanished down their capacious gullets. Such a feast might continue for several days and nights, after which the gorged mountain men set out once again into the wilderness for what might be a meatless period of days or even weeks.

The rigor of their lives kept them always lean and fit, despite the orgies they participated in. They were seldom ill, and even the manifold wounds and injuries incident to their work seldom incapacitated them for any length of time. They often practiced skinning-knife surgery of a horrifying kind in removing arrowheads from a comrade's body; in other cases the barb was allowed to remain imbedded in the flesh until a visit to civilization enabled them to submit to more expert medical aid.

Why they did not succumb to infection is a mystery, for they seldom washed even their bodies, to say nothing of their clothing. When the lice that customarily infested their garments grew too troublesome, they took off their clothes, spread them on an anthill, and let the ants do the rest.

On the rare occasions when one of these wild men of the mountains was seen in civilization, or was encountered by Easterners at some rendezvous, he was often mistaken for an Indian. He had the shy wildness of the red man, his taciturnity in strange surroundings, his dark coppery complexion. The trapper's dress was indistinguishable from that of the Indian: antelope-hide hunting shirt and breeches, with leggings of smoked buffalo hide, perhaps a gay handkerchief tied around his head to hold back the shoulder-length hair, moccasins of buffalo or elk hide, and the ensemble covered with a bright blanket or a tanned buffalo robe. His entire dress was ornamented with beadwork and similar Indian finery.

In the mountain country his "possibles" or "fixin's" consisted usually of a few articles indispensable to his occupation or existence: flint and steel, a blanket or two, a skinning knife, a "bait box" in which to carry beaver musk, rifle, powder horn, bullet pouch, tobacco and pipe, and a small quantity of salt for curing meat. Stretching frames for the hides he secured with his precious traps were kept in camp. A saddle and bridle for his horse completed his meager equipment.

Since trapping was done only in the spring or fall, the men of the mountains came to maintain winter camps, where they whiled away the long snowbound months with feasting, yarn-spinning, and repairing their gear for the coming season. Among their own kind they were less restrained than usual, and in the safety of the camps they relaxed the vigilance they found necessary during their solitary periods. Among them were a few college graduates from eastern universities, although the great majority were illiterates from the backwoods of the frontier. In the long months of idleness these latter were sometimes taught to read and write by their more enlightened fellows. Shakespeare's works were read aloud to appreciative audiences (what they made of these is open to conjecture); stories like *Robinson Crusoe* held the adventurous men of the mountains spellbound; and the few tattered newspapers which came into their hands were passed on until they were worn out.

At winter's end the trappers split up into small groups for the spring hunt; some went alone into the mountain country; others, accompanied by their Indian "wives," set out for the creeks and rivers of the plains. Because of the average trapper's superior economic position, he was much sought after as a husband by the Indian girls of the plain and mountain tribes; even the daughters of chiefs were glad to marry a white man. They were, in many cases, better treated than they might have been among their own people, and sometimes real love matches occurred. Oftener, however, the arrangement was a temporary one which was terminated at the trapper's convenience—sometimes with tragic results, for some of the Indian girls fell deeply in love with their alien mates and committed suicide when they were cast aside.

In late June or July occurred the great event of the trappers' year: the rendezvous. From all the mountain passes, creeks, and rivers of the Northwest came the trappers and their squaws, the native tribes, and the traders from civilization with their long pack trains laden with goods from "outside." Gamblers, eastern authors in search of material, and various camp hangers-on often accompanied the pack train on its journey from St. Louis, Independence, or another remote civilized center.

In some sheltered valley the traders spread their goods out on the green earth and awaited the coming of the fur-laden trappers. As the rendezvous gradually filled with all the motley population of the wilderness, the scene became one of turbulent animation. The picturesque and colorful costumes of the trappers, Indians, and squaws made bright splashes against the somber backdrop of the Big Horn or the Wind River Mountains. Hundreds of horses, mules, and dogs added to the din and confusion, as the celebrating crowds milled about seeking news, greeting old friends, and exchanging accounts of the season's happenings.

A few lucky souls might have letters or packages awaiting them from families in the East; others, rich for the moment, plunged recklessly into the gambling games that were being conducted on every hand. Crowds of whooping trappers gathered about the buffalo-hide poker tables and watched their comrades wager lordly stacks of rich beaver pelts. Liquor ran like water.

For other diversions there were the ancient sport of "wrasslin'," horse races, marksmanship contests, and wild, half-savage dances. Indian drums and the weird sound of native flutes were heard continually as the drunken trappers whirled their drunken squaws in clumsy capers. For trappers in search of a wife to accompany them in their travels, young captive Indian girls were sometimes offered for sale. Others, more interested in replenishing their gear, bought powder, ball, traps, and other necessaries from the traders—always, of course, at outrageous prices.

Many of the men, hungry for the luxuries of civilization after long months in the wilds, paid fantastic sums for sugar, chocolate, and coffee. Tobacco of the coarsest sort was two dollars a pound. But most potent of the trader's arguments was, as usual, his liquor. In exchange for his alcohol he was able to obtain most of the furs offered for sale at a figure highly profitable to himself.

Savage fights, tragic losses, and scenes of revolting debauchery were common at the rendezvous. Yet there was in this odd wilderness pageant a peculiar fascination which brought men back year after year to its tumult, its prodigious follies, its sudden turns of fortune, its color and romance and strange comradeships.

But the days of the mountain men were numbered. Rivermen were learning more and more each season of the mighty Missouri's secrets. Year by year they kept pushing back the head of navigation upstream until at last they reached the mountain country itself and ended forever the romantic era of the lone mountain man and the rendezvous.

Chapter 7

FIREBOAT-THAT-WALKS-ON-THE-WATER

wwwwwwwwwwwwwwwwwwwwwwwwwwwwwwwwwwwwwwwwwwwwwwwwwwwww

"With no ordinary sensations of pride and pleasure, we announce the arrival, this morning, of the elegant STEAMBOAT INDEPEND-ENCE, Captain NELSON, in seven *sailing* days from St. Louis, with passengers, and a cargo of flour, whiskey, sugar, iron, castings, etc., *being the first Steam Boat that ever attempted ascending the Missouri.* The grand *desideratum,* the important fact is now ascertained, *that Steam Boats can safely navigate the Missouri River.*"

That was in the spring of 1819, and half a century later men still were trying to find a way to navigate the river safely. But the *Independence* had proved it was not impossible to navigate, however unsafe it might be; and before the summer of that same year was far advanced, one of the strangest craft ever seen on western waters nosed her way into the Missouri's yellow current.

A United States military mission under the command of Major Stephen H. Long had been commissioned to explore the river, set up army posts along the stream at strategic points, and prepare scientific reports on the country. Four steamboats were to carry the expedition, which included on its roster famous scientists, botanists, and painters as well as military personnel; no fewer than nine keelboats completed the formidable flotilla. But it was the *Western Engineer,* flagship of the expedition, that was calculated to strike terror into the hearts of the simple red men.

A description of this unique craft appeared in the St. Louis *Enquirer* in 1819: "The bow of the vessel exhibits the form of a huge serpent, black and scaly, rising out of the water from under the boat, his head as high as the deck, darted forward, his mouth open, vomiting smoke, and apparently carrying the boat on his back. From under the boat, at its stern, issues a stream of foaming water, dashing violently along. All the machinery is hid. Three small brass field pieces, mounted on wheel carriages, stand on the deck; the boat is ascending the rapid stream at the rate of three miles an hour. Neither wind nor human hands are seen to help her;

97

and to the eye of ignorance, the illusion is complete that a monster of the deep carries her on his back, smoking with fatigue, and lashing the waves with violent exertion."

Small wonder that "Long's Dragon" excited the awe of the savages as she proceeded on her leisurely way up the turbulent Missouri to Council Bluffs! Her three companions were less fortunate. The *Thomas Jefferson* was wrecked on a snag, first of more than four hundred steamers that were to succumb to the Missouri's dangers; the *Expedition* and the *R. M. Johnson* failed to reach the appointed rendezvous and tied up for the winter.

The venture was a decided failure from the point of view of the government, and Congress called for an investigation of the two hundred and fifty thousand dollars that had been expended in financing it. Cholera decimated the troops stationed at the few river posts that were established along the way, and nothing came of the expedition's grandiose plans for a minute exploration to the head of navigation. Major Long indeed was so disgusted that he returned to the East and gave the name of "the Great American Desert" to the country that had so humiliatingly frustrated him— an epithet that the northern plains were some time in living down.

But the experiment had proved one thing to the canny fur traders at St. Louis: steamboats could ascend the river to its upper reaches. Astor's American Fur Company, with its principal headquarters in New York City, was quick to see the financial benefit that would result from steamboat service to its far northern outposts. Pierre Chouteau, a member of the group that managed the St. Louis branch of the company's trade, urged the construction of a specially equipped steamboat for use in the upper valley, and in the summer of 1831 the *Yellowstone*, first of the company's river steamers, set out toward the river for which she was named.

Her maiden voyage carried her only as far as the present site of Pierre, South Dakota, but the following year she reached Fort Union at the mouth of the Yellowstone. George Catlin, the eminent painter of western scenes, was a passenger on this history-making trip, and his account of the fear induced among the Indians by the steamer's appearance is worth reproducing.

"If anything did ever literally astound and astonish the natives, it was the appearance of our steamer, puffing, and blowing, and paddling, and rushing by their villages, which were on the banks of the river. . . . We had on board one twelve-pound cannon and three or four eight-pound swivels, which we were taking up to arm the Fur Company's fort at the mouth of the Yellowstone; and at the approach to every village they were all discharged several times in rapid succession, which threw the inhabitants into utter confusion and amazement.

"Some of them laid their faces to the ground and cried to the Great Spirit; some shot their horses and dogs, and sacrificed them to appease the Great Spirit, whom they conceived was offended; some deserted their villages and ran to the top of the bluff some miles distant; and others, in some places, as the boat landed in front of their villages, came with great caution and peeped over the bank to see the fate of their chiefs, whose duty it was, from the nature of their office, to approach us, whether friends or foes, and to go on board. Sometimes in this plight, they were instantly thrown, neck and heels, over each other's heads and shoulders—men, women and children, and dogs, sage, sachem, old and young—all in a mass, at the frightful discharge of the steam from the escape pipe, which the captain of the boat let loose upon them for his own fun and amusement.

"There were many curious conjectures among their wise men with regard to the nature and powers of the steamboat. Among the Mandans some called it the 'big thunder canoe,' for when some distance below the village they 'saw lightning flash from its sides, and heard the thunder roll from its big pipe.' Others called it the 'big medicine canoe with eyes.' It was 'medicine' or 'mystery,' because they could not understand it; and it must have eyes, said they, for it sees its own way and takes the deep water in the middle of the channel."

The following year, 1833, the company sent the *Yellowstone* upstream with a companion vessel, the *Assiniboine*, and accompanying the expedition was a distinguished European traveler who was to preserve invaluable records of scenes and history on the upper river. Maximilian, Prince of Wied, whose book, *Travels in the Interior of North America*, was a result of this journey, brought with him the gifted artist Karl Bodmer, whose paintings of Indian life, river craft, and early wilderness scenes are among the best available of the vanished steamboat and fur-trading era.

Maximilian, Bodmer, and Catlin were but the forerunners of a long list of distinguished personages who were to visit the upper river valley in the steamboats of the fur companies. Audubon was another famous painter to arrive on the scene in one of the first boats. A notable tosspot as well as a gifted artist, Audubon found an amiable cupmate in Kenneth McKenzie, *bourgeois* of Fort Union. Visitors at the fort remarked that the artist was oftener in his cups than engaged in depicting the wild life of the region.

Once the pioneering work of the American Fur Company had proved the value of the steamboat, the industry grew in a short time to remarkable proportions. It was not many years before a hundred great steamers were plying the river in a single season, making it such a highway of life and movement as must have seemed almost unbelievable in the midst of the untouched wilderness that flanked the stream's banks.

The country along the Mississippi had been fairly well settled before the advent of the steamboat; but along the Missouri there was no white settlement for thousands of miles; and the procession of lordly steamers, laden to their guards with freight and passengers, churned through a solitude where savage men ruled and lived as they had for centuries.

The steamers of the upper river were not the gilded and ornate leviathans of the lower reaches, for they faced difficulties in navigation that made any extra weight or draft out of the question. The average boat measured about two hundred and twenty feet in length, thirty-five feet in width, and carried five hundred tons of freight. She was built with a flat bottom and was of shallow draft, drawing about three feet of water empty and about four feet when laden. And sometimes even that was too much, for the tricky Missouri, filled with shifting sandbars, kept the boat walking on her stilts half the time.

That great skeptic, H. L. Mencken, has related in his memoirs that he was forty years old before he learned that it was actually a fact that Missouri steamers had stilts. As a lad he had been told, along with several other boys, of steamers that climbed over sand-bars; and he and the other boys promptly decided that the gentle-man who told them this whopper was the biggest liar they had ever met. But the Missouri boats did have stilts, and used them, too. The rivermen had a name for this odd practice. They called it "grasshoppering," and one of the early river captains has explained why:

"When she became lodged on a bar, the spars were raised and set in the river bottom, like posts, their tops inclined somewhat toward the bow. Above the line of the deck each was rigged with a tackle-block over which a manila cable was passed, one end be-ing fastened to the gunwale of the boat and the other end wound around the capstan. As the capstan was turned and the paddle-wheel revolved, the boat was thus lifted and pushed forward. Then the spars were re-set farther ahead and the process repeated until the boat was at last lifted over the bar. From the grotesque re-semblance to a grasshopper which the craft bore when her spars were set, and from the fact that she might be said to move for-ward in a series of hops, the practice came to be called grass-hoppering."

One amusing story of the shallow Missouri concerns a steamer that was attempting to grasshopper its way over a sandbar in the fashion described. Her engines were straining, her paddlewheels churning madly, and every member of the crew was holding his breath as the vessel crept inch by inch over the bar. A "wood-hawk" living in a solitary cabin on the riverbank chose this moment to come down to the stream's edge for a pail of water. As he turned away with a brimming pail, his action caught the captain's eye.

"Hey," roared the fuming skipper, "you put that water back!"

EVEN Mark Twain, who loved the Mississippi as a mother, was obliged to confess that Missouri pilots were in a class by them-selves. The difficulties of navigating the Mississippi were as noth-ing compared to the problems posed by the Big Muddy, with its treacherously shifting channel, its lethal "sawyers," and its in-numerable sandbars. And Missouri pilots had frequently to per-

101

form their piloting miracles while dodging Sioux bullets that zipped through the walls of the pilothouses.

Running the Missouri at night was out of the question and even in the daytime there was scarcely an instant when the pilot dared lift his hand from the wheel. As the editor of the Sioux City, Iowa, *Register* wrote in 1868: "Of all the variable things in creation the most uncertain are the action of a jury, the state of a woman's mind, and the condition of the Missouri River." The mournful cry of the leadsman was seldom heard on the Smoky Water; instead of a lead, a sounding pole manned from the boat's bow was sufficient to plumb the depths of this shallow river. And often the pilot needed nobody to tell him the stream's depth, for he could feel the boat's timbers scraping the bottom beneath. Missouri boats, because of the shallow water and frequent bars, were not rigid craft; often the timbers of a steamer would bend and yield as much as two feet in crawling over a bar.

The crew of an upper river steamboat numbered usually from thirty to forty men, many of them ex-keelboatmen whose profession had vanished with the advent of steam-powered craft. Taken all in all, they were as hard a lot as their predecessors on the river, and it took a tough captain and mate to keep them in any semblance of order. The logs of the old steamers give ample evidence that human life was held cheap by the masters of the boats and that discipline was maintained by methods reminiscent of the flogging days of the sailing ships.

One steamer sent two men out in a yawl to sound a passage on a stormy day. The yawl overturned and the unlucky two were drowned. "We recovered the yawl," says the ship's log laconically. A short time later the captain again ordered the small boat out for soundings and the men, quite understandably, refused to go. "But," remarks the ship's chronicler, "a club soon brought them to their milk." On another day the logkeeper casually reported that the boat's engineer had brained one of his helpers with a wrench. And on the occasion of a brief stop to bury one of the chambermaids who had died, he closed his entry with the remark: "She makes the fifth one we have lost so far on this trip."

In the early years of the steamboat traffic each boat could make only one trip a season, and each journeyed only to its own company's upriver post. The annual departure from St. Louis was a momentous and gala event. There were often a hundred or more passengers bound for the Indian country on various errands. Missionaries, generals, traders, clerks, *engagés,* perhaps a painter and a scientist or two; delegations of Indians returning from visits to Washington or St. Louis; almost certainly a couple of gamblers, immaculate and soft-spoken, who would disembark quietly after a few days and take the next boat back to civilization with well-filled pockets; buckskin-clad hunters, trappers, and traders with long flowing hair; and soldiers bound for the frontier outposts.

A final drunken brawl lasting for several days was customary for the crew and the rougher element among the passengers. Then, with a salute of cannon and a rattle of musketry, the steamer cast off her lines and stood out into the river for the long summer's voyage.

Once the drinkers had recovered from their hangovers and the forecastle was cleared, the interest of all on board was occupied for several days with a contest among the crew for the championship of the boat. Butting, kicking, biting, and gouging, with no holds barred, the merry roustabouts persisted until one of them had conquered the rest, whereupon the winner was awarded a red sash and the title of "King of the River." Frequently it was an honor earned at the expense of an ear, several teeth, or even an eye. "A more bull dog affair no one need wish to see," was the opinion of an old river captain who witnessed a grudge fight between two of these river roughnecks.

The coming of the steamboat created difficult situations for some of the officials of the upriver posts who had married into Indian tribes for purposes of improving trade relations—or for less mercenary reasons. Now that such novel and elaborate means of transportation were available, many of the officials' wives wished to take a trip into the wilderness to see the romantic outposts where their husbands spent so many months of their time.

A letter addressed to one of these gentlemen is preserved in the "Fort Pierre Letter Book": "Mrs. Picotte and Mrs. Kipp have intimated to me their intention of coming up in the steamboat. I have no doubt that your lady when she hears it, will also wish to come, and as there is every possibility of her doing so, would it not be well for you to dispense with the society of at least some of your present companions?"

At the upper river posts the annual arrival of the steamboat was an event of even greater moment than its departure from St. Louis. All through the long winter and the early months of spring the men of the fort awaited the coming of the boat with its news of civilization, its fresh faces from the outside world, its load of supplies for the next season. When, on some unexpected day, she hove in sight at last, black smoke pouring from her funnels and shrill blasts echoing from her 'scape pipes, the sleepy atmosphere of the post became one of anthill activity. The fort's cannon fired a resounding salute which the steamer answered; the boat, crowded to her guards with curious passengers who waved greetings, made for the landing; and from all the buildings of the post swarmed the picturesque company of the fort—Indians, trappers, storekeepers, artisans, clerks. And the dignified *bourgeois* of the post was not often the last of the rush.

But all too brief were these glimpses of another world to the lonely men of the upriver posts. A few days, at most, were all that could be spared before the boat must cast off and be back on her way downstream. A sudden fall in the river might trap her upstream and force her to stay until the following spring; hence little time was wasted in unloading the cargo, acquainting the *bourgeois* with his necessary instructions, and reloading the vessel with the year's catch of furs.

While officials of the company entertained each other at unaccustomed banquets of rare delicacies brought in from St. Louis, the *engagés* and roustabouts worked 24-hour shifts making the transfer of goods and cargo. A last celebration aboard the steamer marked the completion of the work, and the steamer stood out once more into midstream for the race against the falling river back to St. Louis. The post, after this brief contact with the brilliant world outside, settled down again for another year of toil and blizzard and danger and terrible isolation.

FIREBOAT-THAT-WALKS-ON-THE-WATER

IT WAS the mischievous red man who caused the upper river pilots their uneasiest moments. The record of three consecutive days, picked at random from the log of the *Robert Campbell's* voyage from St. Louis to Fort Benton, will give some notion of the pilots' troubles when the Sioux were in an ugly temper.

Sunday, July 5, 1863.—Weighed anchor at daylight. Had just gotten under way when the Indians fired on us, but done no serious injury to anyone, but frightened some few. We lay abreast of the *Shreveport* last night, about twenty-five yards distant. *Shreveport* had landed to wood when the Sioux made a charge, but the captain cut the line and backed out. We fixed a breastwork, ran by, saw none of the red devils. Had to spar some today. Anchored 9:30 p.m.

Monday, July 6, 1863.—Weighed anchor at daylight. The whole country was on fire last night, but a heavy shower came up and spoiled Mr. Injun's fun. They are on all sides of us and some rare sport may be expected soon. Weather cool. River falling. Landed at wood pile. . . . Made very fair time today. Anchored on a bar.

Tuesday, July 7, 1863.—Got our anchor aboard and left at daylight. Weather beautiful. River falling. *Shreveport* ahead. Saw no signs of Indians this morning until 11 a.m., when a large war party was discovered on the south bank. They were in the timber and wanted to come on board. The yawl containing seven men was sent on shore. When it landed some jumped in and shook hands and others fired and killed three men and wounded another. Yawl returned; both boats instantly opened fire on them, killing and wounding several of them. They beat a hasty retreat.

The steamer's log does not tell the whole story of the "Battle of the Two Boats," however, for the excellent reason that the captain of the boat, Joseph La Barge, was to blame for the trouble.

Alexander Culbertson, famous fur trader from Fort Benton, was aboard the *Campbell* at the time and warned Captain La Barge that any attempt to send the yawl ashore would mean a fight, but La Barge stubbornly insisted on sending the men ashore to meet the Indians.

The warriors approached the yawl with gestures of friendship; several climbed into the boat and sat waiting for the men to cast off for the return trip to the steamer; others on the bank watched the white men narrowly. Suddenly a brave notched an arrow to his bow and took aim at the men in the yawl. He was fired on from the steamer and the battle was on. An Indian drove his lance into the body of the nearest white man in the prow of the yawl; two others of the crew were mortally hit by bullets and a third was seriously wounded. The steersman dived overboard and, keeping the yawl between him and the Indians on shore, swam out toward the steamer, pulling the boat along with him.

The war party disappeared as the *Campbell* made her way upstream toward Fort Union, which she reached on July 9, two days later. They dared not go ashore for either wood or food. "Buffalo plenty," wrote the logkeeper, "but the Indians are too bad for us to kill any." And at the fort itself, "The Sioux are around here so that the people at the fort dare not go out to hunt." A report, probably quite exaggerated, that they had killed twenty-eight Indians and wounded forty-seven in the "Battle of the Two Boats" brought only this fervent comment from the keeper of the *Campbell's* log: "Hope it is true!"

FIREWOOD was a continual worry on the upper river, especially during those times when the Indians were on the warpath and lurking in the timbered bottoms along the banks. The average steamer burned from twenty to thirty cords of wood daily; cottonwood, though not a particularly good fuel, was most abundant and formed the principal firewood used on the river. In cases of serious shortage driftwood was sometimes gathered. Abandoned forts, posts, or other buildings along the river's banks were torn down and used for firewood by the first steamboat to pass by—a practice which accounts for the fact that virtually all of the once unnumbered outposts are completely vanished today; even the sites of many of them are unknown.

During the early voyages wooding was done by the boat's crew, but with the growth of river traffic professional "woodhawks" began to appear along the banks to establish woodyards where stands of timber were heaviest. Theirs was a perilous life. It was a common occurrence for a steamboat to put in at a woodyard and find the hawks dead and scalped, and the surrounding timber infested with savages who were prepared to inflict the same fate on any who ventured ashore.

Yet the savagery was not all on one side. One of the early woodhawks on the upper river was George Grinnell, who located near the post of Fort Union. He came originally from Maryland, served as a spy for the Union forces in the Civil War under General Philip H. Sheridan, and was honorably discharged from the Army of the Potomac. In 1865 he traveled with a military wagon train over the prairies from Fort Snelling in Minnesota to Dakota Territory, which was only then beginning to be opened up for settlement.

Settling near the mouth of Dry Fork Creek, he became a woodhawk and solitary wilderness dweller who hunted in winter along the Missouri or made brief gold-seeking forays into the nearby hills during the slack of the steamboat season. He took to drink and became surly and antisocial, soured perhaps by his bleak life. And somewhere in his wanderings he met and acquired Josephine.

Josephine was a slim and appealing half-breed girl, talented and educated far above the station of her red ancestors—and, for that matter, far above the station of George Grinnell. But in that day and society she was a squaw nonetheless, and with Grinnell she lived a life of drudgery, abuse, and terror.

She may have loved George Grinnell. Or, more likely, she was too afraid of his drunken beatings to dare attempt to leave him. At any rate she lived with him, bore him a son, and suffered his curses and abuse for five years. Even in the rough community of the frontier, Josephine had the sympathy of the better element.

One day Grinnell came home from a nearby post and attacked his wife brutally, beating her about the head with the butt of his pistol. She wrenched herself free and fled toward a clearing where several settlers were breaking land. Grinnell, too intoxicated to pursue her afoot, mounted his horse and rode the frightened girl down in a field, where he toppled from his horse in his struggle with her.

For several minutes they wrestled together on the ground. The settlers came running to the girl's aid, but before they could intervene, Grinnell stiffened and lay still.

107

While they raised the girl to her feet, one of them examined the fallen man. George Grinnell was dead. A watch had been suspended from his neck by a sliding leather thong; in the struggle Josephine had clung to this, and Grinnell had died of strangulation.

With the hard practicality of the frontiersman, one of the settlers said simply, "Let's go get a drink."

At the tiny settlement nearby a coroner's jury held a brief inquest over the body. Their verdict was laconic and legally unique. It said merely that "George Grinnell came to his death through an act of Almighty God, by the hand of His agent, Josephine Grinnell."

IN THE month of June 1837 the American Fur Company's steamboat *St. Peters* came upstream on her annual voyage, laden with a cargo such as the Indian country had never seen. Aboard her were several cases of smallpox.

These cases could have been isolated, but the company officials were negligent. The Indians insisted on boarding the boat, because they knew she carried goods for them, and at Fort Clark a Mandan Indian made away with a blanket infected with the dread smallpox virus. Farther upriver at Fort Union an attempt was made to keep the Indians at a distance; but the red men, knowing of old the ways of government officials, feared they were to be defrauded of their goods and refused to scatter over the prairie as they were advised. Next, the commander of a company fort, one Jacob Halsey, decided to vaccinate the assembled Indians and "have it all over in time for the Fall trade."

It did not occur to this amateur practitioner that it might be dangerous to inoculate the previously unexposed Indians with material taken directly from the cases aboard the steamboat. Picture, then, his innocent surprise when twenty-seven squaws out of thirty he had "vaccinated" fell ill with particularly malignant and fatal forms of the disease. Possessing no racial immunity to smallpox, they succumbed to the disease sometimes within twenty-four hours. The infected survivors fled in every direction from the fort. Terror-stricken and unaware that quarantine or isolation was the only hope for the remaining Indians, they carried the disease far and wide to yet uninfected tribes and villages.

When in late summer the epidemic had run its course, seventeen thousand Indians had perished among the tribes of the upper valley: Blackfeet, Assiniboins, Mandans, Arikaras, Crows, and Sioux. The villages of the friendly Mandans were reduced to thirty families. The Sioux, who were more hostile and so more widely scattered, suffered least of the northern plains tribes.

An eyewitness to this terrible disaster reported: "The atmosphere, for miles, is poisoned by the stench of the hundreds of carcasses unburied. The women and children are wandering in groups without food, or howling over the dead. The men are flying in every direction. The proud, warlike, and noble-looking Blackfeet are no more. Their deserted lodges are seen on every hill. No sound but the raven's croak and the wolf's howl breaks the solemn stillness. The scene of desolation is appalling beyond the power of imagination to conceive."

Large numbers of Indians, believing the disease to be a visitation of the evil spirits upon them for their sins, drowned their wives and children and then plunged into the river themselves. A grimly human touch was recorded by another observer: "Many of the handsome Arickarees, who had recovered, seeing the disfiguration of their features, committed suicide; some by throwing themselves from rocks, others by stabbing and shooting. The prairie has become a graveyard; its wild flowers bloom over the sepulchres of Indians."

This decimation of the northern tribes struck the fur trade a ruinous blow, for it left few fur gatherers among the Indians to carry on the far-flung trapping and hunting activities the trade entailed. More effectively than by force of arms, the Indians' power was broken—for purposes of war as well as peaceful commerce—and the way was further opened for an increase in the white man's penetration of the river's upper reaches.

As THE steamboat traffic increased on the upper river and knowledge of the wild Missouri's devious ways grew, the steamers were able to penetrate farther and farther upstream. For many years

Fort Union at the mouth of the Yellowstone remained the farthest point of navigation; this was gradually extended into Montana until, in 1859, Captain John La Barge drove the *Chippewa* within fifteen miles of Fort Benton—3560 miles from the sea and 2565 feet above sea level! No vessel in the world's history had ever accomplished such a feat. The next few years saw the head of navigation moved to Fort Benton itself, and in 1866 the *Peter Balen* forced her way thirty-six miles above the fort, the farthest point any steamboat was ever to reach.

The decline of the fur trade had begun in 1832 when the beaver hat went suddenly out of fashion; the smallpox epidemic of 1837 made further inroads into it; later the increasingly hostile attitude of the Indians and the outbreak of the Civil War threatened to end permanently the romantic era of the steamboat on the river's upper waters. Without an active fur trade there was no need for the steamboat traffic. But the discovery of a new kind of wealth in the northwest wilderness made the steamboat more useful than ever. For in southern Montana, near the extreme headwaters of the mighty Missouri, men had begun to prospect for gold.

It was on Gold Creek between the present cities of Helena and Missoula that François Finlay, also called "Benetsee," made the first strike in 1856. John White struck it rich on Grasshopper Creek—the future site of the town of Bannack—in 1862. A party prospecting along a tiny creek in 1863 came upon one of the richest bonanzas in the history of placer mining—the famous Alder Gulch deposits; within two years more than ten thousand miners had rushed to the diggings, and the town of Virginia City was one of the flourishing gold camps of the West. A year later John Cowan made the strike of Last Chance Gulch where the city of Helena now stands, and the rush to the Montana fields was on in earnest.

The languishing steamboat trade on the upper river came into its own again and in the space of five years had reached tremendous proportions. Fort Benton, within a few hundred miles of all the richest gold strikes, became overnight a great inland seaport. For a thousand miles through the unpeopled wilderness of Dakota and Montana the surface of the river was flecked with graceful boats bound upstream with freight and passengers for the gold camps.

Hiram Chittenden has given us a vivid portrait of the upper river scene in these gold-rush days: "To one set down in the unbroken wilderness, it would have seemed marvelous and wholly inexplicable to find this river filled with noble craft, as beautiful as any that ever rode the ocean, stored with all the necessaries of civilization, and crowded with passengers as cultured, refined and well-dressed as the cabin list of an ocean steamer. Certainly here was a most extraordinary scene, flashed for a moment before the world and then withdrawn forever. . . .

"Some statistics have survived showing the magnitude of the steamboat business on the river during those years. In the year 1865, 1,000 passengers, 6,000 tons of merchandise, and 20 quartz mills went to Benton. In the year 1867, 40 steamboats had passed Sioux City before June 1 on their way upriver, carrying over 12,000 tons of freight, most of it for Benton. In 1866, one boat, the *Luella,* carried downstream $1,250,000 worth of gold dust. The profits of a successful voyage were enormous. In 1866: the *St. John,* $17,000; the *Tacony,* $16,000; the *W. J. Lewis,* $40,000; the *Peter Balen,* $65,000. Freight rates from St. Louis to Benton were 12¢ a pound. The fare for cabin passengers was $300. The master of the boat got $200 a month; the clerk, $150; the mate and engineer each $125. But the pilots received as high as $1200 a month."

Boom prices in the river trade were reflected in the prices charged at the teeming gold camps of the territory. The *Montana Post* in 1865 reported that "Tom White has reduced the price of a bath to $1.50 and states that he is determined to bring it down to the lowest possible figure." In the year 1867 it was estimated that rents were higher in Helena—which, by the way, once boasted more millionaires per capita than any city in America—than in New York City's downtown district.

Shortages of supplies, as well as shrewd corners on the local market, sometimes sent prices to fantastic heights. Flour sold at eighty dollars a sack in one camp during a temporary shortage;

in another, angry miners seized the available supply and rationed it at what they deemed a fair price, rather than submit to the extortionate charges of the owners of the stock.

Distant as the camps were from any fountainhead of law and order, it was inevitable that crime should flourish and the wicked prosper. Shootings, stabbings, robbery, and road-agentry grew apace as the scum of the western population flocked to the gold towns. Brawls, bred of bad liquor and the fact that every man carried a gun, produced an average of a murder a day in some of the camps. Saloons picturesquely named the Miner's Delight, the Nugget, and the Eldorado vied with each other to attract the trade of well-heeled miners on the loose. Gambling and the attractions of prostitutes were features of many of the saloons; others added "reading rooms" to draw the trade of news-hungry prospectors who might not have seen a newspaper for months. Over one of these rooms, in Helena, was this sign: "Don't forget to write home to your dear old mother. She is thinking of you. We furnish paper and envelopes free, and have the best whiskey in town."

In the early 60's there came into southwestern Montana a soft-spoken, mild-mannered gentleman named Henry Plummer, who in due time became a leading citizen and was elected sheriff of Alder Gulch. The gulch needed a sheriff, too. In the space of a few months more than one hundred men had been waylaid and robbed or murdered; the criminals seemed to possess an uncanny sense of where and when to strike to obtain the richest hauls and avoid the forces of the law.

Mr. Plummer's qualifications for his office were not too carefully examined; it was neither polite nor healthy to inquire too closely into the past of men in the mining camps, even though they sang,

> Oh, what was your name in the States?
> Was it Thompson or Johnson or Bates?
> Did you murder your wife
> And fly for your life?
> Say, what was your name in the States?

FIREBOAT-THAT-WALKS-ON-THE-WATER

But so bold and arrogant did the gang, known as the Innocents, finally become that honest citizens began to look askance at Mr. Plummer and his pretensions as a law officer. A bit of detective work soon brought the truth to light: Henry Plummer was a notorious desperado who had previously been run out of half a dozen western towns and was himself the leader of the Innocents.

As a youth, he had murdered a man in California but was pardoned in the mistaken belief that he was dying of tuberculosis. Instead of taking to his bed, Plummer embarked upon a career of robbery and murder that soon made California too hot to hold him. Fleeing to Washington, the ingenious desperado sent back to California a faked account of his death which successfully covered his tracks for a time. It was shortly after his "death" in Washington that he turned up in Montana and organized the Innocents, undoubtedly the most murderous band of cutthroats that ever terrorized a western community.

Among his henchmen was the notorious Joseph Slade, whose bloody record of violence and murder had made his name feared all through the West. Another was Boone Helm, a degenerate savage from Kentucky, who was not only a murderer but a cannibal as well, according to well-authenticated accounts. Such tough killers as Whiskey Bill Graves, George Ives, Red Yeager, and Buck Stinson were other gunmen who followed Plummer's secret leadership.

Hanging out in mountain hideouts which they called "she-bangs," the gang learned through Sheriff Plummer all the inside information concerning gold shipments and other likely hauls passing out of the mining country. And Plummer saw to it that the forces of the law were far away whenever the gang was about to make a raid on a bullion-laden stagecoach or a group of dust-rich miners in some lonely mountain pass.

Even when the facts became known to the honest element among the miners it was difficult to get men to act, for so well organized and so feared were the Innocents that many were afraid to join the Vigilantes who planned the destruction of the mob.

A leak in the Vigilantes' plans would have meant instant death to the men involved.

But the plan went off without a hitch. A few swift forays and the gang was effectively broken. A mass hanging of six men in Virginia City was enlivened by the comments of Boone Helm, last of the six to stretch rope. "There goes another one to hell," Helm would comment, as his pals were one by one strung up before him. When at last his own turn came, he shouted like a true Southerner: "Every man for his principles! Hurrah for Jeff Davis!"

In all, the Vigilantes sent to the gallows more than twenty desperadoes of the band of Innocents, including Henry Plummer, the suave leader, and the murderous Joseph Slade, who died weeping on his knees and begging for his life. The camps were made safe for honest miners once more, and the great fleets of river steamboats continued to pour men and supplies into the Montana mining country.

But this was the last great resurgence of steamer traffic on the Upper Missouri. The westward movement of the railroads cut off the steamboat trade relentlessly, as their railheads crept farther and farther upstream. As supply boats for the military in the campaigns of the 70's against the Sioux and Nez Percé Indians, the river boats experienced a brief revival and wrote a last brilliant chapter in the history of the northern plains. But with the coming of the railroads their usefulness was ended.

Today not a single steamer plies the waters of the Upper Missouri where three quarters of a century ago they were queens of the upriver trade. There is no river traffic, for that matter. The iron horse has supplanted the steamboat as completely as the steamboat supplanted the keelboat of an earlier vanished day.

Chapter 8

THE FOUNDING FATHERS

∿∿

"What do we want with this vast worthless area, this region of savages and wild beasts, of shifting sands and whirlwinds of dust, of cactus and prairie dogs? To what use could we ever put these great deserts or endless mountain ranges, impenetrable and covered to their base with eternal snow?"

It is not unlikely that these words of Daniel Webster, and of others who believed as he did, had something to do with the haphazard and reckless fashion in which the American nation dissipated the wealth of its western public domain. Whatever the cause, the immense folly of our public land policy and the wastage of the national substance began almost before the ink was dry on the Declaration of Independence. That policy, with all its attendant evils, was not to come to an end until the last of all our "vast worthless area" was expended—too often under a tragically misguided system of sale, gift, or distribution whose effects it may take decades to undo. If, indeed, the harm can ever be undone.

Beginning in 1776, land warrants were issued by the states to veterans of America's armies in partial compensation for their services to the nation. The warrants were transferable, and most of the soldiers sold them at a discount to land speculators who profited mightily in later years.

Following the Mexican War, bounty warrants with a face value of a dollar and a quarter an acre were purchasable for as little as fifty cents an acre. Eastern speculators obtained huge areas of the public domain during the 50's and 60's, and in the westward rush that followed the Civil War they were able to dispose of their holdings at prices ranging up to ten dollars an acre. Hundreds of thousands of acres of the public lands passed out of the people's hands into the hands of the speculators; in exchange the government got nothing at all, and the soldiers whom the warrants were supposed to aid often received only a fraction of their value. Fraud and forgery were widespread; during one boom period fraudulent

warrants for more than a million acres of public land were in circulation.

The Preemption Act of 1841 did little to remedy the situation.
The head of a family, a widow, or a single man over twenty-one
could obtain title to 160 acres of the public domain—provided
the claimant built a dwelling place on the land, made adequate
proof of settlement, and otherwise complied with the government's
regulations. He was obliged to swear that he had never obtained
a preemption grant previously; that he did not own 320 acres in
any other state or territory; that his intention was not to sell the
land; and that he had no commitment of any sort to transfer his
claim to anyone else. He was then allowed to buy the claim at its
appraised value—a dollar and a quarter an acre was the usual
price.

This open invitation to loot the lands of the American people
was even less successful, from the public's point of view, than the
infamous warrant system had been. There was no practicable
means of making sure that the claimant had furnished truthful
replies to the government's questions. And the vast distances of
many of the claims from any government land office made it
highly inconvenient for the federal officials to verify the declaration that a dwelling had actually been erected and that the claimant was really living on the land.

Every professional witness and perjurer within traveling distance of any land office found offers for his services, once the
loopholes in the Preemption Act became apparent to land-greedy
speculators. Often there was not even a pretense of taking up
residence after the required oath had been sworn. Speculators employed rascals by the dozens to preempt and later deed the land
back to them.

Some preemptors went to fantastic extremes to defraud the
government. Portable houses mounted on wheels were constructed
and hauled from claim to claim, so that witnesses could honestly
swear that they had seen a bona fide dwelling house on the prem-
ises. The size of the dwelling was set at a minimum of "twelve by
twelve" feet by some land offices, and canny preemptors were
known to build tiny houses twelve *inches* square and then swear

116

roundly that they had constructed a dwelling "twelve by twelve" on the property.

Preemption was still the method by which the public domain was being carved away in great slashes when the first claims were filed in the land of the Dacotahs. The Western Town Company of Dubuque, Iowa, tried as early as 1856 to establish a townsite near the present city of Sioux Falls; but the red men promptly gave them orders to decamp, and the Iowa boomers returned to Sioux City. The following year, however, they were back again and established a claim of 320 acres. A second group, the Dakota Land Company, took possession of a half section in the same area. This company, chartered by the Minnesota legislature and headed by the governor of Minnesota Territory, gave the name of Sioux Falls City to their imaginary metropolis—which became the first permanent white settlement in South Dakota.

In 1858, a scant two years later, a visitor to the area wrote: "We soon began to look about for locations, but found that lands for a long distance in all directions were claimed and foundations for log cabins already on the ground." This was, of course, in direct violation of the Preemption Act. The Iowa and Minnesota companies hoped to secure control of the lands surrounding their townsites; then when the influx of settlers began, the holders of the properties would reap a profitable harvest.

But it did not work out that way in most cases. There was a tendency on the part of latecomers to dispute the validity of these fraudulently owned preemptions; many of them settled on the filed lands and later successfully defended their claims in court. Others successfully defended them by force of arms. When the Indian treaty of 1858 threw the lands open to white settlement and the big rush into what is now southeastern South Dakota began in 1859, the warfare was for a time open and bloody; but in the end the smaller settlers won—despite the fact that many frauds and highhanded thefts of public land went unpunished.

The Homestead Act of May 1862 gave a tremendous impetus to the flood of emigrants that was already pouring westward. This new measure gave to every man or woman, competent or incompetent, 160 acres of the public domain absolutely free, save for a nominal filing fee of eighteen dollars. The red tempest of the Civil War hampered the full operation of the law during the first few years after its enactment, but once the great national storm was over, a virtual army of homesteaders made their way in successive migrations toward the free western lands that stretched away untenanted to the base of the Rockies.

THE huge territory of Dakota, organized in 1861, originally included not only the present states of Montana and North and South Dakota, but slices of several neighboring states as well. It covered three hundred and fifty thousand square miles and was the largest territorial organization in the United States. Its total population, aside from Indians and mixed-bloods, was 2402 persons—an average of a fraction of one white settler for every one hundred square miles!

But these early empire builders had a fierce faith in their country's future and, in certain cases, eminently practical suggestions for causing the land to grow and prosper. Moses K. Armstrong, a member of the first territorial legislature, has left an account of one such suggestion:

"My seat was near a frontier member and desperado, by the name of Jim Somers, who some years afterward was shot dead for jumping a claim near Chamberlain. He was a giant in frame and as daring as an Indian. On one occasion he got on the warpath in Yankton, and rode on horseback into a saloon and shot the sheriff. I remember vividly the only speech Jim made in the legislature. It was short, but full of fire and threats of vengeance against all who should dare to vote against his bill legalizing marriages between white men and squaws. Jim and his cannon were both loaded that morning, when he arose with blood in his eye, and swore that he would blow out all the brains of the assembled lawmakers if they killed his bill. He declared that what Dakota needed was less brains and more children, and he struck his fist on the desk and moved that the legislature adjourn and take Indian wives and go out populating the country."

In the far western part of the territory, at the time this oration on eugenics was being delivered, there was coming into being an even more cogent reason why the country was soon to be populated. The rich gold strikes in the Montana country were being made, and men were flocking to the new camps by the thousands. And to the south, on the battlefields of the Civil War, was occurring a curious circumstance that was to have a permanent effect on the history of the Northwest.

Grant, the stubborn besieger, was hammering at the gates of Vicksburg. Inside the city, under the command of the Confederate General Pemberton, were thirty thousand Southern troops who on July 4, 1863, laid down their arms and surrendered to the Northern forces. Grant, instead of taking them prisoner, exacted an oath that they would never again take up arms against the Union, and then released them. Since most of the Southerners' homes were in territory occupied by Federal forces, they were unable to return to their domiciles; thousands of them went northwest to the newly discovered gold fields, prospered, and became "galvanized Yankees."

The state of Montana has been strongly Democratic ever since, thanks to these settlers from Pemberton's army, and also to thousands of other Southern soldiers who took the same way out when captured on other battlefields. Indeed, when Montana was made a part of Idaho Territory in 1863, before it became a territory in its own right, the federal judge was forced to exert his official powers to prevent the transplanted Confederates from naming the principal town of the territory after the wife of Jefferson Davis!

But in eastern Dakota, in the early 60's, there was nothing to attract the gold-seeking Southerners, and the present states of North and South Dakota were settled largely by land-seekers of Northern extraction. William Jayne, the territory's first governor, had been Abraham Lincoln's personal physician in Springfield, Illinois; he was rewarded with the post of governor almost immediately after Lincoln's first inauguration. Unlike many of his successors, he proved to be an excellent administrator. An item, tantalizingly brief, which appeared in a territorial newspaper of the time indicates that he understood the temper of his constituents and how to deal with them in the approved frontier fashion: "A real executive fist fight took place last night, at the Hotel d'Ash, between the governor and Hon. Jesse Wherry, late receiver of the land office. Hair-pulling, choking, striking, blood-spitting, and pugilistic exercises were the order, which were performed with grit and relish."

In the files of the territory's early newspapers, by the way, one can find traces of an interstate rivalry and bitterness that has all but disappeared today—except perhaps in California and Florida. Iowa editors were allegedly guilty of dissuading emigrants from settling in Dakota, and Dakota's frontier newspapermen made the ink fly over this dastardly practice:

Northern Iowa hates southern Dakota as the devil hates daylight. Why? Not because we ever abused or slandered that state or in any way spoke disrespectfully of its people. Still, all the little hungry newspapers along the line of the Fort Dodge and Marshalltown road are continually howling in the ears of immigrants the most pitiful lies concerning the "barren, desolate, God-forsaken land of Dakota." We cannot see why the grumbling denizens of the wind-warped and clapboard towns of Iowa should borrow so much trouble about Dakota and her people, unless it be because we are independent enough to mind our own business and refuse to beg or steal, but go on steadily improving day to day in all that makes a people content and prosperous. We will bet a load of frozen Iowa potatoes, for which we paid four dollars a bushel, that more new buildings have been erected in Yankton in the last eight months than in any town of equal size in all northern Iowa. If newspaper abuse and indignant lying is all that Iowa has in store for us, the sooner we open our trade in some other direction the better it will be for the whole Northwest.

A few weeks later Moses K. Armstrong, territorial representative of Dakota, felt obliged to take notice of further attacks from the east. "A few of the northern Iowa papers have gone stark mad at Dakota," Armstrong declared. "They roar like Goliahs struck with slung-shots. They are mad—frothing mad. They bite their own tongues, pull out their own hair, tear their ragged garments, and stamp upon their granger hats with wooden shoes. They throw up their red nostrils and snort like gored bullocks; they paw up the wild prairie around Fort Dodge, smash down the only cabin between that place and Webster City, while down at Dubuque the *Times* declares that 'frozen potatoes were raised in Iowa last year.' A great country is northern Iowa, and astonishing must be the race who live in Dubuque, if by a freak of grammar or of the soil, they can raise frozen murphies in the summertime. This beats the Fort Dodge prairie, where the cows give blue milk and the wind whips the long-tailed pigs to death.

"They would like to see our territory fill up and pour its trade and travel down through Iowa, but they want immigrants who come here to go round by the Red River of the North or Bering Straits, or some route by which they can't be seen 'coming to Dakota.' . . . In less than two years northern Iowa will see us rapping Dubuque over the knuckles with the golden key to the Black Hills, and shaking our dust and nuggets in the streets of Chicago!"

This, as it turned out, was an optimistic boast, for a few months later, in the summer of 1862, the remaining Sioux in the state of Minnesota rose up in a bloody revolt against the white settlers of the region. The causes were the same old ones that had always brought about war between the races: broken treaties, unfair treatment, and mutual distrust. But now, with the white men locked in a titanic struggle between two sections of their own nation, the Indians thought they saw an opportunity for successful revolt.

It was a brutal and terrible conflict while it lasted, and when it had been suppressed thirty-eight of the Indian ringleaders were hanged in a mass execution at Mankato, Minnesota. The surviving Indians fled to Dakota, where their presence emptied the scattered white settlements almost overnight.

Although Fort Abercrombie in eastern Dakota was besieged for a time, and some forty settlers were killed throughout the territory, the expeditions of Generals Sully and Sibley, which followed the Indians into Dakota from the south and the east, effectively smashed for some years any military power of the Sioux. Their confidence restored, the Dakota men and women soon returned to their homesteads.

A minor result of the episode was a revival of the clamor for statehood—intensified by the ignominious flight of the territorial officials who left the country at the first rumors of warfare. Newspaper correspondents excoriated the carpetbaggers from the East who never set foot in the territory unless absolutely necessary, and who disappeared from sight when danger threatened:

These brave and "loyal" dignitaries, at the first approach of a red man, are the first to leave the country; and with such rapidity do they fly, pale and breathless, that a boy could play marbles on their horizontal coattails. And on they go, governor, secretary, judges, attorney general, clerks, in one wild panic-stricken express train of "loyal" officials. The people became frightened and looked for Indians and officials, but could see nothing of the latter but their vanishing coattails disappearing on the far shore of the Big Sioux River. Safe in Sioux City, under the protection of a battery, and four military companies, these "loyal" officials, like rats in a haystack, stick their heads from under their wives' multitudinous crinoline and whisper, with white lips, "Are they coming?"

This was an old story to the people of the territory, who had protested repeatedly to the government, asking that they be given officials appointed from their own country, instead of Easterners who knew nothing of Dakota and her people, and cared less. "Out of three judges appointed for Dakota and paid by the government a salary of eighteen hundred a year," declared Representative Armstrong, "not one of them is to be found in the territory. Where are they? They are back in the states, where they have been for the last year, drawing their salaries as judges of Dakota. Have they gone to war? No, not one of them. Are they saving the Union? Not by any means. They are seated in their Eastern homes, carefully bagging the government's dollars."

Thanks to President Lincoln, these officials were soon brought to account. They were required to submit quarterly affidavits setting forth the length of time they had spent in the territory in the discharge of their duties—such affidavits to be found good and sufficient before their salaries would be forthcoming.

THE Indian danger was now temporarily ended, the settlements had regained their lost populations, and a steady stream of new land-seekers was pouring into the rich bottom lands along the

Missouri and its tributaries in southeastern Dakota. A correspondent of the time wrote:

The roads are lined with immigrant teams, and our green hills and plains are covered with the droves of cattle of new home-seekers. On every hand, by almost every grove and brookside, can be seen the smoke arising from the newly erected claim cabin of some hardy immigrant who has come to open a farm under the Homestead Act. This law has been a godsend to Dakota, and from its effects, in less than two years, the whole Missouri Valley will ring with the clatter of invincible enterprise. Nowhere in the West are more desirable farming lands to be found than along the valley of this stream.

This bumptious confidence was a tragic error which the people of the Upper Missouri Valley are only now beginning to comprehend. The Homestead Act, far from being a "godsend" to the territory, was actually to become a source of infinite exploitation and misery.

The principal defect in the Homestead Act was that it made successful farming seem simple and the acquisition of riches an inevitable result. It did not require more than the breaking of ten acres of the 160-acre grant, the building of a flimsy shack for a "home," and a brief period of residence before the land was given absolutely free to the new owner. Experience or aptitude in farming was not considered at all, nor was the ability of the claimant to buy necessary equipment. And most important of all, the nature of the land and the climate was disregarded. Thousands of people who had never owned a bit of property in their lives were deluded into believing that the mere title to such a vast tract of land would automatically give the owner a handsome living.

And lack of capital was no deterrent. One estimate of the day stated that a sod house could be built for two dollars and eighty cents—an estimate that was but slightly inaccurate, if at all. Only fourteen dollars of the eighteen-dollar fee had to be paid down; the balance was not due until final "proving up."

Like the Preemption Act, the homestead laws were freely broken. Many homesteaders proved up as quickly as possible, then sold the land to the highest bidder. Or they mortgaged it for the biggest sum they could secure, never intending to redeem the pledge. And scoundrels devised shrewd schemes for using the law for their own ends.

In the town of Fargo, for example, a saccharine and pious banker named E. Ashley Mears demonstrated his faith in Dakota by establishing a chain of banks throughout the territory for the purpose of engaging in the mortgage-loan business. Many of the homesteaders who had taken up land for speculative purposes, or those who had found the life uncongenial, were easily persuaded to sign mortgages for far larger sums than the astute Mr. Mears actually advanced to them. Since they had no intention of redeeming the mortgages, they did not hesitate to sign for a thousand or fifteen hundred dollars—although they actually received five hundred dollars or less.

When Mears had acquired as many of these extraordinary papers as he could obtain, he took a trip east, selected a prosperous community, and settled there as a resident. He soon became a respected citizen and a pillar of the community church. Once he had ingratiated himself with the pastor of the church and the leading members of the congregation, Mears began to unload his mortgages. His chain of banks in Dakota continued to pay interest on them for a year or two before going broke—but by that time Mears had departed for greener pastures, leaving the minister and his shorn flock almost as insolvent as Mears's own banks.

As IN any newly organized and growing territory, there were large sums to be made from the townsite, county-organization, and capital-city rackets, which flourished for years in the Northwest to the detriment of the citizenry in general. The railroads were building into the new country from the east, and advance knowledge of projected townsites and railroad routes was as good as money in one's pockets. Seats in the territorial legislature were eagerly sought after—not for the salaries which went with them, but for the inside information and other emoluments that enabled many an early legislator to get rich on townsite speculations or outright bribes from railroads seeking special privileges.

Dakota's early legislatures were scarcely models of parliamentary decorum and dignity. From far-off Pembina in the north-east corner of the territory came fur-clad legislators who were sometimes forced to travel part way by dog team. Frontier desperadoes like Jim Somers came armed with knife and revolver into the legislative chambers. There were cultured and polished eastern gentlemen, too, men with legal degrees from the finest American universities, who doubtless looked down their noses at the rough backwoodsmen who sat with their boots on their desks, "eating boiled eggs with their jack knives" during the deliberations. Norwegian immigrants who knew hardly a word of English sat in stolid uncomprehension through much of the proceedings.

A picture of the strenuous election campaigns has been preserved for us by the ready wit and prolific pen of Representative Armstrong, one of the few Democrats to win a seat in Dakota's first legislature. He once made a campaign tour a hundred miles up the Missouri River from the capital at Yankton to a trading post kept by General C. T. Campbell, "a rip-roaring Democrat," who had made elaborate preparations to entertain his colleague. An Indian war dance, a feast of dog meat, a shooting match, and plenty of liquor opened the festivities, after which the general made a speech of welcome.

Armstrong, who was to follow the general, was not encouraged when someone in the crowd fired a revolver shot that knocked off the general's hat and broke a bottle on the shelf behind him. "But," wrote Armstrong, "he went right on speaking, bareheaded, and finished in fiery eloquence. He then proposed that I lead the way to the speakers' stand and invite the thirsty crowd to select their poison."

Armstrong, not wishing to offend such hotheaded voters as these, led the way "to make the attack on the shining array of decanters. Our band struck up and played a lively tune for the Indians, who pronounced it 'heap noise, plenty brass, big thunder.' As things began to get exciting, I drew the general aside, and suggested that when the next shooting scene was to take place I would retire to the side wings of the stage for prayer and inspiration. I told him I did not come there to be shot at—that I came to catch ballots, not bullets. He blurted out with an oath, saying:

"'Now, Armstrong, don't be a damned coward. I brought you

up here to show these Democratic hyenas the kind of stuff you are made of. If you show the white feather you are a dead duck with this crowd. You should have done your praying before you crossed the county line—

> You must bare your breast and tell 'em to shoot
> And you'll get the vote of every galoot!'

"I followed the old general's stage practice and got the votes."

After this unnerving experience, Armstrong continued north to Pembina, some four hundred miles away, where Joe Rolette, famous early pioneer of Dakota, took over the direction of the campaign. In a two-wheeled Red River cart, a vehicle made entirely of wood whose creaking could be heard for miles, the representative campaigned for a week among the people of the Red River Valley. These carts, despite their crude construction and the fact that they were drawn by a single ox over rough virgin prairie, were effective distance-coverers, if Armstrong's testimony is to be credited. "The ox would take a pacing rack, or trot," he wrote, "and would go thirty miles a day. At night we had meetings in the log houses in the woods, winding up with a dance, a feast of pemmican meat, maple sugar, rabiboo and red rum. Those were times of wild jubilee, mirth and merriment."

The town of Sioux City, Iowa, strange as it may seem, was the headquarters for all the Dakota politicians during the important campaigns in the Sioux Valley, where most of the territory's people lived in the days of the first elections. It was in the Iowa city, according to Armstrong, that the candidates and speakers would "load up with patriotism and firewater, and charge across the Sioux to attack the bewildered voters with spread-eagle speeches, torch-light parades, fife and drum, and bottles labeled firewater. These campaign parties traveled in cavalcades made up of men on foot, on horseback and with band wagon. The musicians were to furnish the music and do the fighting at the meetings, the lawyers were to make the speeches and do the lying, the voters were to furnish the cheers and do the drinking, while the candidates were to do the bragging during the campaign and to pay the bills and do the swearing after election."

The amount of "treating" and the consumption of liquor by the men of the frontier in that lusty age make present-day statesmen seem teetotalers by comparison. They were less hypocritical about their conduct, too, than are the politicians of a more conventional age; often their drinking bouts were held on the very grounds of the territorial capitol, where the carousing continued until dawn.

Again we have the testimony of Representative Armstrong: "I happened to cross the street one morning at peep of day, and there I beheld, around a smouldering camp-fire, two lusty legislators holding a kicking cow by the horns, and a third one pulling his full weight on her horizontal tail. On each side of the milkless heifer sat two councilmen flat upon their unfailing foundations, with pails in hand, making sorrowful and vain attempts at teasing enough milk from the farrow quadruped for their final pitcher of egg-nog. Off on one side lay a corpulent representative, sprawled upon his belly and convulsed with laughter. And there in front of the scene stood another eloquent law-maker, with hat, coat and boots off, making a military speech, and appealing to the sympathies of the cow, in behalf of her country, to give down."

BY ALL odds the most conspicuous citizen of Dakota, from territorial times well into the present century, was a gentleman of variegated and peculiar talents named Alexander McKenzie—otherwise known as the Bismarck Boomer, Alexander the Great, and in later years as the Boss of North Dakota.

The scope of his machinations was by no means confined to Dakota. His adventures in the far north during the period known to history as "The Looting of Alaska" earned him a brief sojourn in the custody of the federal authorities at San Francisco. It is too far outside the scope of this book to recount the story here; but interested readers may find the tale, told with more or less fidelity to fact, in Rex Beach's Alaskan novel, *The Spoilers*. Alec McKenzie will not be difficult to recognize, for he wears the thinnest of disguises, his fictional cognomen being "Alec McNamara, the Boss of North Dakota."

McKenzie's beginnings were humble and unpromising. He first

came to Dakota as an employee of Don Stevenson's wagon train in 1867. The train was used to carry military supplies to the outpost at Fort Rice, and young McKenzie, only seventeen years old at the time, became a dispatch carrier between Forts Rice and Buford.

Five years later he returned to Dakota with the coming of the Northern Pacific Railway, in whose employ he had charge of tracklaying from Fargo west to Bismarck. With the passing of the years he became the Northern Pacific's unofficial representative, lobbyist, and political manipulator in Dakota—whose early legislatures were dominated by the railroad interests.

He was the very antithesis of the fat political boss made famous in countless cartoons. Tall, handsome, and possessed of unbounded physical courage, yet quiet and soft-spoken, he was a natural leader of men and an adroit practical psychologist; he knew how and where to dispense gifts and favors to the best advantage— a quality which gave him a reputation somewhat of the Robin Hood type.

But never was Good Samaritan reputation less deserved, for he was ruthless, when necessary, in the exaction of favors in return. One frontier editor whom he was able neither to buy nor coerce, found his plant smashed and his printing press dumped into the Missouri River by "unknown" vandals. Men who opposed McKenzie's wishes sometimes awakened one day to find a coffin resting on their front porches—a delicate hint that their conduct was displeasing to the Boss.

Yet McKenzie, more than any other single man, was responsible for the development and early growth of Dakota. He advertised and aided the territory in many ways, though his motives were not in the least altruistic. He dealt heavily in state and county securities and in lands, and it was to his own direct advantage that instrumentalities whose securities he held should prosper.

With all his objectionable traits, he seems to have been a most personable and likable individual. Even his enemies gave him grudging admiration and spoke of his friendly qualities, his unobtrusiveness, his generosity, and above all, his damnable effectiveness! An editor in southern Dakota, lamenting the fact that McKenzie had just brought about a political coup in which the editor's locality had suffered, nevertheless paid Alexander the Great the coin of high praise.

Alec was not a delegate himself. He never is, or rarely is. He poses, smiling and serene, on the convention floor, and gayly proceeds to figure you out of your boots. What is the secret of his success? Ah, there are more secrets than one, and it must be admitted that they are for the most part open ones. In the first place, Alexander McKenzie is personally a man you would like. Tall, broad-shouldered, and of full proportions, with light sandy hair and mustache, and the round ruddy face of the good-humored Scotchman, Alexander the Great, of the North, is everybody's friend on principle. There is not a political or "public" enemy, to adapt a word to my meaning, who stands without the pale of the adroit chieftain's speaking acquaintance. He can slap them all on the shoulder and sit down to a confidential chat . . . Alec understands human nature, and always rubs fur the right way. With the same clear insight into the human breast, he is free-handed to a degree. He always carries a roll of bills, of which the smallest is the V denomination, and spends his money so freely and with such evident relish, that one fancies that some of the virtuous innocents from south Dakota, who now and then get taken in, secretly wish, at the bottom of their hearts, that there were only more chiefs like him—like the merry, merry Modoc in the land of the Dakotahs. McKenzie is always ready for a trade, and if he does not get the best of it he generally manages to make the other side feel that he is well pleased for the time being. He pays the highest market price for everybody and everything he gets, and knows just exactly how to approach things and people. Alec McKenzie is the type of rustler who takes the world as he finds it, and employs the methods in use to his own advantage. He is generous to his friends and friendly toward his enemies, and upon the whole about as well-liked personally as Ordway is detested.

Nehemiah Ordway, the gentleman referred to in the closing sentence, was at the time territorial governor of Dakota, and a bird of notably different feather from McKenzie. Ordway was from New Hampshire: a tall, white-bearded, handsome, pious, covetous old sinner, with an icy New Englandish look of astonishing rectitude. He had served in Washington for twelve years as sergeant at arms of the House of Representatives before receiving his appointment as governor of Dakota, and rather fancied himself as an astute politician. McKenzie, with his usual acumen, allowed Ordway to nurture this illusion, while he adroitly used the governor for his own ends; then Ordway, once he had fulfilled his usefulness, found himself on the short end of one of McKenzie's masterful double crosses.

These two ill-suited companions, united only in their cupidity and unscrupulousness, decided that the territorial capital, located at Yankton in the far southeastern corner of Dakota, should be moved to another part of the territory. There was, in fact, excellent reason for the removal, for the northern part of Dakota was rapidly filling with settlers, and Yankton was an out-of-the-way and inconvenient location. Yankton citizens themselves recognized the inevitability of the change.

In plotting the removal McKenzie was not primarily moved by considerations of personal profit. The Northern Pacific Railway quite naturally desired the relocation of the capital somewhere on its own right of way; the city of Bismarck, in north-central Dakota, was its choice, and McKenzie, as the railroad's unofficial —though well-paid—representative, undertook to effect this selection. But he did not trouble to confide these facts to Governor Ordway.

Instead, the governor was allowed to believe that the capital would be located at an almost empty townsite known, strangely enough, as Ordway, where the governor owned virtually all of the land. So eager was the greedy old gentleman to get his clutches on the wealth that was sure to be his if the capital was located there, that he completely neglected to keep an eye on Alexander the Great of the North.

The governor became McKenzie's slavish tool; often he would not even sign bills passed by the territorial legislature until McKenzie had approved them. The acme of his dependence on the Boss came when Ordway, who was a physical giant, taller than McKenzie, allowed McKenzie to act as his bodyguard. Threats had been made against the governor because of certain shady manipulations he had engaged in, and Ordway, who was as timid as he was covetous, actually refused to appear in public without the genial Alec, who feared nothing, in attendance. To Dakota frontiersmen, who despised a coward even more than they did a horse thief, this was the last straw.

McKenzie had laid his plans well, and in the final days of the 1883 legislative session Ordway was probably more in McKenzie's custody than under his protection. All the powers of the Boss's persuasive genius—to say nothing of the virtually bottomless depths of his campaign purse—were exerted to make certain that his secret bill would pass when it came to a vote. This ingenious measure deprived the residents of the territory of any voice whatsoever in the selection of their new capital; instead, it empowered the governor to appoint a capital commission of nine members, with exclusive power to name any site they might choose. On the last day of the session, with many lawmakers absent and others napping, McKenzie's henchmen railroaded the bill through the legislature, a vote to adjourn was quickly taken and passed, and the bill went to Governor Ordway, who hastily affixed his signature before anything unforeseen might happen.

The howls that arose from the bewildered and angry people were loud and lusty. Almost without exception the newspapers denounced the affair as a shameless theft, conceived in iniquity and born in bribery.

So bitter was the feeling in southern Dakota that the desperate citizens of the Yankton area threatened to prevent the commission from carrying out its duties. The bill provided that the commission must meet, organize, and adjourn in the city of Yankton. Members of the commission were warned not to come near the town on pain of personal violence; they were shadowed and every precaution was taken to prevent their meeting at any place near Yankton, from which they might make a swift foray in order to fulfill the terms of the law.

But Alexander the Great was too sharp to be outwitted in this way. By devious routes he summoned the commission members to Sioux City, Iowa, where his railroad connections enabled him to secure a special train with dimmed lights and a faithful guard and crew. It was three o'clock in the morning when the darkened special pulled out in the direction of Yankton. The railroad superintendent in charge of the Yankton yards had arranged to have the switches set and spiked, in order that the special might have a clear track for sudden flight. Shortly after five in the morning the train slid unnoticed into the city limits of Yankton, the commission was hastily called to order, elected its officers, and adjourned a few minutes later as the special rolled stealthily out of the limits of Yankton once more.

It was a long time before McKenzie ceased to be the object of bitter vituperation from angry Yankton citizens. Other towns of the territory were only slightly less hostile, and McKenzie did not dare to locate the capital at Bismarck immediately. Instead, he visited every principal town in the territory, inviting them all to make bids for the new capital and thus stirring up intense rivalry among them. He soon had them fighting furiously for the capital site: Fargo against Jamestown, Mitchell against Chamberlain, Huron against Pierre.

Actually, of course, this whole procedure was a farce, but so successful were the Boss's tactics that by the time Bismarck was named most of the sting of defeat was removed for the losing cities by the comforting thought that their rival neighbors had lost too.

As for Ordway and the town named after him, both were gracefully lost in the shuffle. Probably McKenzie convinced the governor that it would look too suspicious to name Ordway the new capital, and pacified him with a few lots in the city of Bismarck and with vague promises of election to the Senate—which, of course, were never fulfilled. But Ordway seems never to have realized how McKenzie had used him; or if he did, it was not until so many years afterward that he was unable to take any revenge for it.

THE credit for this notable coup should not go entirely to McKenzie. The vast power of the railroad he represented gave strength to his position and placed ample funds in his hands. Today, when the once great railroad monopolies are largely tamed and have their teeth drawn, it is difficult to realize the unlimited power they formerly exercised—particularly in the new territories of the Northwest, where their merest whim could make or break any frontier town or district.

Men along the fringe of the new lands talked constantly of "when the railroad gets here," where its townsites would be located, and how their particular community might derive some advantage from its coming. When the government, in 1864, made the stupendous gift of fifty million acres of public land to the Northern Pacific Railway, it could not foresee the future difficulties that were to arise from this gargantuan gratuity. From Lake Superior to Puget Sound the Northern Pacific received each odd-numbered section of the public lands for a distance of twenty miles on each side of its right of way in the states and a distance of forty miles in the territories. To compensate the road for any lands already settled, there was an additional "indemnity grant" of ten more miles on each side of the primary one.

It is unquestionably true that the coming of the railroads sharply speeded up the settlement of the Northwest. Passenger fares that were ten cents a mile in 1866 dropped rapidly to seven cents, then to five, and down to two and one-third cents by the close of the century. New towns came into being almost daily as the railroads pressed their way westward, while hopeful little communities left off the track withered and died almost as rapidly. Rivalry among the frontier towns reached such a point that pitched battles were fought and the towns bankrupted themselves by offering excessive sums to the railroads in return for routing the tracks through their communities.

This latter practice, needless to say, was encouraged by the railroads; local newspapers, often bought by the railroad companies, whipped up public interest and advocated the issuance of county bonds to induce the railways to pass through their cities. Sometimes more direct methods were used. Jay Gould, of unsavory memory, stood on the platform of his private car at Columbus, Nebraska, and told the townsfolk he would "make the grass grow in the streets of Columbus" unless the desired bond issue was forthcoming. Such threats were not empty talk, either, for more than one prosperous community was turned into a ghost town for daring to fight the railroad interests.

In some cases a particularly cruel fraud was perpetrated upon the frontier towns. In exchange for the issuance of county bonds to be turned over to the company, the railroad would sign a contract agreeing to construct a road through the town—with the stipulation that the bonds were to be turned over when the "first train" arrived or when the roadbed was "ready for traffic." Once the company had secured the bonds, the unlucky town was left holding the sack—for the "first train" was often the only one, and the roadbed that was "ready for traffic" was a cheaply constructed grade that never carried any of the traffic for which it was ready.

Intelligent men throughout the territory were not blind to these abuses, but the great economic power of the companies, their ability to crush any town that opposed them, and their profligate use of the free pass made them virtually unassailable. They controlled territorial conventions and legislatures with ease; bills aimed at correcting some of the more flagrant abuses were quickly killed through the efforts of such stalwart allies of the corporations as Alexander McKenzie and his followers. Even legislators who were opposed to the dominance of the railroads could scarcely be induced to vote for a law abolishing the giving of free passes to public officials. In Dakota it was brought up time and again before a majority could be mustered to pass it.

Since most of the territorial legislators were men of moderate means, the pass system was an effective aid to McKenzie and his gang. Political conventions were duly attended by the McKenzie henchmen, who rode free on the trains and were furnished rooms, meals, liquor, expenses, and other gratuities by the machine; while those delegates who opposed the McKenzie Ring received none of these things, and often did not attend conventions because they could ill afford the cost. McKenzie, with a convention packed with faithful pass-holders, was usually able to obtain the results he desired.

When other methods failed, there remained the usual contemptible tricks of the shady politician. In the North Dakota legislature of 1907 the abolition of the pass system was a primary legislative aim. Usher L. Burdick, a member of the house of representatives, who later served long and honorably in the national House, was one of the sponsors of the antipass bill. He noticed that one member who was pledged to vote for the bill, a fine and upright man from Traill County, had suddenly lost all interest in the measure.

Burdick, knowing the man to be unbribable, pressed him until the member broke down and revealed the true state of affairs. The opposition had arranged to have a woman visit the Traill representative on some pretext or other. No sooner had she entered his room than she slipped out of her coat—which proved to be all she had on—and flung herself at the astounded representative, while the gang took a picture from the open door. Moth-eaten as this dodge was, the member, when shown the photograph, consented to vote against the bill rather than have the picture sent to his wife and family.

The distracted legislator finally consented to allow Burdick to make the affair public, which he did the next day on the floor of the house in such scathing fashion that the antipass bill went through the house by a whopping majority. But the gang must have had other evidence quite as potent as the faked picture in its hands, for the senate defeated the measure, and not until the 1911 session was the pass system at last outlawed.

It was still in full flower when Dakota Territory celebrated the laying of the new capitol cornerstone at Bismarck on September 5, 1883—a great year for the Northern Pacific in more ways than one, for it was that same year that their road was completed to the Pacific Coast. Four sections of the special train chartered by Henry Villard, president of the road, brought prominent Americans and foreigners from all over the United States and the world. The British and German ambassadors, Generals Grant and Haupt, Marshall Field, James J. Hill, Joseph Pulitzer, Carl Schurz, Noah Brooks, Joseph Medill, and A. H. McClure were among the distinguished guests. James Bryce in his classic work, *The American Commonwealth*, has given his impressions of the occasion, and even this sober Englishman seems to have fallen under the spell of the oratory of the day.

"I happened in 1883 to be at the city of Bismarck in Dakota when this young settlement was laying the corner-stone of its

Capitol, intended to contain the halls of the legislature and other State offices of Dakota when that flourishing Territory should have become a State, or perhaps, for they spoke of dividing it, two States. The town was then only some five years old, and may have had six or seven thousand inhabitants. [Actually it was eleven years old and had nearer twenty-five hundred inhabitants.] It was gaily decorated for the occasion, and had collected many distinguished guests. . . . By far the most remarkable figure was that of Sitting Bull, the famous Sioux chief, who had surprised and slain a detachment of the American army some years before. Among the speeches made, in one of which it was proved that Bismarck was the centre of Dakota, Dakota the centre of the United States, and the United States the centre of the world, and that Bismarck was destined to be 'the metropolitan hearth of the world's civilization,' there came a short but pithy discourse from this grim old warrior, in which he told us, through an interpreter, that the Great Spirit moved him to shake hands with everybody.

"However, the feature of the ceremony which struck us Europeans most was the spot chosen for the Capitol. It was not in the city, nor even on the skirts of the city; it was nearly a mile off, on the top of a hill in the brown and dusty prairie. 'Why here?' we asked. 'Is it because you mean to enclose the building in a public park?' 'By no means; the Capitol is intended to be in the centre of the city; it is in this direction that the city is to grow.'

"It is the same everywhere, from the Mississippi to the Pacific. Men seem to live in the future rather than in the present; not that they fail to work while it is called today, but that they see the country not merely as it is, but as it will be, twenty, fifty, a hundred years hence, when the seedlings shall have grown to forest trees."

Today, in 1946, sixty-three years later, Bismarck is a town of fifteen thousand people. And the capitol is still a mile from the center of the city.

MONTANA, which became a separate territory in 1864, had capital-city troubles of its own. There was no Alexander McKenzie to rob the people of their right to vote on its location, but there were the copper kings, Marcus Daly and William Andrews Clark, leading citizens of the rival communities of Anaconda and Helena, to spend sums beyond the wildest dreams of McKenzie in a senseless battle over the capital site after Montana had been admitted as a state in 1889.

C. P. Connolly in *The Devil Learns to Vote* estimated that Daly must have spent two and a half million dollars in his vain effort to establish the state capital in Anaconda, while it cost Clark and his supporters four hundred thousand dollars to assert Helena's superiority as the logical location. It was money wasted in any case, for the votes of Montanans in general were probably not affected one way or the other by the huge sums expended in bribes or propaganda.

The vast wealth which had become concentrated in the hands of a few men as a result of the discovery of "the richest hill on earth" at Butte, had already begun to work its evil effects on the destiny of Montana when the state constitution was adopted. The mining interests were able to fix firmly in the state constitution a system of mining taxation so outrageous in its unfairness to the state and its people that one wonders how they dared advocate it publicly. And when William Andrews Clark decided in 1899 that his presence in the United States Senate would be a national asset, bribery and political corruption reached a depth in Montana that has perhaps never been equaled by any state in the Union in all American history.

United States senators were at that time still elected by the state legislatures, and Clark set out with cold, calculated, shameless chicanery to accomplish his purpose. The price offered for a legislator's vote ran as high as twenty-five thousand dollars. Fred Whiteside, an honorable member of the body, took thirty thousand dollars, then rose from his seat next day to denounce Clark and his methods, after which he gave the bribe money to the state treasurer. Instead of a storm of indignation, there was a hastily contrived move to oust Whiteside from his seat—a move which, because of a technical question, was successful.

On the day the legislature met to select Montana's United States senator, the galleries were packed with citizens who knew to the dollar the bribe each member had accepted. As the legislators rose, white-faced, from their seats to cast their votes for Clark, the crowd hooted and called out the amount Clark was known to have paid them: "Ten thousand dollars!" "Five thousand!" "Twenty-five thousand!"

Here, surely, was a scene for the hand of a master political satirist—the prostitution of democracy by a cynical multimillionaire and a handful of venal politicians, consummated before the eyes of the helpless citizenry. But not all the legislators were venal; thirteen members of the senate rejected sums that totaled two hundred thousand dollars. Nor were the citizens of Montana entirely helpless; Clark's election was later successfully challenged in the United States Senate and he was forced to resign.

Giant Anaconda, the great copper trust which is controlled by the Standard Oil Company and which has taken two and a half billion dollars from Montana's resources, uses methods less direct today. But no less effective, in many instances. The wealth of Montana's mines, like the profits of Dakota's grain produce, has been employed to control its legislatures, its courts, and its press. Anaconda, like its serpentine namesake, has held an entire state in its copper coils while it slowly crushed the life from Montana.

In North Dakota, an almost entirely agricultural state with no great mineral resources to fall into the hands of a few men who could then dominate its government for their own selfish ends, the people of the state found a way, in time, to oust the McKenzie Ring from power and institute a political regime of their own. Its sister state to the west has not yet found a way. North Dakota is luckier than Montana.

SIX years after James Bryce witnessed the optimistic dedication of the territorial capitol, the city of Bismarck was again the scene of a political gathering. This time it was for the purpose of adopting a constitution for the newly created state of North Dakota. Again there were spread-eagle speeches and hopeful predictions of metropolitan greatness. There were so many of them, in fact, that the gloomy words of a bearded government geologist who briefly addressed the convention went almost unnoticed.

The geologist was John Wesley Powell, and the words of his mouth were mighty—although they received either no mention at all in the newspapers of the day, or simply a curt dismissal as the views of a chronic pessimist.

"The state of North Dakota," Powell told the delegates, "has a curious position geographically in relation to agriculture . . . In the western portion all dependence on rains will ultimately bring disaster to the people . . . They will soon learn in the western portion to depend upon irrigation and provide themselves with agencies for the artificial fructifying of the soil with water. In the eastern part they will depend on the rainfall, and in the middle portion they will have a series of years when they will have abundant crops; then for two or three years they will have less rainfall and there will be failure of crops and disaster will come on thousands of people, who will become discouraged and leave . . . That is the history of all those who live on the border between humid and arid lands. Years will come of abundance and years will come of disaster, and between the two the people will be prosperous and unprosperous, and the thing to do is look the question squarely in the face . . .

"There's almost enough rain for your purposes, but one year with another you need a little more than you get. It is flowing past you in the rivers . . . All other wealth falls into insignificance compared with that which is to come from these lands from the pouring on them of the running streams of this country. Don't let these streams get out of the possession of the people. If you fail in making a constitution in any other respect, fail not in this one. Fix it in your constitution that no corporation—no body of men—no capital can get possession and right of your waters. Hold the waters in the hands of the people . . . You should forbid the right to acquire property in water. The property should be in the land, and the right to the water should inhere in the land and no company or individual should have property in the running streams. Such a provision will prevent your great agricultural resources from falling into the hands of a few."

John Wesley Powell knew whereof he spoke. In 1878 he had filed in the congressional library a government report setting forth the resources and economic possibilities of the western plains with what today seems uncanny prescience. He warned of the drought years and the inevitable deterioration of the soil if practices already begun on the plains were allowed to continue—overgrazing of lands and plowing up of semi-arid territories unsuited to cultivation.

But his report went beyond mere warning. It included a model plan for a western agricultural and pastoral society that would fit the nature of the land and develop eventually a social structure to harmonize with the country's resources and the needs, both cultural and economic, of its people. But the empire builders, the exploiters, the boosters of the West had no time for visionaries like Powell. Not only in North Dakota were his painstaking findings disregarded; other states in the northern plains, to some of which the warning was even more applicable, paid no heed either.

Powell and his assistants had gone about their business in a workmanlike fashion. They had studied rain cycles, soil samples, and the native grasses of the northern plains. Basing his predictions on the results of these findings, Powell came to the conclusion that intensive farming practices should never be established on the dryland plains of the Upper Missouri Valley. Wet years would be succeeded by dry years, and no man could predict their order, occurrence, or duration. Twenty inches of rainfall annually was the minimum necessary for sustained successful agricultural cultivation, and nowhere in the upper river valley was the annual average that high.

The natural hay of the prairies—the bluestem and buffalo grass —Powell and his assistants found admirable for grazing purposes, but they discovered, too, that overgrazing would quickly reduce it to uselessness, especially if livestock was confined within fenced pasturage. Their gravest warnings, however, were against the danger of breaking the natural sod cover and applying intensive agricultural methods to the land.

Powell hit hard at the Homestead Act, with its limitation of 160 acres to each settler: ample in a country of sufficient rainfall, but an invitation to failure in the semi-arid regions of the northern plains. In his plan for a balanced economy of the land he advocated irrigation to produce hay for feed and to grow garden produce, and suggested 2560 acres as an ideal land unit for the average settler's tract. "A quarter-section of land alone will be of no value," he wrote. "The pasturage it will afford will not suffice to maintain a herd that even the poorest man will need for his support."

The government did not listen to this sound advice. It did increase the acreage a settler might acquire from 160 to 320 acres—an increase so slight as to be of little value—but in the same breath it added a requirement that one eighth of the land thus obtained must be planted to agricultural crops within three years after the land entry had been made and must thereafter be kept in continuous cultivation. The breaking of the plains against which Powell had warned was thus established by governmental fiat, and the destruction of the Northwest's economy began.

It is interesting to contemplate what might have been the destiny of the northern plains had Powell's model plan for their development been followed. He advocated a topographical surveying of the land, rather than the orthodox method of township division which might place all available water within one man's holdings and deprive his neighbors of their own essential supply. And he recommended that the land be kept free of fencing, that cattle be grazed communally over vast stretches of pasturage—a procedure which would have curtailed effectively the ruin of western grasslands from overgrazing.

Under such a system of sparse population and large tracts of land, Powell further suggested, residences of settlers could be grouped to provide social and cultural unity and lessen the otherwise high costs of administration. Under such a plan, community development of necessary services could have been achieved without costly county organization, which has been a financial headache to the Northwest states for half a century.

Powell was a prophet of astonishing accuracy, but none of his recommendations were put into practice. The land was homesteaded and plowed; the pasturage was fenced and overgrazed; the surveys were made after the township plan, and water rights were misused and stolen; bankrupt counties struggled to provide services for scattered tenants. When the wealth of the northern plains began at last to blow in choking dust storms over the gutted land, state and federal planners, sixty-five years too late, strove to bind up the Northwest's wounds and turn it back to soil practices and a way of life for which nature fitted it.

But all these things were far in the future when Powell addressed North Dakota's convention in 1889. In eastern Dakota bonanza farming was making giant strides; rainfall was almost up to the twenty-inch average in those districts, and tremendous yields of wheat were being raised on the new mechanized farms of the Red River Valley. All the signs of the times made it appear that Powell was wrong and the boosters were right. The 70's and 80's had brought into the Upper Missouri Valley a veritable tide of northern European immigrants. One third of the population of North Dakota today is of Norwegian stock. And this curious fact is largely the result of the work of a single man.

CLENG PEERSON was born with the roving blood of Viking ancestors in his veins. It was as if the Voice that spoke to Peer Gynt out of the darkness had spoken, too, to Cleng, saying: "Go roundabout, Cleng Peerson!" And Cleng went roundabout. He traveled through Scandinavia, France, Germany, and England before, in his restless fashion, he set sail from Norway for America in 1821 to seek out the New World's possibilities as a place of settlement for his people.

For three years Cleng wandered over the hills and plains and valleys of America's frontier lands. He walked alone beneath the drifting shadows of the clouds and made his solitary bed under the sky and the twinkling stars; he saw the lush meadowlands and the great forests; he picked up his living as best he could; and in the year 1824 he took ship for Norway to tell his friends what he had discovered.

Cleng was a persuasive fellow, and the very next year the sloop *Restoration* sailed for America with the first shipload of Norwegian immigrants to come to the New World since Leif Ericson and Thorfinn Karlsefni touched there in the gray of antiquity eight long centuries before.

Cleng, in the meantime, had preceded the group to arrange for

142

the selection of a proper site for settlement and to continue his investigation into the country's advantages. Cleng Peerson had found his life's work. In the decades that followed he made trip after trip back and forth across the Atlantic, persuading and leading new waves of Norwegian immigrants toward the Promised Land that was America. He wandered to and fro over the vast reaches of the frontier, seeking out desirable locations for settlers. From Illinois to Wisconsin, back to the Illinois prairies, on to Missouri, to Iowa, and then to Texas Cleng traveled. He planted Norwegians in the bosom of the earth as Johnny Appleseed planted trees.

Cleng Peerson never saw the country where his people were to settle in the greatest numbers, but it was his direct influence which has made the northern plains the dwelling place of so many Scandinavians. Some of his followers had already made their way into the land of the Dacotahs before the old Viking breathed his last in Texas in 1865.

O. E. Rölvaag, in his moving novel *Giants in the Earth,* has told, and superbly, the story of the Dakota immigrants' fight against drought and prairie fire and hailstorm and plague and awful isolation. For every Beret whose mind snapped under the strain of unaccustomed privations there was a Per Hansa who died with his eyes still set toward the west. And for every Per Hansa there were thousands who stood like dark Norway pines against every storm until at last the wilderness was beaten.

To Hamlin Garland life on the Dakota frontier was a futile struggle in a dreary, brutalizing environment; his stories are stark, true portraits of frontier life. Yet, perhaps because he was too close to the struggle, or perhaps because he was at heart as much a Boston Brahmin as was Francis Parkman, he missed something which Rölvaag saw with simple clarity: there was an epic there.

Yes, there were giants in the earth in those days. But there were ordinary men, too.

Chapter 9

GIANTS IN THE EARTH

∿∿∿

Yankton, August 8.—Thor Ericsson, a Norwegian immigrant farmer who homesteaded about thirty miles north of here several years ago, was brought into town last night and lodged in the local calaboose by the Sheriff. He is charged with having murdered his wife and his two small children, after which he tried to take his own life. Ericsson is a slight, blond, inoffensive-looking man, speaking almost no English. When questioned he could give no reason for his fiendish act.

Thor Ericsson was born in a tiny fishing village on the western coast of Norway, where the black, beetling cliffs look down on wind-whipped fiords. With patience and years of hard work he might have acquired a boat of his own and become a captain among the fishermen, but his heart was not on the sea. He came of landed folk, and in him was a love for the earth and the feel of the earth. He wanted, more than anything else, a farm of his own, and cattle, and a snug home for Karen and the little one. He and Karen talked it over.

America, now. There was a land where a man could stand straight and be a man, and independent. His friends in Minnesota had written to him that rich farm lands were to be had free from the government: lands that had never known the plow and were broad and rolling, unlike the stony soil of Norway, where a poor man had no chance to get land anyway. Why, in America, his friends had written, a man could have as many rich acres free as would make a manor at home!

So Thor talked and dreamed, while Karen clutched their little blonde daughter to her and thought fearfully of the tales of wild Indians and fierce beasts she had heard. But there were the pamphlets distributed by the steamship companies in the village, Thor reminded her. They did not speak of such things. They told of cheap rates for passage to the new land and of the wonderful opportunities there. And in the end Karen did as women have done since time began: she nodded her head sadly and followed the desire of her man.

When Thor had scraped and saved and borrowed the money for their passage and the long journey across the country to the new lands, they took ship from Christiania harbor. Thor, scanning the vessel with the practiced eye of the professional sailor, thought her ill-found and dirty; she was not at all like the luxurious ships the steamboat companies' advertisements had told about. But he held his peace as she beat her way outward into the heave and surge of the North Atlantic, for she was taking him to America and freedom; and under her forefoot was the Swan Road of Thorfinn Karlsefni and Eric the Red.

Weeks in the fetid, crowded hold under the smoky lanterns did not lessen his enthusiasm, though Karen and little Inga grew thin and pale. Cheer up, said Thor, it will be better soon. Don't mind these seasick landlubbers all around us. Soon we'll be in America. But he wondered, privately, as the ancient sailing ship wallowed in the gray, smoking swells, whether they'd make it before the old tub foundered.

New York was a nightmare, a bedlam, a babble of foreign tongues and faces. Uniformed officials shouted at him, seized his papers. Then, in a moment of quiet, a soft-spoken, friendly man approached and spoke to him in Norwegian. It was good to find a friend. The man helped him, aided him with the officials, told him just what he must do. Had he had his money changed into American money yet? No? Well, that must be done at once. The kindly stranger offered to see to it for him, and Thor gave him two bills from the greasy little roll of money he kept pinned inside his jacket.

He waited, an hour, two hours, with a sick, growing sense of what had happened. Karen sat holding little Inga and looking at him trustingly. Thor cursed, hoarse angry oaths at his own stupidity and helplessness. What a simpleton he was! To lose his money like a greenhorn before he had been in America a single day!

There was nothing to do but tell Karen, who only looked at him in mute reproach. Then he tried to tell his story to a uniformed man who muttered impatiently something that sounded like "Dum Norskies," and explained that he could do nothing about it. Thor counted his slender funds and thanked his stars the loss had been no greater.

So everything was not good about this country, after all. A man had to look out for himself. Well, he guessed he could do it, now that he'd had his lesson. But his face burned at the thought of how he had been taken in.

As THE immigrant coaches thundered across the continent, Thor and Karen and Inga marveled at the majestic breadth and richness of the land. Great cities, and broad rolling plains dotted with herds of cattle or covered to the horizons with shimmering fields of grain. Then the cities grew smaller and gave way to tiny prairie villages that were farther and farther apart. The train rushed along through mighty virgin forests that reminded Thor of the pine-clad mountains of Norway; at last they were in Minnesota.

Thor's friend Hans met them at the St. Paul depot, looking tall and fine in his American clothes. He had a job with the railroad, helping to build the tracks that were thrusting westward, and he was full of news and enthusiasm. He brushed away Thor's thanks. He had great news for them. Dakota was the place to go now. The railroad was building out into the new territory; rich lands were there for the taking. He, Hans, would take them into his home temporarily until other arrangements could be made. Everything would turn out fine yet.

Two weeks later Thor stood on the rolling Dakota plain, looking out over the virgin acres, rich with native grasses, which were soon to be his own. Under the direction of the locator he had picked out his claim—for a fat fee, to be sure, but it was certainly worth it—and with the help of neighboring settlers, who had arrived a few weeks before him, he had set about building the sod hut that would be his and Karen's and Inga's first home.

Thor worked from dawn till dusk, driving himself to the point of exhaustion, for he wished to send for his family as soon as possible. They were still at Hans's, in St. Paul, and he was already longing for Karen after an absence of only a few weeks. He chuckled to himself as he laid the fresh-cut sods row upon row. What was that proverb of his old grandmother's in Norway? *One hair of a maiden's head pulls stronger then ten yoke of oxen.* Indeed, it was true!

It was early in May when Karen and little Inga came, and Thor, with the proud light of the landholder in his eyes, showed them his new possessions. Although they were tired from the long ox-team ride over the rough prairie, Thor could see they were impressed. It was green with spring, and there was soft air and emptiness and sky, and the upturned lovely faces of pasqueflowers; his claim of a hundred and sixty acres seemed like land without end, and surely where such rich grass grew, wheat would flourish like the green bay tree.

But Karen's face grew troubled when she saw the rude sod hut, like the cave of a wild beast in the earth, and the endless running sweep of the prairie, tossing in lonely waves like the sea, unbroken even by a single stunted tree.

Thor roared with laughter when she asked him timidly about neighbors. Of course they had neighbors! There were a Swedish farmer and three other Norwegian families not more than a few miles away. And the new settlement, where there were at least fifty people, was only nine miles distant. But look at the earth he had already plowed! Feel how rich it was to the touch! Not much of his land had been broken yet, but just wait a few months and then look at the ground where he had already plowed and sown. Why, it would yield scores of bushels to the acre! They had told him so at the settlement.

THE hot summer months came and went, and the ten acres of corn and potatoes behind the strip of plowed firebreak stood straight and green in the gathering dusk when Thor looked out one evening from his sod-shanty doorway and saw in the distance a flickering, unearthly glow that seemed to reach from horizon to horizon. The acrid tang of smoke came to his nostrils on the rising wind. He knew suddenly, without quite knowing how he knew, that it was the dreaded grass fire of the prairie. A shout brought Karen and Inga running outside.

There was no need to explain. With the speed of the wind the lambent curtain of fire was racing toward them across the sun-dried prairie. Thor thought with a sinking heart of the two oxen grazing a half mile away. But it was useless even to think of rescuing them from this roaring enemy which could outrun the fastest horse. Besides, they must make sure that the crop was saved.

They watched with caught breath as the racing flames reached the firebreak, paused, and divided. Here and there a tiny tongue of fire leaped over into the margin of the ripe corn. Thor called his little fire brigade into action. Using blankets soaked with water, they fell to beating down the stray flames that sprang up here and there. The firebreak had done its work well; a few minutes and the last of the tiny blazes was extinguished. The prairie fire was now only a red glow on the horizon once more, and all around them lay the blackened earth, save for the little circle of green life within the firebreak. They had saved the precious crop.

Next morning before the others were awake, Thor rose early and took his ax with him out on the ravaged earth where he had tethered the two oxen. They stood where he had left them, with eyes seared tight shut by the burning heat and the cooked flesh hanging in strips from their tortured bodies. They were still alive, and they staggered on trembling legs and bellowed weakly. Two swift merciful blows from the ax and they were put out of their pain. Thor shivered slightly as he looked down at their fallen bodies. The prairie was a cruel foe . . . And now, somehow, he must replace them . . .

At the settlement Thor found that it was not too hard for a man to get credit. True, he must sign papers, and interest rates were high, but when the crops came in the years to follow, those things would easily be taken care of. They could live through the winter, and next year when he would have many more acres broken and sown, the debts would be paid.

Thor worried over the debts more than Karen knew, for soon there would be another mouth to feed in his little family. He made arrangements to take Karen into the settlement, where the only doctor in the region lived; but one evening in early November, two weeks before they were to make the trip to the settlement, the skies darkened suddenly, the wind rose to a keening gale that swept down from the north, and on the crest of the gale rode the blinding blizzard of the prairie. Drifts piled in four- and five-foot depths on the windswept plain and buried the sod hut to its gables as blizzard followed blizzard in the succeeding days.

Thor kept a lamp burning in the dugout's lone window and ventured out only to the sod barn a few yards away to feed his oxen. A journey to the settlement was unthinkable. And on the night when his wife's labor began, there were only Thor and little frightened Inga to keep vigil. Near midnight they heard a feeble scratching at the door. When Thor flung it open to the gale, a man, blue-lipped and ghastly, crept in with a broken hand, asking news of his father, whom he had lost in the storm. Guided by Thor's lamp, he had found the house. Thor could offer him no hope for his father out in the storm, but his presence steadied Thor.

They did what needed to be done throughout the long night of pain, Thor and the stranger with the broken hand and little Inga, alone with the wonder and the terror of creation; and when the gray dawn broke over the housetop the prairie had given a life for the one it had exacted of the stranger's father, lost in the white smother outside. Two days later, when the storm was over, the man went away. Thor never saw him again. He had not even learned his name.

THAT spring Thor worked long hours behind the new ox team he had bought. Where the roots of the tough grass lay too thick and matted, he and the neighbors helped each other with the heavy breaking plow borrowed from the settlement and drawn by five yoke of oxen. This year he sowed wheat. The money would take care of his debts, with something left over. As the days passed he looked out proudly over the acres of grain already coming up green in the spring sunlight.

It was late in June when the plague struck, a plague straight out of the pages of the heavy brass-bound Bible from which Thor read to his family each evening before bedtime. It came in disguise, masquerading as a welcome rain cloud that blotted out the sun and cast its great shadow over the land. But as the cloud drifted nearer, Thor heard a low, humming sound like the beating of distant wings; the great gray mass resolved itself into millions of locusts which swooped down on the green crops and covered the whole prairie with a crawling, hopping, shimmering blanket. The incessant sound of myriad crunching mandibles on the tender stalks roused the family to futile action.

They beat at the loathsome invaders with clubs, pounded with sticks on kettles to create a din and so frighten the voracious creatures away; they set fires that were smothered in a few moments by the very juice of the frying creatures. And still they came, in a stream seemingly endless, blighting the grass and the green crops, stripping the bark from the trees Thor had planted as a windbreak, gnawing hoe and ax handles to slivers.

Thor heard later seemingly impossible tales of the terrible plague, yet the tales were true: how trains had been halted by crushed millions of grasshoppers that made the rails slippery as grease, while trainmen shoveled the creatures away in great scoops and sanded the tracks before they could continue; how other millions had perished in the Missouri River and washed up on the banks in foot-deep windrows whose stench could be smelled for miles; how the fish of the streams and the domestic fowl of the barnyards had gorged themselves for days on the repulsive creatures until their flesh was inedible, so strong was the taste of the locusts they had eaten.

There was no defense against such a foe, and Thor saw with helpless despair the very food for his family's mouths disappearing down the insatiable maw of the invader. Not till the last living spear of growth had been ravaged did the enemy depart. Then, as if moved by a single mind, the creeping horde one day rose into the skies and disappeared toward the horizon, its great drifting shadow moving like a blight over the land it had devoured.

Thor and his neighbors talked it over. They were not beaten yet. They could get work in the settlement for wages; they could gather buffalo bones and haul them eastward to the railroad for sale. Next year the plague might not return.

And it did not return. Instead, the crops came up green and flourishing in the spring, and June passed without the feared descent of the creeping locusts. But as summer lengthened, the sun hung like a burnished ball in the cloudless sky, and tiny dust-devils whipped through the fresh-turned sod. Day after day the settlers scanned the sky in vain for the dark rain clouds which never came; the wheat drooped and turned brown and the prairie grasses themselves parched in the furnacelike heat.

Late summer brought blinding dust storms—only another added burden, for by now the crops were gone anyway. A neighbor's wife hanged herself in the barn one day, her mind unhinged by the unaccustomed hardships and the immeasurable loneliness of the prairie. Others began to move away that fall. There was no use battling this land, they said. They would go back to Minnesota. Maybe their relatives and friends there would help them to get a new start. The railroad was slow in coming, too, now that times were hard, and the womenfolk refused to live longer in the wilderness, with not even a sign of civilization to break the isolation and monotony of their bleak lives.

Thor looked grim and vowed that he would hang on. Once when the last of his neighbors drove by in his laden wagon to tell him that he too was leaving, Thor lost his temper and cursed the man savagely for a coward. That fellow Ericsson is a crazy man, the departing farmer told people at the settlement, and spoke truer than he knew.

But Thor stayed. Again he worked as a day laborer in the settlement, but most of his wages, which he had hoped to spend for seed, had to go instead to pay the notes he had signed with the men at the village, with interest at 20 per cent. They talked differently now, these men who had been so optimistic and helpful a few seasons before: unintelligible talk about hard times, and interest, and notes, and a desperate new thing called *Panic*.

But the next summer nature was kind. The locusts stayed away, and the rains came, and at harvest time the wheat stood tall and golden in the sun. In a week, now, it would be ready for cutting.

That afternoon, as Thor was mending harness in the sod barn, his work was interrupted by a pattering sound that grew suddenly into a roar like the drumming of thousands of steel-shod hoofs. He rushed out into the yard, to be met by a hurricane of blows that momentarily blinded him. The hot afternoon air had turned icy cold. Great pelting balls of ice, large as walnuts, leaped and rolled impishly as they struck the earth at his feet. It was the dreaded hailstorm of the prairies.

Thor thought of the ripe wheat, and knew that it was being beaten flat, crushed, soaked, ruined, a total loss. Unless he could again find work at the settlement, it meant starvation for his little family. He could not waste a single hour. When he came into the house and Karen saw the look in his eyes she wisely said nothing; she watched him from the doorway as he trudged away on foot through the late afternoon sunlight toward the settlement nine miles away.

So absorbed was Thor in his thoughts that he did not at once notice the absence of life as he came into the outskirts of the little hamlet. Not until he halted in front of the village store and saw the boarded-up door and the bare shelves did he realize that the town was empty of people. He broke into a clumsy run, making his way along the single block of crude frame buildings and peering stupidly into the dirty windows. The buildings were deserted, tenantless as if men had not been here for ten years, instead of the ten days since he had last been in the village.

He shouted and bellowed in his frenzy, calling to someone to answer him. He ran through the dusty streets, smashing open doors and prowling through the vacant shacks searching for some explanation for this fearful disaster; but the hamlet was deserted; its fifty people had vanished without a trace.

Thor could not know that three days before, a farmer and his son had been killed by a band of marauding Indians as they were putting up hay near the town; that the farmer's wife had escaped to carry the news to the settlement; and that the knowledge of the Indians' presence had emptied the village overnight. The people had loaded their goods and all their belongings and fled to Yankton twenty miles away, where there was a large enough population to make possible a defense against the Indians. Nobody, in the sudden panic, had thought to send word to the Norwegian immigrant who lived nine miles away across the Indian-infested prairie.

Thor was seized by a sudden blinding terror. It was like witchcraft, this terrifying disappearance of a whole community. It was as if some evil troll had cast a spell over the village, destroying all life, or worse still, rendering the people of the town invisible and disembodied. As he stood there in the settlement street in the gathering darkness, something snapped in the mind of Thor Ericsson. He shambled off into the darkness, stumbling and muttering to himself. A rainstorm, coming on the heels of the hail, beat at his head and shoulders as he trudged unseeing the long nine miles back to his lonely homestead. It was almost dawn when he returned and let himself quietly in the door. His wife and the children were asleep. Outside, the storm was over.

He hesitated only for a moment. He took the butcher knife from the kitchen table and cut the throat of his infant son. He cut the throat of his little daughter. He crossed the room on trembling legs and cut the throat of his sleeping wife. Then he slashed with the dripping knife at his own neck.

A LONE horseman, stopping by in the early morning hours for a drink of water, found him unconscious on the floor in a pool of his own blood. Dragging him out into the sunlight, the horrified rider yoked Thor's oxen to the farm wagon and carried the unconscious man into Yankton. After receiving medical aid he was taken to the territorial jail, where he crouched in a corner of his room, a gibbering creature with haunted, insane eyes.

Yankton, August 8.—Thor Ericsson, a Norwegian immigrant farmer who homesteaded about thirty miles north of here several years ago, was brought into town last night and lodged in the local calaboose by the Sheriff. He is charged with having murdered his wife and his two small children, after which he tried to take his own life. Ericsson is a slight, blond, inoffensive-looking man, speaking almost no English. When questioned he could give no reason for his fiendish act.

Chapter 10

THE SPOILERS

Once there was a Mountain That Stood on Its Head.

It's a tale they tell in the Black Hills country, where the stern faces of Washington, Jefferson, Lincoln, and Theodore Roosevelt look down with granitic frowns from the sculptured shoulder of Mt. Rushmore. So you can be sure the story is true. Because the man doesn't live who'd dare to tell a lie with the Father of His Country towering over him, sixty feet from chin to forehead.

They say it was Hels Helsen's fault to begin with. Hels was Paul Bunyan's foreman, and they had come down together to South Dakota to log off the queerest forest that ever grew. This was the timber that covered the Mountain That Stood on Its Head. Hels Helsen, the Bull of the Woods, was put in charge of the job, because Paul Bunyan had other things to do—and that was when the trouble all began. Hels, the Big Swede, was a hard worker, but he couldn't hope to keep up with Paul—and on a ticklish job like this one, something odd was bound to turn up.

You see, the Mountain That Stood on Its Head was two miles high and a hundred and twenty-seven feet broad at its top, which was covered with a heavy stand of timber. High Springs, which bubbled out of the ground to form Lofty River, was in the center of the broad plateau, and at the edge of the mountain, where Lofty River leaped into space and fell to earth two miles below, was a mighty waterfall called Niagara.

But that wasn't all. The Mountain That Stood on Its Head cast a vast shadow over the plain beneath, and on its slopes, which slanted down and inward, the trees grew upside down. It was this forest of upside-down timber that caused Hels Helsen, the Big Swede, all the trouble. His loggers began to complain when he ordered them to string cables from tree to tree for support and log off the slopes of the mountain with their heads pointing down to earth. The lumberjacks complained that all the sawdust fell into their eyes and mouths; the blood ran to their heads; and, worst

154

of all, their *snus* boxes kept falling out of their pockets. Hels Helsen was stumped. The loggers weren't getting anything done under these strange conditions, so the Big Swede went to talk to Paul Bunyan.

"Yumping Yesus," said the Bull of the Woods to Paul, "Aye tank ve skall move camp, Meester Bunyan. Dese logger can't hang oopside down no longer."

But Paul Bunyan had already figured out how the job should be done, and he let forth a mighty roar that brought the loggers leaping from their bunkhouses.

"Come along," said Paul. "I'll show you how to log off this upside-down timber!"

Hels Helsen and all the lumberjacks followed Paul to the Mountain That Stood on Its Head, marveling meanwhile at the mighty double-barreled shotgun that Paul carried over his shoulder. His belt was studded with cartridges loaded with blasting powder and filled with bullets made of two-foot sheets of steel. The barrels of the huge shotgun were used later by Paul as smokestacks for one of his sawmills.

At the Mountain That Stood on Its Head, Paul leveled the weapon and pulled the triggers. There was a roar like thunder and the flying sheets of steel tore through the upside-down trees, cutting them through at the base and dropping them earthward, where they stuck top side down in the ground. Paul kept at this work all day long, until the forest that grew upside down was completely leveled and the loggers were able to go to work right side up once more.

But the Big Swede, Hels Helsen, was not to be outdone by Paul Bunyan. Hels determined to show the jacks he knew a thing or two himself, and next morning he set out alone for the Mountain That Stood on Its Head. Clambering up the mountain's slope and over its rim onto the flat plateau above, Hels set to work tearing up the great pine trees with his bare hands.

When Paul Bunyan caught sight of this unorthodox method of logging, he made a mighty leap at the mountain's rim two miles in the air, caught hold of it with his big hands, and drew himself up on the mountain's top, where the Big Swede was hard at work. A moment later they charged each other with roars of rage that could be heard in the distant Minnesota forests.

The loggers left behind in camp crawled into their bunks and covered their heads at the sound of the battling giants hurling each other to the earth and trampling the huge pine trees into splinters. The ground rolled and trembled underfoot as if from an earthquake. Great pieces of the mountain's edge broke off as the warring loggers drove each other back and forth. From dawn to dusk and all through the black night their fierce cries and the sound of mighty blows echoed over the countryside.

At dawn the next day there was one last rock-shivering reverberation, and then silence. The concussion overturned all the bunkhouses, and when the bewildered loggers crept out from under the ruins a few minutes later, they saw Paul Bunyan approaching, bearing on his broad shoulder the unconscious form of the Big Swede. As Paul dumped the Bull of the Woods on the ground, Hels opened one battered eye.

"Aye tank aye behave now, Meester Bunyan," he said.

But there was nothing left of the Mountain That Stood on Its Head. The heavy calked boots of Paul and the Big Swede had trampled it into a mass of blood-stained clods of earth, which are known today as the Black Hills. High Springs was gone, Lofty River was gone, and the great waterfall known as Niagara was gone, too. But Paul Bunyan had always liked the name *Niagara*. So he gave it later on to a little rapids somewhere up in New York State along the Canadian border.

James Stevens, author of *Paul Bunyan*, has more or less verified this version of the Black Hills' formation, but there are other versions too. Some old lumberjacks declare that the Hills are nothing more than the grave of Paul's famous Blue Ox, Babe—who, it will be remembered, was forty-two ax handles and a plug of tobacco between the eyes.

Babe in a moment of carelessness had swallowed a red-hot stove—that same huge stove which had a griddle so large it was kept greased by nine small Negro boys who skated over it with hams strapped to their feet. Once Babe had got his breath he lowered his head, flung up his tail, and set out bellowing in the general direction of South Dakota, with Paul Bunyan in close pursuit. But it was too late for Paul to help. Far out on the prairies Babe fell crashing to earth and died—of heartburn, probably.

The fountains of Paul's great deep were broken up and he rained floods of tears that made the Missouri River. Since it was impractical to dig a grave for so huge a beast, Paul heaped rocks and earth on the mighty bulk until it was completely covered. And in the fullness of time the mountain became dimpled with grass and covered with great trees; the creeks eroded deep gullies and canyons in its mass; and so the Black Hills were formed.

There are a number of intransigent scientists, however, who disagree with both these explanations and declare that the Hills are considerably older than Hels Helsen or even Paul Bunyan. It was ages ago in geologic time, they say—far back in the morning of the world—when some mighty convulsion of nature first thrust the giant batholith of the Hills up from the level land.

The Hills were old when the Rocky Mountains were not yet a fold in the North American continental mass; were old when the Alps and the Apennines first upreared their heads; were old when the Caucasus and the ancient Pyrenees were born; stood as they stand today when the mighty Himalayas were a swampland and Mesozoic monsters swarmed and spawned in the slime of the tidal beaches.

For millions of years the Hills have been rising, and it is by no means certain that the process has even now been arrested. This tremendous movement, extending over immeasurable periods of geologic time, has accomplished strange things. The deepest and oldest strata now form the upper surface, so that the Hills are a veritable paradise for archaeologists; the fossilized bones of dinosaurs and other prehistoric forms of life may be found in almost · every exposed outcropping of rock. And hidden in the seams and folds of this extraordinary formation are veins of rich gold-bearing ore.

IT WAS in 1874 that General Custer and his Seventh Cavalry, stationed at Fort Abraham Lincoln near Bismarck, Dakota Territory, set out for the Black Hills to investigate rumors that gold was to be found there. The Black Hills were Indian territory, promised to the Sioux for "as long as the grass shall grow or the waters run." If gold was really there, it would be the duty of the government to protect the Indian hunting grounds from a white man's rush. But if it was there in large quantities, the government would be interested in obtaining title to the land and moving the Indians to a new home; the panic of '73 was at its nadir and a big gold strike would provide a welcome economic palliative.

On French Creek, near the present town of Custer, the expedition discovered unmistakable signs of gold in large quantities. The fact was supposed to be kept secret, but within a short time the news was all over the West and hundreds of men had started for the Black Hills. To the credit of the government it must be said that an attempt was made to halt them; United States troops actually turned back numerous parties bound for the Sioux hunting grounds.

But it was a futile and halfhearted gesture. The wild and unsettled nature of the country made the military's task virtually impossible in any case. After an unsuccessful attempt to make a treaty with the Sioux by which they would relinquish the Hills, the troops were withdrawn and the lands were thrown open to gold-seekers. Unquestionably public opinion in favor of the move was almost irresistible; but, also unquestionably, it was a brutal and shameless violation of the Indians' rights.

Upon the withdrawal of the troops, white prospectors by the thousands swept into the peaceful domain of the Sioux and made of it a scarred and unlovely countryside, barren of game and inhospitable to its rightful owners. In the cool fashion of the Anglo-Saxon, the miners who were occupying the Indians' lands made up purses and offered two hundred dollars for each Sioux scalp delivered to them. Slowly but inexorably the Sioux were driven back, disillusioned and embittered, many of them to join the sullen Sitting Bull, who sulked in majestic silence on the rolling plains to the west. They were learning, in hardship and hunger, the worth of the conqueror's word.

The white man had sown the wind. Custer and his Seventh

Cavalry were to reap its harvest in blood and agony a scant twenty-four months later.

The first wave of gold-seekers poured into the southern portion of the Hills, near where Custer's expedition had made the original discovery. The town of Custer City, which sprang up as if by magic, had a population of seven thousand before the year was out.

But the big strike was yet to come. John Pearson, a Yankton prospector, ranged far to the north seeking signs of gold in the unexplored Indian country. In the fall of 1875 he one day came upon a gulch filled with dead timber, the result of an earlier forest fire. And John Pearson struck it rich! He had discovered famous Deadwood Gulch, one of the richest diggings in mining history; the mother lode of the Homestake mine alone has since yielded more than three hundred million dollars in gold.

Pearson managed to keep his discovery a secret until the following spring; then, when news of the fabulous strike got abroad, the rush to Deadwood Gulch began. Custer City miners left the town at the rate of a thousand a day for the new diggings; within a week where there had been a city of seven thousand there was left a hamlet of only a few hundred persons.

By the summer of 1876 Deadwood Gulch was a teeming gold camp of twenty-five thousand people. From one end to the other of the long narrow canyon stretched a makeshift city: one hell-roaring, gun-fighting, whiskey-drinking, gold-digging mass of humanity crammed into a single continuous street that stretched for miles along the canyon floor.

All the floating population of the West descended on this last of the great gold strikes in the continental United States. Gamblers, prostitutes, miners, gunmen, dance-hall girls, speculators, merchants—yes, even a preacher—flocked to the new Eldorado of the West. Forty-niners from far-off California mingled with greenhorns and tenderfeet from all the eastern states. Names famous all over the West were there: Poker Alice, Wild Bill Hickok, Calamity Jane, Bedrock Tom, and California Jack. Preacher Smith, come to spread the Gospel among the lost souls of the diggings, found only part-time need for his services and was obliged to spend weekdays doing carpenter work to augment his income. This stalwart champion of the Lord's work was later killed by Indians, but his memory is kept green by a re-enactment of his deeds and death each year at Deadwood's *Days of '76* celebration.

Fantastic and colorful names blossomed among the rough characters who affixed titles to this virgin country. Nigger Gulch, Shirt Tail Gulch, Two Bit Gulch, and Bob Tail Gulch were names given to Black Hills canyons. The miners named their claims with a fine disregard for the civilized amenities of nomenclature. The Mother De Smet, doubtless named in honor of that fine old wilderness priest, Father De Smet, was a fair sample. Easterners and government map-makers alike were horrified at such sturdy western place names as Stud Horse Canyon and Stinking Water Creek.

There was ample entertainment available in Deadwood, and not only in saloons, hurdy-gurdy houses, gambling dens, and bawdy houses. The Bella Union Theater boasted seventeen curtained boxes, although they were made of rough logs. Ordinary seats were constructed of wooden slabs laid atop stakes driven into the bare earth. The first piano in the gulch, brought in by ox team from Bismarck in an arduous two-month trip, graced the stage of the Bella. Ticket prices ranged from two and a half dollars to five dollars. A troupe of traveling players who brought *The Mikado* to the gulch were amazed when the show ran for a hundred and thirty nights. Deadwood's most famous theater, the Gem, was known from coast to coast in its heyday, and an astonishing array of famous actors of the time appeared before appreciative audiences of roughly clad miners.

For the elite of the town there were less frivolous and more educational activities. Literary societies, a popular fad of the day, were common, as were traveling "lyceums" and lecturers. Dancing clubs, amateur theatricals, and card parties provided other diversions for those who did not care for the more lusty entertainments.

To satisfy the miners' insatiable appetite for gambling, almost every form of chance-taking was available. Chuck-a-luck, roulette, fan-tan, draw and stud poker, faro, and euchre were some of the commoner games. Horse races, cock fights, prize fights, dog fights—and even, in some of the western camps, bull fights—were everyday occurrences on which huge sums were wagered.

The notorious gambler and gunman Wild Bill Hickok met his end while gambling in Deadwood's famous No. 10 saloon. Known throughout the West as the Prince of Pistoleers, this soft-spoken ex-theological student was one of the more personable and law-abiding of the many murderous characters who then passed as "heroes" on the frontier. Most of his alleged twenty-seven killings had been accomplished in the service of the law as a frontier marshal; but the evidence indicates that he was no more averse than the next desperado to shooting a man in the back to satisfy his own personal pique or whim.

It is only in Hollywood movies that famous gunmen give their enemies fair warning by confronting them in daylight in the town streets. Actually the reputations of virtually all the famous killers of the West were made by quite other means. A common practice was to hide in a dark alley, after first screwing up one's courage with whiskey, and then shoot the victim in the back with a thoroughly lethal weapon that would give him no opportunity to return even a dying shot. In short, the methods of the famous desperadoes were the methods that cowardly murderers have always used since time began.

The outlaw elements of Deadwood, fearing that Wild Bill might be made marshal of the town—for he did sometimes work on the side of the law if the price was right—bribed Jack McCall to assassinate him. Jack, in the approved fashion, fortified himself with whiskey and entered the No. 10 saloon, where Wild Bill sat playing cards with his back to the door—though he should have known better.

He held aces and eights in his hand and was probably contemplating a raise when McCall stepped up behind him and shot him in the back of the head. The bullet passed clear through Wild Bill's skull and lodged in the wrist of the man seated opposite him. This man thereby became famous for the rest of his life. He refused to have the slug extracted and spent the remainder of his existence making dramatic entrances into gatherings throughout the West with the loud announcement: "Gentlemen, the bullet that killed Wild Bill has come to town!"

For Wild Bill was dead, all right. And all over the western country today aces and eights are known as "the dead man's hand."

McCall was tried by a jury of miners—a jury well packed with the men who had paid him three hundred dollars to assassinate Hickok—and acquitted. Later, however, he was seized by the federal authorities, tried, and hanged for his crime. His plea of double jeopardy was disregarded, for the federal court held that a local jury had no jurisdiction in a case where a crime was committed in federal territory.

ANOTHER famous Deadwood character lives on in the romantic mythology of the West. They called her Calamity Jane.

From the Texas Panhandle to the bonanza strikes of Deadwood and Alder Gulch her name was on men's lips, and the tall tales of her deeds were legend while still she lived. Eastern writers who had never been beyond the Alleghenies seized eagerly on the stories of the western lady fire-eater and wove tales of her daring exploits that made her name a household word along with Buffalo Bill's. Modern authors and Hollywood scenario writers have perpetuated the legend, until today Calamity Jane is a heroic figure in the pageant of our western folklore.

The true story of her life is a drab caricature of the glamorous career invented by herself and fitted with trappings by numerous biographers. Actually, as Bill Nye once put it, "Hard luck and Martha Jane Canary always went hand in hand."

The principal facts of her career are not hard to trace, although there are some discrepancies in the several accounts of her earlier years. According to Calamity's own version, given in her autobiography, *The Life and Adventures of Calamity Jane*, she was born Martha Jane Canary in Princeton, Missouri, in 1851. Other writers give the year of her birth as 1850 and the place as Ohio, whence her family moved to Missouri while she was a small child.

Her mother was Charlotte Canary, a handsome young woman whose husband had reputedly rescued her from a brothel in the hope of reforming her. Charlotte, however, proved to be singularly unimpressed by the reformer's arguments; and the staider elements of the little Missouri village were horrified by the spectacle of the young Mrs. Canary smoking cigars, drinking whiskey, and cursing loudly and publicly all who disapproved of her conduct. Her husband, a rather ineffectual young farmer, was either unable to curb Charlotte's lusty appetites or became finally reconciled to his fate. At any rate, during the rush to the Montana gold fields in 1865, the Canary family joined the hopeful caravan traveling north.

Calamity's own story states that her mother died in Montana in 1866, after which she and her father moved to Salt Lake City, where the luckless reformer soon followed his unreformed mate into eternity. Another version has it that Charlotte divorced her unsympathetic spouse and opened a bawdy house appropriately called "The Bird Cage" in honor of the Canary name. Here the fifteen-year-old Jane assisted her mother in entertaining such custom as was available.

In any case, the legend of Calamity Jane had its inception soon after her appearance in Salt Lake City in 1867. There is little of truth in her own version of the career that was to make her name a byword, but since many biographers have accepted her story, and in some cases even embellished it further, a brief review of its salient points may be of interest.

After the death of her mother, she relates, she spent a brief time following the construction camps of the Northern Pacific Railway, which was then extending its steel tentacles across the continent. Next, according to her highly fictional account, she made the acquaintance of General Custer and became a scout for the United States Army at Fort Russel. She began to dress as a man during this period, and participated in several campaigns against the Indians in Arizona and elsewhere.

"I was considered," she writes modestly, "the most daring and reckless rider and one of the best shots in the Western country."

Among the more hazardous exploits she recounts is how she saved Captain Egan from a band of hostile savages, and how the captain, in gratitude, christened her "Calamity Jane" in recognition of her talent for making felicitous appearances when matters were at their most calamitous.

Calamity describes in her little book how she accompanied General Custer and his famous Seventh Cavalry when they were ordered to the Black Hills in the middle 70's. But for an illness brought on by incredible hardships suffered while carrying important dispatches, she might have been present at the Seventh's tragic defeat in the Battle of the Little Big Horn. It was shortly after this that she met Wild Bill Hickok and accompanied him to Deadwood, where she became a pony-express rider between Deadwood and Custer City. Badmen were wise enough to steer clear of her path, however, "for, being a well-known rider and a good shot," it was quite apparent that any attempt to molest the lady rider would have been tantamount to suicide.

When Wild Bill Hickok was shot by the gunman Jack McCall, Calamity's righteous anger knew no bounds. Cornering the culprit in a Deadwood butcher shop, Jane seized a cleaver and forced the cringing badman to throw up his hands. But McCall survived to expiate his crime legally, for Calamity discovered at this strategic moment that she had left her shootin' irons home on the bedpost. "I would have killed him on the spot," she confides, had it not been for this baffling circumstance.

To sum up Calamity's flamboyant account: She left Deadwood in 1877, later prevented a robbery of the Overland Mail, nursed a camp of six miners through a smallpox epidemic, and helped the Seventh Cavalry construct Fort Meade and the town of Sturgis. The next year she became a prospector and afterward a bullwhacker on the route between Fort Pierre and the Black Hills. Later she homesteaded, ran a roadside tavern, moved to Texas in 1885, married, and remained there until 1889. She then became a hotelkeeper in Boulder, Colorado, and finally returned to Deadwood in 1896.

Calamity's autobiography ends here, with her return to the haunts of her earlier days. Its basic facts have been accepted by many writers of more enthusiasm than discernment, and her adventures have been more or less faithfully portrayed in a half dozen Hollywood movies. The facts are less romantic.

Calamity's accounts of her U.S. Army connections and her duties as a scout and dispatch-carrier are, of course, completely without foundation in fact. It is true that she lived in many of the frontier towns described in her story, but her services to the Army were in a quite different capacity from that mentioned in her book.

Her story of Captain Egan's naming her Calamity Jane is a case in point. Captain Egan's only recollection of her was that he had once ordered her off a military reservation under his command for reasons of "discipline." Contemporary records indicate that she was recognized for what she was even among the rough and generous natives of the mining camps. The ridiculous falsehoods that filled the Deadwood papers at the time of her residence there in 1887 prompted one angry miner to take up the pen in his hairy fist and pour out his wrath in a letter to the editor of the Deadwood *Daily Champion*:

As far as her solid merit is concerned she is a fraud and a dead giveaway. A hundred waiter girls or mop-squeezers in this gulch are her superior in everything. She strikes out and lays around with a lot of bull-whackers and road agents like an Indian squaw. But everybody in the Hills knows her, largely through newspaper accounts which have made her famous. Her form and features are not only indifferent but are repulsive. It makes me tired to see so much written about such a woman.

Citizens of Deadwood who knew Jane well describe her as a common harlot—and one of such coarse and forbidding appearance as to frighten away all save the tipsiest miners. In Montana her boon companion was Madame Bulldog, who is described by the Montana *State Guide Book* as a Livingston harlot who "tipped the scales at 190, stripped." After which it adds blithely, "And stripped she was most of the time."

Calamity's claim of being Wild Bill Hickok's sweetheart was an infamous slander—a fact which Calamity herself admitted in her declining years—for, whatever else may be said of Wild Bill, he was at least fastidious. At the time of the smallpox epidemic in the gold fields, court records of the district indicate that, far from performing the offices of a Good Samaritan, Calamity was actually before a justice of the peace for jack-rolling a drunken miner to the tune of thirty dollars.

In short, virtually every adventure related by this bedraggled creature in her "autobiography" was nothing more than a figment of her imagination. Upon her return to Deadwood in 1896, Calamity, who by this time had become a western institution, became a member of the burlesque troupe at the famous Gem theater, but her stay there was brief. The manager objected to her conduct, as well as to her disconcerting habit of improvising bawdy lines at random moments during the performance. She next signed a contract to exhibit herself in Kohl and Middleton's circuit of dime museums, where she gave a short lecture on her adventures, peddled photographs of herself, and hawked copies of her autobiography.

Clad in fringed buckskins and armed with two huge six guns with which she was obviously unfamiliar, she caused so much amusement among the customers that the venture was canceled. After another fling in show business at the Pan-American Exposition in Buffalo, she became embroiled in a drunken fight and Buffalo Bill gave her train fare back to Billings, Montana.

In her final years she traveled about from town to town in the West, selling pictures of herself dressed in scout garb and cadging drinks and lodging as best she could. She spent a short time in a Montana poorhouse after falling ill at Bozeman, and upon her recovery drifted back to her old stamping ground at Deadwood.

Penniless, her health broken by years of dissipation, and of such fearsome and forbidding visage that she could no longer practice her profession, she found herself unwelcome even in the tough dives of the Black Hills. A handful of kindly citizens paid her expenses during the few months left to her of life. She died in a cheap boardinghouse at Terry. At her funeral in Deadwood the whole town turned out to follow her coffin to Boot Hill, where she was buried beside Wild Bill Hickok.

Her own story, the praises of numerous biographers, and the final accolade accorded her by Hollywood have probably made her place secure as the epitome of those bold and adventurous women who followed the forward movement of the frontier. Perhaps it is better so. In the imperishable story of the West, legend has made her what she most desired to be, but never was, in real life.

WHILE Calamity, Wild Bill, and all the motley population of the Black Hills camps were manufacturing their own peculiar forms of history, more serious events were shaping in the tragic struggle of the red man to cling to his last strongholds of freedom. General Sherman, who said that war was hell, proceeded to prove it in a letter to Ulysses S. Grant concerning the Indian question: "We must proceed . . . against them, even to their extermination— men, women and children. Nothing less will reach the root of the case." But not all army generals were, like Sherman, more blood-thirsty than the savages themselves. When General Crook was asked if he did not find the Indian campaigns hard work, Crook replied: "Yes, they are hard, but the hardest thing is to go out and fight against those who you know are in the right."

General Crook's statement of the Indians' position was quite correct. They were completely within their treaty rights in insist-ing upon the retention of the Black Hills as their home. Further, they were within their rights in remaining on the Montana prairies where they were molesting nobody, despite the government's plea that they come in and let themselves be settled on reservations.

But eastern railroads wished to build into Montana; white men wished to settle there; hence it became necessary to manufacture an excuse that would enable the Army to interfere. This the gov-ernment proceeded to do with enviable diplomatic finesse. An order was issued to all Indians off the reservations to return to those reservations by January 31, 1876, or be classified as "hos-tile." This ingenious order was issued in December 1875. It was an exceptionally severe winter, and the couriers bearing the mes-sages did not get through to the tribes in many cases. Many were hundreds of miles away and could not possibly have returned by the appointed date even if it had been summertime. Perhaps some just didn't want to return—and they were within their treaty rights to refuse, if they so desired.

But the proper diplomatic forms had been observed, thousands of Indians were declared hostile who had never heard of the order, and the campaign of '76 was ordered into preparation. The white men were jubilant, and in the Black Hills, that summer of '76, the miners were still offering two hundred dollars apiece for Sioux scalps.

But far to the West, in Montana, the Sioux were busy taking scalps themselves. We call it Custer's Last Stand. Actually, it was the last stand of the Sioux Nation against the irresistible force of the encroaching white man.

Chapter 11

THE WHIRLWIND

The river steamer *Far West* bucked in the yellow current and tugged at her moorings. It was in the sultry month of June 1876, and the *Far West* had nosed her way to the mouth of the Little Big Horn, where she lay awaiting orders from General Alfred Terry. A week had passed now, and somewhere in the rugged interior Terry and his United States troops were ranging the wild Montana prairies in search of the elusive Sioux.

Captain Grant Marsh, skipper of the *Far West*, paced her deck and cursed the delay of the long-awaited courier. The hot June wind of the last few days had borne to his ears, now and then, the distant crepitation of rifle fire, but there had been no word from the commander.

As Marsh stared out impatiently over the hazy prairies, the tangled growth at the stream's edge parted suddenly. A lathered, plunging pony slid to his haunches on the riverbank, as the rider jerked him to a stop and signaled that he wished to board the vessel. It was a Crow scout, in the last stages of exhaustion.

On deck, the Indian squatted and traced on the clean white boards a group of dots. Looking up at Marsh, he spoke the Crow word for "white men." Marsh nodded to indicate that he understood. Around the group of dots the Indian traced a second group, which he labeled with the word for "Sioux." Again the captain nodded. Then the scout leaned forward and with a dramatic sweep of his hand brushed out the inner group of dots.

Captain Marsh gasped in horror and disbelief. But the scout's pantomime drama was true. And in that primitive fashion the story of the greatest military disaster in the history of our Indian wars was first reported: the annihilation of Custer and his entire immediate command in the Battle of the Little Big Horn.

For a clear comprehension of the Custer battle, it is best to begin with certain provisions of the Indian treaties of the preceding

169

decades by which the red men had been persuaded to cede a portion of their dwindling lands. Besides guaranteeing the Indians their remaining land in perpetuity, the government was to issue to them certain goods at specified seasons: foodstuffs, blankets, and other supplies.

But the Indian traderships under which the government distributed this largess to the Sioux became riddled with graft. The agencies were covertly for sale to the highest bidder. The trail of the scandal led to high places in Washington: to the families of Cabinet members; to Secretary of War Belknap, who was impeached, and resigned rather than face an investigation; even, it was darkly whispered, to Orville Grant, brother of the President.

General Custer, stationed at Fort Abraham Lincoln near Bismarck, Dakota Territory, had become aware of the corrupt conditions. Several New York newspapers investigated and exposed the vicious system under which the Sioux were being mulcted. Then Custer, always rash and impetuous, made accusations that helped to bring on the famous "Belknap Scandal"—which, in turn, paved the way to the terrible responsibility that is Custer's before the bar of history.

Summoned to appear before a congressional committee, the dashing general made charges far more sweeping than he was able to establish, though there is little doubt today that most of them were well founded. The gentlemen in Washington and elsewhere who conceived such stenches in the public nostrils as the Whiskey Ring, the Gold Scandal, and the infamous Crédit Mobilier would scarcely have scrupled at swindling ignorant savages.

But President Grant, loyal to his friends and appointees, refused to believe any of them less honest than himself, an error of judgment he was to regret bitterly in later years. When Grant learned that Custer's testimony had cast a shadow of suspicion upon his own immediate family, he was furious. A soldier to the core, he took a soldier's revenge: Custer was deprived of his command and expressly forbidden to accompany the expedition which was preparing to crush the Sioux.

This was a bitter blow to Custer, for the order touched him at his weakest point—his inordinate love for the limelight. At the last moment General Terry, who commanded the expedition in Custer's stead, secured permission for the disappointed general to accompany him. It was a gesture Terry was later to regret.

On the morning of May 17, 1876, Terry and his command moved out of Fort Abraham Lincoln. With characteristic generosity Terry had placed Custer in command of his old regiment, the Seventh Cavalry. The leathery creak of polished saddles, the jingle of accouterments, the heavy lumbering of wagon trains mingled with the strains of the regimental tune "Garryowen," as the two-mile-long battle array swept out of old Fort Lincoln with flags astream.

Only one accredited newspaper correspondent was authorized to accompany the expedition: Colonel C. A. Lounsberry of Bismarck, editor of the Bismarck *Tribune* and special correspondent for James Gordon Bennett of the New York *Herald*. Even this was a concession, for General Sheridan had directed Terry to take no correspondents with him. "They always make trouble," said Sheridan gruffly, with the professional soldier's classic distaste for having on hand any witnesses able to talk in case he should blunder. But illness in Lounsberry's family made it necessary for him to remain at home at the moment of departure, and in his place he sent Mark Kellogg, a young employee of his who knew much of Indians and frontier warfare. "Man-who-makes-the-paper-talk" Kellogg was called by the admiring Sioux, to whom the art of writing was a source of constant wonder.

General Sheridan had planned the campaign at his headquarters in Chicago. It was a three-pronged attack that could not possibly have failed had it been executed properly. Terry was to move west from Fort Abraham Lincoln, General Crook north from Fort Fetterman in Wyoming, and General Gibbon from Fort Ellis in Montana. The Sioux were massed in the vicinity of the Big Horn River, where the three prongs of the attack were to converge, suppress any resistance, and escort the Indians back to their reservations.

It was past the middle of June when Generals Terry and Gibbon established contact with each other at the confluence of the Rosebud and Yellowstone rivers. Though they knew nothing of it, one arm of the triple attack had been thwarted already. General Crook had been met and thrown back by a huge force of well-armed Indians under the leadership of the famous Chief Crazy Horse. Crook retired and encamped, but, with the country between him and his colleagues swarming with hostiles, he had no means of communicating to them the unexpected numbers of the enemy. Terry and Gibbon thought the Indians numbered no more than a thousand or fifteen hundred. Actually, estimates of the huge camp were later set at ten or twelve thousand men, women, and children—or perhaps two thousand to three thousand warriors.

Terry and Gibbon, confident that they had more than sufficient strength to overwhelm any number of Indians they might encounter, decided to prosecute the campaign as scheduled in spite of Crook's absence. The generals held their council of war aboard the *Far West*, the supply steamer which Captain Marsh had brought upstream to the military rendezvous from Fort Abraham Lincoln. Major Reno, scouting a few days before, had come upon a fresh Indian trail that appeared to lead toward the Little Big Horn River. It was agreed that the trail had probably been made by the large body of Sioux they were seeking, and the strategy of an enveloping movement was threshed out by Custer, Gibbon, and Terry. Marsh was ordered to take his vessel to the mouth of the Big Horn and then proceed, if possible, up that stream to the mouth of the Little Big Horn.

The plan was clear. It was the afternoon of the twenty-second of June when Yellow Hair and his Seventh Cavalry cantered off over the tawny prairies into the pages of history.

It is not difficult to reconstruct today the tragedy of that summer afternoon on the brown sloping hills above the river which the Sioux called the Greasy Grass. From Major Reno and his surviving men we have most of the story of what took place after Custer and the Seventh Cavalry took leave of Terry and Gibbon. General Terry had given Custer his written orders, bearing principally upon what action should be taken concerning the Indian trail discovered a few days before by Major Reno:

"It is, of course, impossible to give you any definite instructions in regard to this movement; and were it not impossible to do so, the department commander places too much confidence in your zeal, energy, and ability to wish to impose upon you precise orders which might hamper your action when nearly in contact with the enemy. He will, however, indicate to you his own views of what your action should be, and he desires that you should conform to them unless you shall see sufficient reason for departing from them. He thinks that you should proceed up the Rosebud until you ascertain definitely the direction in which the trail above spoken of leads. Should it be found—as it appears to be almost certain that it will be found—to lead toward the Little Big Horn, he thinks that you should still proceed southward, perhaps as far as the headwaters of the Tongue, and then turn toward the Little Big Horn. . . ."

General Terry doubtless labored diligently over the composition of this bit of military prose. He felt the delicacy of his position. He was in command of an expedition that Custer, with some justice, felt *he* should have had the honor of leading. He knew how thin-skinned the sensitive Yellow Hair was. And he knew, too, that Custer was smarting under the treatment he had received at the hands of President Grant.

On the other hand, Terry could not afford a fiasco. Gibbon and Custer were to meet in the valley of the Little Big Horn and crush the hostiles between them. Cooperation was vital. So Terry, coating the pill of duty with the sugar of flattery, tried to bind the impetuous Custer to a prescribed course of action without giving further offense to his already bruised ego.

The plan was simple. Gibbon was to move upstream from the Little Big Horn's mouth, while Custer moved downstream from its source. Between them they would trap the Sioux. Gibbon planned to reach his destination on the twenty-sixth. Custer, if he followed the route mapped for him by Terry, would reach his at approximately the same time.

AT NINE o'clock on the night of June 24, Custer's scouts bring to the sleeping regiment the news that they have found the Indian trail mentioned in Terry's orders. It leads toward the Little Big Horn, just as Terry has anticipated. There is no "sufficient reason" —not even a flimsy reason—for departing from the instructions laid down by the commander. Should the trail lead toward the Little Big Horn, Terry has written, "you should still proceed southward, perhaps as far as the headwaters of the Tongue, and then turn toward the Little Big Horn." But Custer, strangely distraught, at once summons his officers for a conference in his candlelit field tent.

What thoughts race through Custer's mind that night we can only guess. That he is aware he is about to disobey his orders there can be little doubt. He is about to cut his line of march by fifty or more miles—a departure that means the battle will be joined thirty-six hours before Gibbon's column can arrive on the scene. But Custer feels keenly the humiliation imposed upon him by the President, and here in his grasp is an opportunity to recoup his injured reputation, to steal a march on the superiors who have replaced him as commander, and to gather for himself the glory of a great victory. A victory that will make him the hero of the hour and restore his lost prestige. The temptation is irresistible.

A brisk command from Yellow Hair, and the column is ordered to set out at midnight under forced march on the trail of the "hostile" Sioux. It is not the first time in history that men are to perish in the red tempest of unequal battle merely because a general is jealous of his reputation; nor, unfortunately, is it to be the last. It is memorable only because of its mystery and drama.

All night long the weary regiment blunders on in the pitch blackness. At nine o'clock the next morning, Custer's scouts report the presence of the Sioux camp, directly ahead of their line of march and on the opposite side of the Little Big Horn River. It is a big camp, the scouts warn. "You are going to have one hell of a fight," says Mitch Bouyer, even though, through the hills and tangled gullies that flank the river's edge fifteen miles away, he has seen but a small part of the village. Custer himself investigates with his field glasses and scoffs that he can see nothing.

Were the rash commander to scout the position properly he

would know that the tipis stretch for miles along the opposite bank and contain the greatest gathering of savage might ever amassed upon the continent. But Yellow Hair is impatient. He dares not waste time, lest Gibbon and his men arrive unexpectedly and rob him of the fruits of singlehanded triumph. The column presses onward.

At noon, when the panting regiment again halts briefly, Custer commits his second serious blunder. Captain Benteen, with three troops, is detached from the main body and ordered to scout south and west in search of Indians. Major Reno and Custer continue forward along the freshening trail of the Sioux. Captain McDougall, with a single troop, is left behind to guard the slow-moving pack train of ammunition mules. Firmly convinced that his scouts are mistaken concerning the existence of a huge encampment of Indians, the commander has violated a cardinal tenet of military tactics. He has divided his forces in the presence of a numerically superior enemy.

It is two o'clock when the first outposts of the Sioux are sighted. A little band of forty Indians flees, as if panic-stricken, before the approach of Custer and his men. Though men and horses are utterly fagged after the long hours of forced marching since midnight, Custer halts only long enough to issue battle orders. Major Reno, with three troops—about 112 men—is ordered forward to the attack. Custer, with the remaining five troops, is to follow and support his onslaught. No attempt is made to recall Captain Benteen; there is not even a brief delay to permit Captain McDougall and the ammunition train to catch up with the forward elements.

Even now, with the great Indian encampment but four miles distant, the obstinate general refuses to verify its existence. Screened as it is from his sight by high bluffs, he remains tragically unaware that the massed might of the great Sioux nation lies awaiting his pitiful handful; that dozens of sharp, hidden eyes have marked his progress all through the long forenoon; that even now, in the wooded gullies, the crafty Crazy Horse, Crow King, and Gall are disposing the ambush that is to engulf him.

Two o'clock. The zero hour. Sweating, tense, impatient troopers.

LAND OF THE DACOTAHS

The muffled chant of Indian scouts, annointed in preparation for death, as they shuffle in solemn prayer dances. The swift, numb whispering of the long prairie grasses. Above it all a brassy, pitiless sky. Suddenly, over the brush-tangled gullies and the tops of low-lying foothills, the silver stuttering voices of cavalry bugles. The lines of lean mounted troopers sweep forward to the assault. . . .

WHAT happened to Custer from the time he disappeared into the tortuous gullies with his 225 troopers has preoccupied historians ever since. It is at best a futile speculation, for the dead cannot speak, and the only living thing found on the field two days later was Captain Keogh's horse, Comanche.

To Reno and Benteen, then, we must turn for the only available stories of the white man's side of the struggle. Reno, following his orders, advanced toward the Little Big Horn River with his troops, covering about three miles before he reached the stream, forded it, and turned northward. His appearance above their village was a surprise to the Indians; they had not been aware of the splitting of the command, for the terrain made their own observation difficult. But as Reno advanced on the village the Indians who had been marking the progress of Custer's troops turned back to meet the more imminent threat. In a few moments Reno's command was confronted by masses of mounted Sioux. "The very earth seemed to grow Indians," Reno testified later.

Dismounting his command, Reno placed his horses in a heavy stand of timber along the riverbank and fought on foot, his extended skirmish line falling back slowly in an arc toward the stream's edge where his right flank was anchored. The friendly Indian scouts who held his left flank broke suddenly and deserted the field en masse. There was nothing left to do but take refuge in the timber, with the river at their backs, and try to hold.

The fighting had been going on for half an hour now, and Reno looked anxiously backward toward the ford for the support promised him by Custer. There was no sign of the dashing Yellow Hair. Their position was rapidly becoming a deathtrap and Reno saw that immediate steps were necessary. Ordering his men to remount, he led them in a retreat upstream in an attempt to reach the ford a mile or two away, but the pressure of the Sioux was too great. The retreat became a rout and the entire command, forced over the river's bank in a welter of threshing men and horses, was compelled to cross where it could. Once across the river, the command took refuge on a high bluff and waited for the assault.

Benteen, meanwhile, after wandering some fifteen miles to the south and west in search of Indians, received a note by courier from Custer ordering him back to aid in the attack. Returning, he came upon the shattered remnant of Reno's command on the blufftop and shared his ammunition with the almost cartridgeless men. A trooper was dispatched to the rear to hurry Captain Mc-Dougall with the ammunition train, while Reno and Benteen discussed the situation.

From their vantage point on the bluff they could see nothing of Custer. Reno's men, shaken by the terrible mauling they had just received, were cursing the absent Yellow Hair for deserting them. None guessed the truth: that even as they spoke, Custer and his entire command lay cold in death.

As the afternoon wore on, the assaults of the Sioux became heavier. Thousands of naked howling savages milled about the hillside, approaching closely enough at times to hurl stones into the cavalrymen's ranks. Each time they were driven back by the fire of the desperate troopers. Dead horses and pack rolls were heaped into makeshift barricades.

The battle raged about the butte for two days and a night before the approach of Gibbon's troops put the Sioux to flight. "They were surrounded by dead, dying and wounded. Men were crying for water, for help, for relief, for life. For twenty-four hours there was no water. The sun was blazing hot, the dead horses were sickening, the air heavy with a hundred smells, the bullets thick, the men falling and the bluffs for miles black with jubilant savages."

On the twenty-sixth, with the approach of Gibbon and Terry, the Sioux fired the prairie and withdrew toward the mountains. Next morning, as Gibbon's column came into view of the be-leaguered and hopeless men on the blufftop, the Bismarck *Tribune* relates that "strong men wept on each other's necks." And well they might. Only by a miracle had they escaped the same dreadful fate that overwhelmed Custer and his men.

OF ALL the millions of words written about the obscure and mysterious Custer battle, it is perhaps safest to take the eyewitness accounts of those who actually saw the struggle and survived: the Sioux. Here is the story of old Paints Brown, as told through an interpreter many years after the famous battle. Paints Brown was no gifted storyteller; so we may reject any suspicion of literary invention in the battle piece of this aboriginal Hemingway.

"The soldiers were first seen by the Indian scouts quite early and when they came in sight of the camp the sun was rather high. It must have been about eight o'clock, for breakfast was over, but the fires were still smoking.

"There was not much excitement and at first we thought it would be better to surrender as there were so many soldiers in the country, but when Custer came in sight there were not so many, and the word was sent around the camp to get ready. We sneaked from our tents through the tall grass to where our ponies were picketed and drew them to us by the long ropes. I was one of the first to mount, but the others followed quickly, and we raced toward the soldiers as the bullets came switching through the grass and through the leaves of the trees. But we were not excited.

"And we fought and the soldiers fought and when we chased the first lot across the river we turned and went for those on the hills. The smoke and dust were very thick—you couldn't see anything and we killed lots of our own men because they got in the way.

"Pretty soon the soldiers started to run and we went after them but it wasn't long before they were all killed or wounded. We couldn't tell who was Custer, we couldn't tell anything; their faces were covered with dust and their eyes and mouths were full of it.

"We found a soldier sitting against the dead body of his horse. He was alive but he had been shot through the belly. He could speak a little Sioux and he said: 'My friends, I am in a bad way, I wish you would take me to a tent.'

"We got off our horses and crowded around and one of us spoke up: 'Why, he is my friend!'

"'Yes,' he replied. 'I was at Standing Rock and at Fort Lincoln.'

"We got on our horses again and two of us reached down and took him under the armpits and tried to lead him away, but he said: 'Oh, I can't walk, my legs hurt!' and then he dropped down and died.

"We were looking around and we found Captain Keogh, but left him alone, for we saw that he wore a scapular and we said that he was a Black Robe man. We dressed ourselves in the uniforms and put on the swords and took the flags and bugles and marched around, and we marched toward Reno that way, too.

"And Reno was up on a hill across from our camp and his men were lying in trenches and they didn't have any water all day and it was very hot. Once in a while a soldier would start down the bluff, a-sneaking through the grass. He'd stop and lie still and then he'd crawl along again and we'd let him get pretty close to the river's edge and we'd shoot him. Once a soldier got clear down to the water and drank and filled some round things with stoppers in them with water and started back, but we played with him and shot him.

"And we didn't see Sitting Bull. He was off somewhere in the hills with the women, I think. We saw Comanche, the horse— the only one that got out of the fight—going toward the river. It was Keogh's horse and it was wounded and it walked very slow. We did not think much about it and let it go and the whites got it. But we didn't see Sitting Bull."

Paints Brown's reference to the wounded animal was prompted by the fact that in later years Comanche was made a pensioner of the Seventh Cavalry. He was never ridden again, but was always draped in black and led with the regiment on parade. Knowing how much store the whites seemed to set by him, old Paints Brown was evidently sorry that they had not finished him off when they had the chance.

As for the slighting reference to Sitting Bull, such remarks are common in many warriors' stories. Although Sitting Bull was a great spiritual and political leader and had been a fair warrior in his younger days, the great publicity he received among white people as a mighty fighting man angered Gall, Crow King, Crazy Horse, and many other really notable warriors. Like white generals in similar case, they never missed an opportunity to take a dig at him. But let us listen further to Paints Brown:

"The soldiers had lots and lots of money and we took it. We knew what the silver was but the paper we didn't know. And the children played with it; they made little tepees out of it and put about one hundred dollars in bills together and made toy shawls, and some of it was bloody.

"And after we saw what we had done some of us thought we would get hanged like the Indians did at Mankato, and some of us thought we would not get any rations if we went back to the reservations, and we heard that the country was full of more white soldiers coming, and we were all scared, so we broke camp next day and left. We traveled at night to the north and camped during the day.

"We sent out our scouts in every direction but didn't see any soldiers. We brought our wounded with us and they died all along the way and we buried them and our hearts were bad. The women also buried lots of trinkets, like rings and things, that we took from the dead soldiers, because we were scared.

"We had done more than we thought we ever could do, and we knew that the whites were very strong and would punish us."

It is an unusual tale, this story of old Paints Brown. It is the bare bones of history, stripped of the rosy flesh of glamour and romance. It is the pathetic portrait of a bewildered and persecuted people, impressed against their will into acts of violence and terrible retaliation. And, very likely, it is as accurate a glimpse as we shall ever get of the Battle of the Little Big Horn.

IT WAS two days after the battle—the twenty-seventh of June—when the Crow scout Curley brought to Captain Marsh and the *Far West*, which lay at anchor at the Little Big Horn's mouth, the story of Custer's fate. Marsh and the other officers aboard the vessel at first refused to credit the tale. But later in the day, as scouts from Gibbon's command arrived at the boat with orders to make her ready for a race to Fort Abraham Lincoln, the disaster was confirmed.

It became Marsh's duty, now, to carry back to Fort Lincoln the wounded of Major Reno's command, and to acquaint the world with what Poet James Foley has called "for stark tragedy, horror and surprise, perhaps the greatest news story ever flashed over a telegraph wire to a stunned and stricken country in the history of the United States." The nearest telegraph wire that could be reached by boat was at Bismarck, 710 miles away.

Gibbon's men, after coming to the rescue of the beleaguered Major Reno and his command and driving off the Sioux, had stumbled upon the shambles of the Custer battlefield. Even hardened frontier veterans were sickened at the sight that met their eyes. Despite the ravages wrought by three days of broiling sun, they could read on the naked swollen corpses the marks of the red man's savage hand.

In a gully nearby, the silent men of Gibbon's column found Captain Keogh's horse, Comanche, his claybank sorrel hide freckled with bullet holes and bristling with arrows like a pincushion. He was the sole survivor of the five troops that had followed Yellow Hair into battle.

Gibbon's troopers rescued the half-dead animal, did a hurried job of partially burying the fallen men, and hastened back to Reno's company of tattered and exhausted survivors. It was slow and painstaking labor, carrying the wounded over the rough terrain to Marsh's vessel. Most of the horses had been killed, and the work was done by hand; the injured were transported over the twisted earth in stretchers improvised from the hides of dead horses.

Captain Marsh, in the meantime, loaded fuel and turned the *Far West* as best he could into a floating field hospital. Great beds of prairie grass were strewn over the deck and covered with tarpaulins; medicine chests were attached to the guards ready for the surgeons' instant use. In the stern a place was made for the suffering Comanche. By the evening of July 3 everything was in readiness.

Just as Marsh was preparing to cast off, General Terry sent a message requesting the captain to call on him. Marsh, describing the incident later, said he had never seen the general so deeply shaken.

"Captain," he told Marsh, "you are about to start on a trip with fifty-two wounded men on your boat. This is a bad river to navigate and accidents are likely to happen. I wish to ask of you that you use all the skill you possess, all the caution you can command, to make the journey safely. You have on board the most precious cargo a boat ever carried. Every soldier here who is suffering with wounds is the victim of a terrible blunder; a sad and terrible blunder."

Thus General Terry, on Yellow Hair's last and most sensational bid for fame. Terry was too much the professional officer and gentleman to condemn Custer publicly, but to Captain Marsh he spoke the bitter truth, and Marsh's biographer has recorded it in the story of the captain's life.

The heroic exploit of Captain Marsh and the men of the *Far West* has never been given due credit in our histories, over-shadowed as it was by the more sensational story of Custer and his regiment. But among old rivermen, who know the horrors of exploding boilers and unseen snags that can rip the guts out of the strongest vessel, Marsh's epic race has become a byword.

Down the narrow Big Horn, through the tortuous Yellowstone, and into the swollen, yellow Missouri, Captain Marsh hurled his throbbing craft, laden with wounded and dying men. It was the evening of July 3 when the *Far West* cast off in the Big Horn, and eleven o'clock on the night of July 5 when she moored at Bismarck 710 miles away—an average of nearly 350 miles a day on partially strange and unexplored rivers.

This was a record unequaled on the Missouri to this day and a race that rivaled the classic Mississippi River stories of the *Natchez* and the *R. E. Lee.* But most important of all, Marsh brought to Bismarck and to Fort Abraham Lincoln a story that was to go down in history as the most dramatic of the decade and give to the New York *Herald* a scoop famous in journalistic annals.

Colonel Lounsberry, editor of the Bismarck *Tribune,* was routed out of bed by Captain Marsh when the *Far West* tied up at the Bismarck landing. Lounsberry's first questions were about the fate of young Mark Kellogg, the reporter he had sent in his place. Silently one of the officers handed him a pouch that had been picked up on the field of battle beside Kellogg's body. It was his dispatch case, filled with notes up to the time of the battle.

"We leave the Rosebud tomorrow," read his last prophetic message, "and by the time this reaches you we will have met and fought the red devils, with what result remains to be seen. I go with Custer and will be at the death."

Colonel Lounsberry, realizing that he had one of the great exclusive stories of all time, waited impatiently for Terry's official dispatches to General Sheridan to be filed over the single wire to the East. Then while the officers and eyewitnesses poured details into his ears, Lounsberry whipped them into narrative form and sent the story crackling over the wire to the New York *Herald*.

At that time an individual sender could monopolize the single direct wire from Bismarck, terminal point of the telegraph line, to St. Paul—as long as he was able to keep sending continuously. Lounsberry drafted the little frontier hamlet's only two telegraphers and with his own printers as assistants composed a 50,000-word story that was to electrify the editorial staffs of the nation, anger the War Department, and seal forever the fate of the unfortunate Sioux.

When the telegraphers ran short of copy now and then, the sweating colonel tossed them a Bible with instructions to start anywhere and keep the wire clear until he could catch up again. All through the night and into the afternoon of the next day he labored at his tremendous task—50,000 words would make a book roughly one third the size of this one—and twenty-four hours later, when the telegraph operators staggered to their feet, cramped and drunken with fatigue, the *Herald*'s telegraph tolls were in excess of three thousand dollars and the St. Paul offices were begging for mercy. But the *Herald* had its scoop. And horrified readers on the Atlantic seaboard were clamoring for vengeance against the Sioux.

LAND OF THE DACOTAHS

THE story exploded in the East with devastating effect. It had been a week of celebration the like of which America had not seen for many a year. At the great Centennial Exposition in Philadelphia and in a thousand other American towns citizens were commemorating the one-hundredth anniversary of the nation's founding. The news of the military disaster was as unexpected as it was unbelievable. It was the most overwhelming defeat ever suffered by professional soldiers at the hands of untrained troops. Then, too, the Boy General with the Golden Locks, as Custer had been known in Civil War days, had captured the popular imagination and the news of his death infuriated the public to fever pitch. Though he deserved only censure for his rash conduct, he became instead the hero of the hour. Thus, by a curious quirk of historical fate, Yellow Hair found in death the enduring fame which had eluded him in life.

Colonel Lounsberry's story broke in the *Herald* on July 6. On that same date several garbled rumors giving the victory to Custer appeared in Utah and Montana papers. These had been brought overland by runners, and some of them received brief bulletin mention in a few eastern journals. Then, to add to the *Herald*'s extraordinary stroke of luck, General Sheridan issued a denial of the story: "It comes without any marks of credence; it does not come to Headquarters; it does not come to the leading papers from special correspondents; it is not given to the press for telegraphing," declared Sheridan. Such stories, he added, "are to be carefully considered."

Frightened by the denial, other eastern papers avoided the story, while the *Herald*, pinning its faith on Lounsberry's reportorial integrity, continued to print fourteen-column accounts of the disaster on July 7 and 8. Some skeptical editors even went so far as to charge that the *Herald* had been made the victim of a hoax—a fact that served only to enhance the scoop when the War Department finally confirmed it.

It will be recalled that Terry's confidential reports to General Sheridan were filed from Bismarck before Lounsberry's story was put on the wire. Why, then, did Sheridan deny that the battle had taken place? The answer is simple.

184

Sheridan was not at his headquarters in Chicago when the reports arrived; he was in Philadelphia attending the Centennial Exposition. Lounsberry's story had already been printed and denied by the general when, late in the afternoon of July 6, Terry's confidential report reached Sheridan after being forwarded from Chicago. Sheridan read the report and immediately handed it to a young man who represented himself as a "messenger boy," with instructions that it be forwarded at once to Washington.

The messenger boy, however, turned out to be an enterprising young Philadelphia reporter, and much to Sheridan's consternation the entire "confidential" report appeared next day in a Philadelphia newspaper. The report gave little inkling, though, of the scope of the disaster; it stated merely that Custer had been killed and his regiment repulsed; but unfortunately, it did place the blame squarely where it belonged—on Custer's shoulders. Terry had not intended that this confidential report should ever reach the public eye; he was too much the professional soldier to wish to blacken publicly the name of a dead brother officer, even though that officer had jeopardized Terry's own career.

On the contrary, General Terry did everything in his power to shield Custer. Before the *Far West* was sent downstream to Bismarck he sent a runner overland to Fort Ellis with a dispatch for public release in which no mention whatever was made of Custer's failure to carry out his part of the campaign strategy. But the telegraph wires at Fort Ellis were out of order, and the confidential report stolen by the Philadelphia reporter had already been given wide circulation when the public dispatch was finally released.

Terry, as a result, was charged with bad faith; he was accused of telling one story to the public and another to his commanding officer privately in an effort to save his own skin. All the evidence indicates that nothing could be farther from the truth.

The newspaper accounts of the battle, composed in haste from sketchy word-of-mouth sources, in many respects were not notably accurate. Almost all the early stories are filled with gruesome details of torture and mutilation of the fallen troopers. The first Bismarck *Tribune* extra, for example, fairly wallowed in gore:

LAND OF THE DACOTAHS

"All dead—all stripped of their clothing and many with bodies horribly mutilated. The squaws seemed to have passed over the field and crushed the skulls of the wounded and dying with stones and clubs. The heads of some were severed from the body, the privates of some were cut off, while others bore traces of torture, arrows having been shot into their private parts while yet living, or other means of torture adopted."

There was no word of truth in any of this—except that they were "all dead." The officers appointed by General Terry to inspect the field and supervise the burial of the dead submitted a lengthy and detailed written report refuting any charges of atrocities. Many of the corpses had been scalped, of course, but that was a practice engaged in by both sides and was only to be expected. It is not far different from the recent practice of American troops in the Pacific, who slit the cheeks of dead Japanese to secure gold teeth for souvenirs.

The Indian wars are within the memory of many living men, yet atrocity stories among the northwest Indian tribes are almost impossible to substantiate. Jacob Horner, the sole survivor of the Seventh Cavalry Regiment that marched out of Fort Abraham Lincoln that May day in 1876, has told me he never heard of a case of torture or mutilation of captives among the Sioux. Sergeant Horner, who is walking the streets of Bismarck today despite his more than ninety years, likewise adds a good word for the Nez Percé Indians against whom he fought in 1877 in Montana. A few of his comrades who were captured spent their time sitting around the Nez Percé campfires playing poker with the Indians until they were rescued.

But men believed the atrocity tales, and the temper of the entire country and the West in particular was an ugly one. Nobody troubled to point out that the Indians were quite within their rights in being where they were; that they were conducting themselves in a peaceable fashion; that their very homes, filled with their women and children, had been attacked without warning by United States troops. No attempt had been made to parley with them to see if they were willing to surrender—as they might well have done, if we can credit Paints Brown's story.

The Sioux were but ordinary men, facing the grim reality of the extinction of their race. They fought in the only way they knew for their lives, their women and children, and their ancestral lands. Perhaps old Sitting Bull, defiant to the last, summed it up best: "Let no man say that this was a massacre. They came to kill us, and got killed themselves."

ALTHOUGH the stories of the day made Custer a hero whose name was on every tongue, the passage of time has somewhat dimmed his luster as a military genius—among historians, if not among the general public. It is time the Custer myth was exploded but, despite the testimony of many competent authorities, it lingers on—perhaps because of the highly fictionalized and widely circulated books written by the Boy General's adoring widow.

Custer's most eminent military apologist, General E. S. Godfrey, has summed up his view of the causes of Yellow Hair's dramatic defeat, and his deductions are quite typical of those of others who have come to the dashing general's defense. Their case should be examined carefully if for no other reason than to clear the name of the unhappy Major Reno, whose life and career were wrecked by the Custerphiles' charges.

"The causes of Custer's defeat," says General Godfrey, "were first, the overpowering number of the enemy and their unexpected cohesion; second, Reno's panic rout from the valley; third, the defective extraction of empty cartridge shells from the carbines."

General Godfrey, to begin with, neatly sidesteps the fact that, had Custer obeyed his orders, the battle would never have taken place. But even leaving entirely aside this rather pertinent matter, the case for the defense remains a shaky one.

First, had Custer done what any competent commander should have done, he would have known the overwhelming number of the enemy. Instead, he attacked blindly, without investigating the size of the opposing force; without bringing up his ammunition supply; and, last but not least, with his command divided into four separate units—none of which knew the whereabouts of the other three. Certainly failure to investigate and properly to maintain his communications is not legitimate excuse for defeat.

Second, Reno's "panic rout from the valley" had virtually nothing to do with Custer's defeat. His handful of troopers were met and thrown back by perhaps a thousand Sioux, while the main body of the Indian warriors maintained the ambush they had prepared for Custer and his command five miles away.

At the court-martial that Reno requested because of the slanderous attacks against him, every officer and man who testified declared that Reno's retreat to the bluff was the only factor that saved them from annihilation. Immediately after the battle the surviving enlisted personnel of the Seventh unanimously petitioned the War Department that Reno be advanced to commanding officer to replace Custer—an accolade they would scarcely have accorded to a cowardly officer.

Said the military court after hearing the testimony: "The conduct of the officers throughout was excellent . . . and there was nothing in his [Reno's] conduct that requires animadversion from this Court." But the slander persisted and persists to this day. One of the lesser tragic aspects of the Battle of the Little Big Horn was the plight of the unfortunate Major Reno, who, as a result of the defamation directed at him, drank himself out of the service and into an untimely grave.

General Godfrey's third cause has some basis in fact. The munitions profiteers of that day were none too fastidious about the kind of equipment they supplied to the military. Dozens of jammed carbines were picked up on the field of battle—mute but grim evidence that many of the surrounded men had died victims of defective arms or ammunition. And yet, Reno and Benteen held the Sioux at bay for two days and a night with the same kind of carbines.

The indisputable evidence in the case can lead only to the conclusion that Custer, contrary to his orders, and hoping that victory would excuse his disobedience, led his men into a death-trap; and until testimony to the contrary is forthcoming, the blame should fall squarely on Custer's shoulders. There was no cowardice on the part of Reno or anyone else. Six hundred men met three thousand equally well-armed men—and the result was inevitable.

188

There is, though, one telling point which General Godfrey might well have made. Some 40 per cent of Custer's regiment were green recruits who had no experience of any kind of warfare, who had never heard a shot fired in anger, and some of whom had had only two or three months of military life. Hardened veterans could not have hoped to bring about a victory under the circumstances; it is small wonder that green troops did not do so. The Indian testimony is that the actual fight lasted little longer than half an hour, and that the Sioux casualties numbered only about forty men—as compared with almost three hundred dead and more than fifty wounded among the white troopers.

THE nation was aroused now and the military was stung into effective action. A few brief months and the Sioux were beaten, scattered in hungry shivering bands across the Canadian border. They had become pariahs and outcasts and there was no longer any question of their "rights" to the lands the nation had promised them. Cattlemen of the south and west had long looked with envious eyes on the lush rolling grasslands of Montana and the Dakotas; a decade after the Sioux defeat saw them firmly entrenched in the Sioux hunting grounds, with great cattle drives from the south bringing in ever more and more animals to the new cattle bonanza.

Foreign and eastern capital poured into the country as news of the fortunes to be made in the beef industry got abroad. Dozens of little cow metropolises sprang up to accommodate the growing population of the region, a population that included not only native Westerners but foreigners and Easterners who followed in the wake of the capital investment they had made in the new, wild country.

Such a mushroom cow town was the little village of Medora in the heart of the Dakota Badlands. But the town's founder was such a character as even the West has seldom seen. Virtually neglected by historians, his fabulous career is little known save among the handful of people who inhabit that portion of western North Dakota where he once made his home. There, however, the Marquis de Mores has become a local legend.

Chapter 12

BADLANDS EMPEROR

Tall, slender, with flashing black eyes and the lithe grace of a polished fencer, he might have stepped from the pages of an Alexandre Dumas novel. In the course of his meteoric career he was duelist, adventurer, financier, international diplomat, and aspirant to the throne of France. Though his grandiose schemes came to nothing and his empire has long since crumbled to dust, he remains one of the West's most colorful, if obscure, frontier figures.

Though his career in America encompassed but three short years and ended before he was thirty years of age, Antoine de Vallombrosa, Marquis de Mores, had in that brief space controlled hundreds of thousands of acres of grazing land in Dakota Territory; become affiliated with the Mellon brothers in financial enterprises; founded the Northern Pacific Refrigerator Car Company; launched a million-dollar packing plant in the wilderness; established a newspaper, a hotel, and a town of several hundred people on the frontier; engaged in duels and been acquitted of a charge of murder; and, finally, lost two million dollars in a cooperative ranching enterprise in Dakota Territory. Aside from this staggering list of activities he found time to live the life of a plains hunter and Old World gentleman simultaneously in his exotic château in the heart of the Dakota Badlands, where he entertained guests of international note in the midst of a trackless wilderness.

It was in Paris, in 1881, that the handsome young Frenchman met Medora von Hoffman, wealthy New York heiress. The Marquis was no impecunious fortune hunter. He was rich in his own right and could trace his family tree back through five hundred years of noble ancestry. It was, rather, a case of love at first sight. Red-haired Medora von Hoffman was not only wealthy but a charming and beautiful girl. As for the Marquis, besides his noble birth and unusual good looks, he was a graduate of St. Cyr, one of the finest swordsmen of France, and a veritable gallant in the drawing room.

It was kismet. They were married at Cannes, in the "Church of the Stained Glass Window," and in August of 1882 the Marquis and his bride set sail for New York City.

The Marquis' fertile brain was teeming with ideas. In this new land, where fabulous fortunes were to be made overnight, he would build up his resources to the point where he could return to France and fulfill his life's ambition, which was to overthrow the French Republic and re-establish the monarchy with himself as king. It was an ambitious project for a man of twenty-six.

In New York the Marquis' father-in-law, Baron von Hoffman, invited him to enter the family banking firm and familiarize himself with the American financial world. But the Marquis had other plans; it was not in the nature of this dashing young adventurer to content himself with sitting in a countinghouse. And he was no fool. He knew what it would take to corrupt an army even in corrupt France. What he wanted was some fabulous project that would return him millions in as brief a time as possible.

Then fate, in the person of the Marquis' cousin, Count Fitz-James, intervened. The count, like so many adventurous Europeans of his day, had come to America to enjoy a hunting trip in the wilds of Dakota Territory. Returning to New York, he described the land to the Marquis in glowing terms, elaborating upon the vastness and emptiness of the territory, the abundance of wild game, and the richness of the soil.

The Marquis listened carefully. He had been studying American business opportunities and had become convinced that a great cattle and packing industry, properly managed, would prove a bonanza for its founder. And De Mores was certain he knew how to manage it.

His scheme, for that day, was breath-taking. Once he found a suitable range he would build his packing plants on the spot, slaughter his animals there, and ship the frozen meats in his own refrigerator cars to his own markets in the East. By keeping the entire program "from range to table" in his own hands, he could cut costs drastically—as well as avoid the huge expense of shipping live animals halfway across the continent to eastern abbatoirs. He would be able to undersell the great packers by such a margin that they would have no choice but to go to the wall. The Marquis would have a corner on the entire industry.

It looked good on paper. All he needed was to locate the proper cattle country. As he listened to Fitz-James, he believed he had found the answer.

In the spring of 1883 De Mores said goodbye to his young bride and departed for the fastnesses of Dakota Territory, ostensibly on a hunting trip, although the actual purpose of his journey was to determine whether the wild land Fitz-James had described to him was suited to his ends. Moving slowly across the great empty Territory of Dakota the Marquis studied the terrain carefully. It seemed admirably fitted to his needs. The rolling grasslands stretched as far as the eye could reach, promising lush, free grazing for the thousands of cattle he could envision on the green plains. There was abundant water in the prairie creeks and rivers.

Then, on the far western edge of Dakota Territory, he came one day upon the awesome grandeur of the Badlands. The Marquis had seen enough. Smitten with the beauty of the country, he remained for three days while he made certain of its natural advantages. Everything was there: feed, water, shelter. He took the train for New York next morning, full of his dream of empire. With his own personal fortune, backed by the support of his millionaire father-in-law, the Marquis set about the organization of the National Consumers' Company. He was a good salesman and there was nothing fundamentally wrong with his idea.

Such men as W. R. Grace, mayor of New York City, Eugene Kelly the banker, Brian Lawrence, Alex Patrick Ford, Henry George, and other prominent citizens were enthusiastic about the Marquis' plan. Perhaps some of them saw only the cooperative side of the project; but others, it must be guessed, could see that the plan had the makings of a very tight little monopoly.

The company was soon organized with a capitalization of ten million dollars, divided into a million shares at ten dollars each. Every shareholder had the privilege of purchasing at company stores, at lowest prices, whatever meat was necessary for his needs. Gone was the middleman, advertised the shrewd De Mores.

The Marquis took immediate steps toward converting his dream into reality. He completed negotiations with the Northern Pacific Railway and the federal government for the purchase of forty-five thousand acres of grazing land in western Dakota Territory. A shrewd manipulator, he gerrymandered his holdings into two long narrow strips on either side of the Little Missouri River, the principal source of water in the country. Thus his acreage effectively controlled hundreds of thousands of adjoining acres, for he possessed the water rights. His dominance was reminiscent of the seignorial control of his noble ancestors in the old days of France. And he had got it all for a paltry thirty-two thousand dollars.

"I like this country," the Marquis wrote to his bride in New York. "There is room to turn around without stepping on the feet of others."

DURING the next few months the Marquis was a busy man. Huge cold-storage warehouses were erected in Bismarck, Fargo, Duluth, Helena, Miles City, Glendive, Brainerd, and Minneapolis; two additional slaughtering plants were built at Miles City and Billings. Other plants were being purchased or constructed in Portland, Seattle, Winnipeg, and Kansas City. Additional holdings were acquired in Chicago, New York, and Boston.

Out on the range land itself, the Marquis selected a site close by the east bank of the Little Missouri River, cracked a bottle of champagne over an iron tent peg, and christened the new town Medora in honor of the Marquise. Men, building materials, and machinery poured into the wilderness by the trainload, and within two weeks a boom town of several hundred people had sprung up.

As operations got into full swing that fall of 1883, the Marquis was slaughtering three hundred animals a day and his eastern food markets were offering frozen meats at prices ruinous to his competitors. The Marquis was overjoyed. He prepared to settle down and watch the golden flood roll in. The Northern Pacific Refrigerator Car Company, which he had established, was carrying his wares to every corner of the nation. Things were looking up in the packing business, and the Marquis turned to other interests.

Into nearby Bismarck that year had come two young Pittsburgh financiers who were immediately attracted by the enterprising De Mores. Their names were Andrew Mellon and R. B. Mellon, and they were buying hundreds of acres of the rich Dakota prairie lands. They had also founded a bank in Bismarck, which had just become the territorial capital. Like the Marquis, they predicted a great future for the country when the influx of settlers should begin, and together with De Mores they founded the Bismarck Loan and Trust Company.

Late that fall another Easterner dropped off the train near the Marquis' estate—a slender young gentleman whom the cowhands described to the Marquis as "a four-eyed dude from New York." It was Theodore Roosevelt, come to Dakota for his health and to attempt to forget the recent deaths of his wife and his mother. Roosevelt was approximately the Marquis' own age, and the two were to see a good deal of each other. Both being domineering and opinionated, they did not always agree, but the young New Yorker was nevertheless a frequent guest at the sprawling 28-room château which the Marquis erected as a frontier home for his family.

Like the Marquis, Roosevelt became enamored of the weirdly beautiful country that is the Dakota Badlands. On this first trip he made tentative arrangements to commence ranching operations there and soon established the Maltese Cross and Elkhorn ranches near Medora, dividing his time for several years between eastern politics and western ranching and hunting. Although he was never one of the really big cattlemen of the region, he entered the business on such a scale that he was able to lose seventy-five thousand dollars at it before he finally disposed of his interests.

The four-eyed dude from New York provided excellent copy even then for the newspapermen of the territory, for he became something of a prairie politician before he had been long in the country, serving for a time as deputy sheriff among other positions. The dull and colorless writing that today passes for reporting in most newspapers has nothing in common with the salty and irreverent prose of the frontier journalist of the 80's. A Bismarck *Tribune* reporter, sent to interview Roosevelt, wrote this thumbnail portrait of the future president:

Theodore Roosevelt, the tenacious and impulsive New York reformer, passed through the city yesterday afternoon en route to his ranch in the Badlands. During his stay he took occasion to brand as a lie the statement that he had expressed himself in favor of Blaine and Logan. "I have not declared myself," exclaimed the impulsive young politician as he adjusted his eyeglasses and puckered up his intense countenance. With a repetition of these facial contortions and a rapid succession of squints and gestures, he assured us of his great faith in Dakota.

DE MORES, meanwhile, with his dream of empire constantly before his eyes, branched out into new fields. He founded a newspaper, the Medora *Bad Lands Cowboy,* the masthead of which announced belligerently that it was published "not for fun, but for $2 a year." When the Black Hills gold fields to the south began to boom, he organized an overland stage route from the Hills to the Northern Pacific Railway at Medora. To help build up the country he purchased twenty thousand acres of wheat land near Bismarck and offered it tax-free for a year to any settlers who would locate there. In Medora he built a church, a school, a theater, and lounging and club rooms equipped with a bowling alley and other means of recreation for his employees and their families.

Medora had become a typical cosmopolitan cattle town of the frontier West. Besides the Marquis and his cousin, Count Fitz-James, the nobility of Europe was represented by Sir John Pender. A. C. Huidekoper, founder of the famous H-T brand and scion of a wealthy eastern family, was a Harvard graduate, and A. T. Packard, editor of the Medora paper, was a University of Michigan alumnus. Laval Nugent, a young Englishman who came to hunt and remained to work, was a son of a member of the House of Lords. Pierre Wibaux, a Frenchman who later amassed a fortune of hundreds of thousands of dollars in the cattle business, lived nearby in a cave scooped out of the virgin earth. He gave his name to the little town of Wibaux, Montana, which had formerly been called Mingusville, after its original founders, Min and Gus. The

Eaton brothers, founders of the first dude ranch enterprise, and C. B. Richards, who later established the Hamburg-American steamship line, were also members of the Medora community.

At the other end of the social scale, of course, were the dregs of the frontier: outcasts, murderers, gamblers, prostitutes, and gunmen. And between the two were average self-reliant pioneers of the Northwest, whom the most illustrious Medoran of them all, Theodore Roosevelt, came to know and love during his years as a Dakota rancher.

The vast enterprises of the French marquis, however, gave to Medora a character unique among western towns of the day. Hundreds of men were brought into the territory to work in the huge packing plant and to supervise the ramifications of the organization. By the summer of 1884 the Marquis was shearing fourteen thousand sheep and grazing tens of thousands of cattle. His competitors were wincing under the lash of his price schedules. Already, though, the storm clouds were gathering—the precursors of a hurricane that was to blow to bits De Mores' mighty empire.

But on the surface everything was tranquil. The Marquis and his attractive wife held open house at their big château, staffed by a retinue of French servants. Eastern blue bloods and foreign titled gentry spent gay summers there, dancing, drinking, hunting, and riding. The Marquis, mannered and dashing in any environment or situation, presided with equal poise as host to visiting diplomats or as guide on the wild prairies. Nor was the Marquise at all out of her element. The Bismarck *Tribune* of September 4, 1885, reported: "The Marquise, wife of Marquis de Mores, has returned from her hunt in the Rocky Mountains, where she killed two cinnamon bears and one large grizzly bear. The accomplished lady, who was a few years ago one of New York City's popular society belles, is now the queen of the Rocky Mountains and the champion huntress of the great northwest."

The Marquis, though, was not popular with his neighbors. The ranchers resented his bland assumption of superiority, his wealth, his titled friends. Many doubted his claim to nobility—or, if they did believe it, considered it an affront to their own openhanded democracy. But worst of all, De Mores began to fence his lands.

196

Owning the water rights, he had the smaller cattlemen completely at his mercy; and it was a grave breach of range etiquette, to say the least, to deprive a neighbor of water for his stock. The stage was set for serious trouble.

It was a lawless land, the Dakota Territory of those days. The Northern Pacific Railway, which in 1883 drove its golden spike to commemorate the spanning of a continent, had to ask for United States troops to protect its track workers from Indians near Medora, in the heart of the Marquis' empire. Rustlers, wolf hunters, and the last of the buffalo hunters still ranged the Little Missouri Badlands, and the hunters particularly were irked by the fences that cut across buffalo and antelope trails in their established hunting grounds.

Perhaps apocryphal, but nevertheless reflecting the spirit of the times, are the stories concerning the appearance of the first trains in the territory. Hard-boiled cowhands, French-Canadian fur trappers, and blanket-wrapped redskins gathered to witness the phenomenon of the Iron Horse. And to gape at the dudes in their quaint hats and sissified clothes.

The first sight of a derby hat proved too much for Hell-Roaring Bill Jones, one of the tough and leathery oldsters who punched cattle in the Medora vicinity. A meek old gentleman, crowned with a broad-brimmed derby, had descended from the train at the Medora station for a timid peep at the new wild country.

Hell-Roaring Bill—also known as Foul-Mouthed Bill—emitted a snort of disgust and promptly blasted the old gentleman's hat from his head with a fusillade from the six gun he habitually wore at his hip. The old gentlman, needless to say, scampered back into the train, leaving his riddled headgear on the station platform. But Hell-Roaring Bill was not satisfied.

"Come back here and get it, you old bastard!" he thundered. "We don't want the God damn' thing in Medora!"

On other occasions, for the edification of the dudes on the train, the cowhands would loose a barrage of gunfire inside the saloon across from the station. Then, while horrified Easterners stared from the train windows, a half dozen or so limp bodies would be carried out and stacked beside the saloon door. The corpses, of course, always came to life after the train had pulled out.

"Gee, mister," asked a popeyed eastern youth after witnessing one of these apparently bloody engagements, "how often do they kill people out here, anyway?"

The native to whom the question was addressed ruminated for a time. Then, shifting his "chaw" from one cheek to the other, he arched a stream of brown liquid through the air and fixed the lad with a wintry eye.

"Only once, sonny," he muttered darkly.

There was gunplay, though, and plenty of it, that did not have its source in the crude risibilities of bored cowhands. The six-shooter was still the "equalizer" of the northern plains, and he was considered a spineless citizen who relied too much on the intervention or protection of the law. In many places there was no law.

When the Marquis began to fence his lands the reaction was prompt and direct. The ranchers got out their wire cutters and slashed the fences apart. Hard words passed on both sides. The Marquis had his fences restrung and the ranchers immediately cut them again. Then one day three hunters, filled to the neckerchiefs with redeye liquor, began shooting up the town of Medora as a gesture of protest against the Marquis' violations of the range code. Bullets were fired into several of the town buildings and into the Marquis' nearby château.

Fearing bloodshed if the shooting was not stopped, De Mores telegraphed to Mandan for an armed posse to handle the gunmen. A deputy sheriff took the next train for Medora, and the Marquis, together with several employees, set out for the station to meet him. They were late, however, and it was the three gunmen who met the deputy. They successfully cowed him, then set out toward the Marquis' domain, with the deputy following at a discreet distance. The Marquis' party and the three exuberant natives met each other, and when the deputy arrived on the scene the smoke of gunfire was still heavy in the air and one of the gunmen lay dead on the ground. Another had a broken leg. The Marquis' clothing had several bullet holes through it, but he and his men were unhurt.

The countryside was up in arms over the incident. In other circumstances the matter might have been overlooked, for it was clearly a case of self-defense, but feeling against the Marquis was too bitter. He was a foreigner in a strange land, and, it must be admitted, a haughty nobleman who despised these cattlemen as *canaille*. He was arrested on a charge of first-degree murder.

The case attracted nationwide attention. The St. Louis *Post-Dispatch* declared patriotically that "De Mores is a titled land pirate and a brigandish foreigner and for smaller offenses than his, better men have tasted the high gallows and the short shrift of frontier justice." The Minneapolis *Tribune* came to the Marquis' defense, prophesying that the *Post-Dispatch* would find itself defendant in a libel suit if it persisted in such attacks. The St. Paul *Pioneer Press* told its readers this was not the first time the fiery Marquis had been in trouble, and described his quarrels (strictly imaginary) with Theodore Roosevelt, "the New York politician who owns an immense cattle ranch near Medora."

But these newspapers were distant from the actual scene of the killing and their information was not notably accurate, to say the least. The light in which the responsible elements of the country viewed the matter was perhaps better summed up in the Mandan *Pioneer*, which was in a position to know the facts of the case:

The *Pioneer* may as well say now as at any time, that its sympathy in the Little Missouri trouble is with the Marquis de Mores. We have here a spectacle of a gentleman of capital endeavoring to bring a vast and fertile piece of country under cultivation. He has a large amount of capital at command. He has seen fit to come to a region that especially needs capital, and he is welcome. The Bad Lands have for years been the rendezvous of a lot of desperadoes, and they are causing a deal of bother. All decent people agree that the desperadoes must go. As surely as civilization must prevail over barbarism, so surely must this desperado element be put down. The Marquis may rest assured that all decent people are with him.

Appearing voluntarily before the justice of the peace, the Marquis was discharged on the ground that the killing was justifiable homicide. Later he was arrested, brought before a second justice at Mandan, and again discharged. But he had powerful enemies;

he was arrested a third time, was indicted, and went on trial for his life at the territorial capitol in Bismarck. The storm of bitter feeling engendered over the affair sobered even the haughty Marquis. He began to see how heartily disliked he was in certain quarters; and though he could have been free under bond, he preferred to await his trial in custody, where he would be safe from over-enthusiastic friends of the dead man.

The Marquis' trial was packed with frontier drama. Altercations and physical encounters marked its progress. At one point the proceedings had to be postponed when the prosecuting attorney was committed to jail for contempt of court. One of the two gunmen who had survived the encounter with the Marquis, a German immigrant named Reuters, alias Wannegan, convulsed the spectators and the court with his account of how he happened to harbor a grudge against the Marquis. He explained in thick guttural dialect that he was a veteran of the Franco-Prussian War, and that when he learned the Marquis was a French army officer he was at once ready to do battle against him.

The trial dragged on before a courtroom evenly divided in its opinion of the Marquis' guilt; and when he was finally acquitted there were ugly rumors of bribery and miscarried justice. When De Mores left the courtroom after the verdict, a friend slipped him a revolver, in case his enemies might attempt to execute for themselves what they thought to be justice. But there was no need for the precaution. During the closing hours of the trial the prosecuting attorney had sought to discredit the Marquis' character by questioning him about his past. Over the objections of the defense he elicited from the Marquis the admission that he had twice killed men in France in duels to which he had been challenged.

But the prosecutor's attempt boomeranged. The crowd of western frontiersmen applauded the statement and it doubtless aided the Marquis' case if it had any effect at all. Nobody, at any rate, tried to take the law into his own hands, and the Marquis was free of the old charge at last.

Slaughtering at the Medora plant had been suspended during the trial, and a few hours after the verdict the Marquis received a telegram from the manager of the company inquiring when they might again resume operations. At the telegraph office the Marquis hastily scribbled the following reply: WILL RESUME KILLING AS SOON AS I CAN GIVE IT MY PERSONAL ATTENTION. DE MORES

The Marquis' attorney, F. B. Allen, scanned the telegram and advised De Mores dryly that he had better put it in his pocket and write another—one that might not be misunderstood by the gun-toting Medora cattlemen. The Marquis chuckled and took Allen's advice, saving the first message for a souvenir.

THE multiple forces which were to overthrow and destroy the Marquis' empire were gathering momentum as spring came again to the Badlands. Of these forces, some were defects in the character of the Marquis himself, some were simply unavoidable physical factors, while others, more sinister, sprang from the scheming brains of the Marquis' baronial competitors.

De Mores, although intelligent and a man of broad vision, was foolhardy, impetuous, and egotistical. He was also scrupulously honest—a quality not particularly to one's advantage in the days before the trust-busting Teddy came to power. The Marquis himself in later years enjoyed telling how he was fleeced by poker-faced ranchers who would sell him a herd of cattle, run them around a butte, and resell them to him a second and third time. But such picayune swindling could never have wrecked an enterprise the size of the Marquis'. It was only when the mighty forces of the great packing companies began to array themselves against him that his unwieldy structure tottered and finally crashed.

The Marquis was no match for the determined, and not always honest, competition he had to meet. How the idea began, nobody seemed to know, but during the second year of the Marquis' enterprise people began to get the notion that his frozen meats were dangerous. It was said that a poisonous preservative was used on them, and the whispering campaign, aided by a number of eastern journals, began to take its toll among the company's customers. Also, although the fact did not become public until long afterward, secret freight rebates were being granted to the Marquis' competitors—thus nullifying one of his principal commercial advantages. Next, the big packing companies, with resources far greater than De Mores could command, turned on a terrific underselling campaign. Their losses must have been great, but they could stand it longer than could the unhappy Frenchman.

There were, besides, several legitimate reasons for De Mores' difficulties. He had plunged into the business on too great a scale. His grass-fed beef was not often of a quality to compete with grain-finished stock. Since he could slaughter only six months of the year, when the cattle were fat, his huge plant stood idle half the time, while overhead went ruthlessly on. And last, but far from least, he committed the cardinal sin of importing sheep into a cattle country. The cattlemen were outraged and the sheep were poisoned by the hundreds.

As misfortune followed misfortune, the Marquis became suspicious even of his friends and neighbors. Since two men who happened to be employed by Theodore Roosevelt had testified against him in his murder trial, he had begun to suspect the four-eyed dude from New York. When a local troublemaker came to him privily and reported that one of Teddy's men had been seen giving money to the two witnesses just before the trial, the Marquis lost all sense of balance and discretion and dispatched a courier bearing a somewhat incoherent note to the future president.

Remarking that "the newspapers print stupid stories about us," which was true, the Marquis charged Roosevelt with influencing witnesses against him and closed the message with a dark hint that in his own country such differences were settled on the field of honor. If he intended to frighten Roosevelt his strategy failed. By the same courier, Teddy returned his answer: "Most emphatically I am not your enemy. If I were you would know it, for I would be an open one and would not have asked you to my house nor gone to yours. Your final words, however, seem to imply a threat. It is due to myself to say that the statement is not made through fear of any possible consequences to me. I too, as you know, am always on hand and ever ready to hold myself accountable in any way for anything I have said or done."

This firm and straightforward missive served to cool the Marquis' fiery mood and he dispatched a second courier with an invitation for Roosevelt to dine with him next day. Teddy readily accepted the invitation, and the source of the difficulty was at once cleared up. Joe Ferris, a Medora storekeeper financed by Roosevelt, had actually given money to the two witnesses before they set out for the trial. But Ferris acted as banker for many cowhands of the community—there was no bank, of course—and he had merely given them their own savings which they needed for traveling expenses. Roosevelt had known nothing at all of the matter. Once it was all explained, the two again became good friends and later saw each other frequently in the East.

The Marquis' difficulties with his real enemies were not so easily solved. In 1886, after three years, he saw that his venture was doomed. But he fulfilled every one of his contracts and repaid all stockholders, then closed his plant with a loss to himself of almost two million dollars. Despite his disappointment he was not bitter. He knew that he was advocating economic and social ideas far ahead of his day, and he still had faith in the fundamental soundness of his plan—a faith that has since been justified by more practical followers in his footsteps.

He hoped that where he had failed, another might succeed. So this generous, paradoxical Frenchman, abandoning his plant and hundreds of thousands of dollars' worth of equipment, placed a sign on the door of the building where his dream of empire lay buried: "Rent free to any responsible party who will make use of it."

His schemes of fabulous fortune in America shattered, the Marquis returned to France. On a hunting trip in India the following year he was struck by the lack of modern industrial development in the interior of the Far East. He hit upon the idea of building a railroad into the undeveloped back country and creating another empire like the one that had failed in Dakota. He organized the enterprise and actually began construction of the railroad that same year, but governmental interference forced him to abandon the project and in 1889 he returned to France by way of the United States.

LAND OF THE DACOTAHS

He stopped at the lonely château in Medora for a brief hunting trip in the Badlands. Like Theodore Roosevelt, the Marquis was curiously exhilarated by that fantastic country.

"Hell with the fires out!" That was what General Sully called the Badlands back in 1864, when he led his U.S. troops through the treacherous gullies and tumbled buttes. But the general, when he delivered that emphatic judgment, was a sick man, jolting over the twisted earth in a military wagon. The hostile Sioux who were sniping at his flanks were more imaginative. In the picturesque imagery of their own tongue they had named the land "Place-where-the-hills-look-at-each-other." But it was the footsore French trappers who were to label the hills for posterity. To them that land of incredible ugliness and beauty was *les mauvaises terres à traverser*, bad lands to travel through.

Hermann Hagedorn, biographer of Theodore Roosevelt, has penned a graphic portrait of the country which the Marquis and his illustrious neighbor found so fascinating: "Between the prairie lands of North Dakota and the prairie lands of Montana there is a narrow strip of broken country so wild and fantastic in its beauty that it seems as though some unholy demon had carved it to mock the loveliness of God. On both sides of a sinuous river rise ten thousand buttes cut into bizarre shapes by the waters of countless centuries. The hand of man never dared to paint anything as those hills are painted. Olive and lavender, buff, brown, and dazzling white mingle with emerald and flaming scarlet to make a piece of savage splendor that is not without an element of the terrible. The buttes are stark and bare. Only in the clefts are ancient cedars, starved and deformed. In spring there are patches of green grass, an acre here, a hundred acres there, reaching up the slopes from the level bottom-land; but there are regions where for miles and miles no green thing grows, and all creation seems a witch's cauldron of gray bubbles tongued with flame, held by some bit of black art forever in suspension."

Not a restful land, precisely, but it had a soothing effect upon the Marquis' ambition-ridden nerves and he spent the time profitably in laying plans for the future. He determined to go at once to

France and enter the political field, which at the time was seething with turmoil.

To the surprise and great displeasure of his family, the Marquis supported the Socialist cause, started a newspaper that attacked Jews as the root of all evil, and in general comported himself after the fashion of a shrewd and scheming demagogue. Although he probably felt little genuine sympathy for the masses, he made himself immensely popular by advocating a housing program for the underprivileged and publicizing governmental graft and corruption.

Parenthetically, the western Stetson hat which he brought back with him from Medora started a new fashion among Parisian *modistes*: a creation for the ladies called "the Mores."

In 1893 the Marquis was among the formidable forces which defeated Clemenceau for the Chamber of Deputies, and the following year, when the Dreyfus case burst upon a shocked populace, he did not hesitate to make political capital of its implications. But the petty bickerings of partisan politics could not hold for long the interest of the dynamic Marquis. His mind turned once more to high adventure and he conceived the idea of organizing all North Africa, together with France, into a vast Franco-Islamic alliance in opposition to the expanding British empire. He could not have espoused a more dangerous project.

He was supported in this venture by a considerable clique in France which actually believed the alliance possible. It has been charged, too, that there were interests in France which, because of his inside knowledge of the Dreyfus case, were glad to get the Marquis out of the country to some place where he could be quietly murdered.

Whatever the facts may be, his activities as a secret agent in the Fashoda Affair proved to be De Mores' last and most fantastic adventure. He was slain in the desert by Tuareg tribesmen. Had he set the stage himself, this swashbuckling French gallant could have conceived no more romantic denouement than that furnished him by fate: death on the North African sands at the hands of yelling desert tribesmen in the midst of dark international intrigue.

LAND OF THE DACOTAHS

The Marquise refused to credit the story that the Tuareg tribesmen were alone responsible for her husband's death. When the government refused to act, she posted a reward herself and eventually two of the murderers were apprehended. The details of the story will never be known, but it was established that the murderers were well paid for their crime and had acted under orders from powerful officials in the North African colonial service.

In the summer of 1903 the Marquise and her two eldest children, Louis and Athenais, made a last pilgrimage to the Marquis' abandoned American empire. The Marquise spent several weeks at the lonely château where she and her ill-fated husband had lived for three happy and eventful years. It was her final journey to America. She died in France in 1921 from injuries suffered while she was a nurse in World War I.

The château as it stands today is symbolic of a peculiar vein of romanticism in the Marquis' character. Though it has been untenanted since the time when he and the Marquise lived there with a retinue of French servants more than half a century ago, it remains exactly as it was in the days before his dreams crumbled to dust.

Until 1936, when Duc Louis de Vallombrosa, eldest son of the Marquis, transferred the property to the North Dakota State Historical Society, the Marquis or his descendants always maintained a caretaker at the deserted château. Its antique furniture, its chests of costly damasks and silver, its ancient wine cellar, wait still in ghostly readiness for the occupants who will come no more. Maintained by the Historical Society, it stands on the bleak Dakota prairie in lonely grandeur—the only concrete remnant of De Mores' once mighty empire, an empty symbol of his empty dreams.

Chapter 13

THE WHITE DEATH

∿∿∿

It was perhaps as well that the Marquis de Mores' venture failed when it did, for conditions in the vast cattle country of the Upper Missouri Valley were moving inexorably toward the disaster of the winter of 1886–87.

The beginnings of the cattle industry had been brought about by the opening of the gold camps and military posts throughout the territory and the necessity of supplying food to these isolated communities. The first beef cattle on the northern plains were simply oxen turned out to fatten on the rich grasses; but early settlers, quick to see the advantages of these unsurpassed grazing lands, soon began bringing in cattle from outside—and so were born the great drives from the Texas plains to the prairies of the Northwest.

Nelson Story in 1866 inaugurated the Texas drives with a herd of six hundred longhorns which he brought north through hostile Indian country over the Bozeman Trail into Montana. The ranges of Missouri, Kansas, and Nebraska had become stocked during the decades of the 1840's and 50's, and Texas cattlemen were penetrating farther and farther north in search of open range country.

Profits were quick, demand for range stock was steadily increasing, and the completion of transcontinental railroad routes was opening the Northwest to large-scale stock enterprises. The Civil War temporarily halted the northern drives, but by the 70's and 80's great herds of Texas cattle were finding their way up the Bozeman Trail and along the Missouri River into the grasslands of the north. Drives from Minnesota onto the Dakota plains also helped to stock the northern cattle lands, and in a remarkably short time the upper river valley from Montana to Nebraska was dotted with boom cow towns and sprawling ranch lands.

Here, surely, was as fantastic an enterprise as the West has ever seen. Herds numbering in the tens of thousands and representing hundreds of thousands of dollars in capital investment ranged over central and eastern Montana and the western Dakotas on millions of acres to which the cattle barons had no shadow of a claim. The great grazing lands were still in the public domain; vast herds owned by foreign capitalists fattened on precious natural resources belonging to the American people. But the native stockmen were not far behind. And out of the peculiar conditions existing in the free-grass regions grew the practices that were later to destroy the industry, and with it much of the region's natural economic balance.

The acreage of the public domain had not yet been surveyed in the Northwest and the men who were moving their herds onto the land could neither lease nor buy from the government. Yet the grass was there, grass that was ideally suited for stock culture; unlike the eastern varieties, it cured into natural hay on the stem and provided feed all winter long, so that during most seasons cattle were able to forage for themselves.

As the pioneer ranchers took possession of the range they evolved their own laws and regulations governing the utilization of the land. Often these were nothing more than the law of the jungle enforced by the six-shooter; in other cases, as under the peculiar institution of the "customary range," they were more or less equitable and successful, particularly in the early days before the country became overcrowded.

The process by which a cattleman took possession of the range he desired was a simple one. A notice published in the nearest newspaper, defining the limits of his range and giving his brand, was all that was necessary. After that, his only problem was to enforce his domination over the appropriated territory and keep out any who might encroach upon his land.

In the fastnesses of the cattle country the enforcement of the range laws was no easy task. That portion of the law making it an offense to drive cattle from their customary range without permission of the owner proved a source of constant bickering and contention. Often the offense was unintentional, for great herds of cattle under the supervision of a handful of men might wander for miles before the fact was brought to the attention of the owner.

No criminal penalty was fixed for rustling or alteration of brands, because this too was sometimes unintentional; but civil damages for three times the value of the cattle thus appropriated were awarded if the injured rancher could prove his case. The faults in this law as it pertained to actual rustlers were many, but to protect honest ranchers who might have branded mavericks mistakenly it was perhaps the best that could have been evolved. And rustlers, as will be seen, were taken care of by other and more effective means.

The law of the customary range, while effective in part, was legally quite without meaning—based as it was on an individual's "right" to a portion of the public domain—and ranchers of a later day found it necessary to protect their "vested interests" in other ways. Violators of the range code found themselves excluded from the common roundup in which all the ranchers of a territory participated; their cattle would not be "worked" by other spreads, and usually the force of public opinion and economic pressure forced the interlopers to go elsewhere.

But this device failed, too, as the ranges became more and more crowded. Instead of being driven out of the country by the roundup boycott, the latecomer instituted his own roundup—well in advance of the common one—and profited mightily by his audacious, if unethical, practice. He was able to round up and brand all the unmarked cattle before his fellow ranchers ever had a chance at them—all too often injuring other men's stock in the process by running them and causing them to lose flesh.

Western stockmen, bedeviled by latecomers who found ways of circumventing their laws as fast as the cattlemen could invent them, tried innumerable devices to protect their squatters' rights —many of them illegal. Under the Homestead Act they had dozens of their employees file on homesteads, with the understanding that the land was actually to be available to the employer for range land; and with the collusion of friendly officials they obtained tracts of the public domain under the Timber Culture and Desert Land acts, by pretending to plant trees and irrigate the land. These measures were not, for obvious reasons, always successful; the ranchers ran the risk of a double cross from the employees in question, as well as possible prosecution for making false statements to the government.

When everything else failed, they actually began to fence the public domain. But the government balked at this brazen violation of public rights, and the fences came down, to the accompaniment of loud curses from the western cattlemen. Now they had but one recourse: with a magnificent disregard for the consequences, they stocked their ranges with such numbers of cattle that there was virtually no room left for encroachment. This deliberate overgrazing was ruining their own—and the public's —ranges, and it provided a paradise for the gangs of professional rustlers who had begun to operate extensively in the cattle country. But the rustler problem was one the cattlemen could do something about.

THERE is a famous western story—perhaps apocryphal and perhaps not—concerning a rustler whose fate was about to be decided by a jury of cattlemen. The jury had no sooner reached the room in which they were to conduct their deliberations than the door was flung open and the sheriff poked his head inside.

"Hurry up, you guys, and reach a verdict," he said. "We need this room to lay out the body in."

Whether or not the actual incident is true, the general spirit of the story is in keeping with the view taken of rustlers in the western country. A horse thief was considered several degrees lower than a murderer, and it was not often that the formality of a trial was resorted to. And *formality* is the proper word; a rustler judged by a cattleman jury was in approximately the same position as a cat would be before a jury of mice. The Huron, Dakota Territory, *Tribune* of August 11, 1883, expressed succinctly the sentiments of the community when it remarked of a certain citizen suspected of rustling: "He will undoubtedly stretch hemp in the course of a few months and we shall be glad to publish his obituary."

A. C. Huidekoper, an old-time ranchman in the Medora vicinity, has described in an unpublished manuscript the trial of a rustler who had been brought to book at Medora. The only at-

torney whose services the rustler was able to obtain was one
Simpson—who had been disbarred and hence was unable to enter
the courtroom. And the bailiff was none other than Hell-Roaring
Bill Jones, under whom Theodore Roosevelt served for a time as
deputy sheriff. But let Mr. Huidekoper tell it in his own words:

"The trial of the rustler was held at Medora. There was great
excitement over it. I think Judge Winchester of Bismarck was to
preside. The court was held in a schoolroom, there being no court
house at the time. The cowboys all came in their boiled shirts.
Foul-Mouthed Bill Jones marshalled them for instructions. 'Now,'
he says, 'don't sit there like a lot of stiffs. Look as if you were
alive. Now I'm going to put a pitcher of water with a tumbler
on the desk for the Judge. There ain't no whiskey in it, so you
needn't sample it . . .'

"When the Judge arrived he seemed much impressed with his reception. He congratulated them upon their intelligent appearance
and impressed upon them the responsibilities some of them would
be called upon to assume as jurors, a duty he hoped they would assume without fear or favor. Bill Jones said afterward that he should
have thought 'the Judge would have strangled when he said such
stuff to a damned lot of boobs.'

"The jury was empaneled, the evidence taken. Simpson couldn't
come into the court room. He sat on the steps outside and coached
his associate from there. His instructions were to object to everything the other side did. After the witnesses had finished, the lawyers delivered their fiery, frothing addresses and the Judge gave
his charge, and then said: 'Mr. Jones, do you have a proper place
where the jury can retire for consultation and where they cannot
be approached?' and Bill replied, 'I have, your Honor. I've been
in New York and I know all about these things.' So the jury filed
solemnly out. Bill took them to the bar-room, ordered everyone
out of the room except the bartender, whom he told must have no
conversation with the jury; then he ordered the bartender to
sling out a drink for the jury and charge it to the county.

"The foreman of the jury, after he had had his drink, suggested
that they return to the court and 'get through with this thing,'
but Bill Jones said 'No.' 'Well,' said the foreman, 'we have con-

victed him.' 'I know that,' said Bill Jones. 'I heard you decide that he was guilty as you came over here, but you've got to put up a bluff at chewing the rag before you go back or the Judge will think that you don't know nothing, and by God you don't!' One of the jury wanted to know how long they would have to stay. 'Well,' said Bill, 'I couldn't let you go in less than half an hour.' 'Can we smoke and drink while we're waiting?' 'Yes,' said Bill, 'you can smoke and liquor up at your own expense, but I got to get you back sober.'

"At the end of half an hour the bartender was ordered to sling another drink at the expense of the county. Before the jury returned, Bill Jones instructed them as follows: 'When you fellers get back, that reading and writing feller will say—Gentlemen, have you agreed on a verdict? Then you, Bob, as foreman, will say—We do. Then he will look at you other fellers and say—So say all of you? Then don't say nothing but bob your heads.'

"After the verdict was delivered, Simpson's associate rushed out to announce the result. 'I knew he was guilty,' says Simpson, 'but go back and take an appeal. Tell the Judge you have two very important witnesses that were held up by high water and couldn't get here.' The Judge took the appeal under advisement and the court was adjourned after a short congratulatory address."

Whether the county of Billings ever paid for Hell-Roaring Bill's generosity to the jury is not known. But the majesty of Justice had been upheld, and Law had come to Medora.

HELL-ROARING BILL's statement that he had been in New York was probably a lie; but it is nevertheless true that he had had some previous experience as a peace officer. He had once been a policeman in Bismarck but had left that employment after beating the mayor of the city over the head with a pistol butt. The mayor, as Bill later explained, didn't mind, but the chief of police took an uncharitable view of the matter and requested Bill's resignation. Theodore Roosevelt has related in his autobiography several amusing instances of Bill's habits and characteristics. An even more interesting commentary, however, would have been Bill's opinion of his part-time deputy, the four-eyed dude from New York.

THE WHITE DEATH

So many biographers of Roosevelt—most of them from New York—have written of Teddy's great skill as a frontiersman, cowboy, horseman, big-game hunter, fisticuffer, and general outdoor he-man that the truth of the matter will probably never prevail. Far from being "one of the boys," he was always known in Dakota as "Mr. Roosevelt," as befitted a man of wealth and social pretensions; and his political reputation even at that early date, plus his aloof demeanor, made any familiarities unthinkable for the great majority of the cowhands. Actually, most of them snickered at him as a greenhorn and had little to do with him. He associated for the most part with their employers—many of whom were Easterners like himself. As for the real cowmen of the West, they respected Roosevelt for what he was and were proud to have him for a friend, but they did not respect him for what he wasn't.

Here is the opinion of one old cowman who knew Teddy well in his brief ranching days: "He didn't know a thing about cattle; he could not catch his own horse out of the cavvy. Roosevelt took part in only one roundup—that of 1885, and here he was simply in the way. He was willing to help but a nuisance anywhere you put him. He didn't have a cowman in his outfit, although he had some who made pretty good hands."

The Roosevelt myth has received able assistance from Teddy himself. One of his biographers, discovering in Teddy's autobiography a false statement concerning his prowess as a schoolboy boxer, has given the ingenious explanation that Roosevelt *wished* it were true so fiercely that he finally convinced himself it *was* true. This generous suggestion scarcely applies in the case of another self-told experience: an account of how he beat with his fists and disarmed a huge bully who had cowed a roomful of Dakota cowhands by shooting up a saloon. No contemporary vouches for it; no record of it appears in any of the newspapers of the day; no old friend ever heard of it.

In a country where everybody knew everybody else, and where such a feat would have been on everyone's lips and earned its hero the respect of western men, the lack of any record except in Teddy's autobiography is suspicious, to say the least. It is noteworthy, too, that the town where the incident took place is un-

213

named. This in a country where there were not more than a half dozen villages within a radius of a hundred miles! The story may be true, of course; it is what one would expect from the man who said: "The bravest man I ever knew *followed* me up San Juan Hill!"

There is another typical Rooseveltian touch in his autobiography: not once in its pages does he mention the Marquis de Mores, who was the leading figure and the most dashing character of the Medora area all during Teddy's residence there. One of Teddy's sons has perhaps given a clue to this omission in his famous quip: "Father doesn't like funerals because he can't be the corpse." Roosevelt's own activities and personality were always overshadowed by the Marquis and his dramatic affairs, and Teddy perhaps did not relish any corpse but himself at his autobiographical funeral.

The Marquis, who was quite as innocent and naive about the West as Teddy was, joined forces with Roosevelt in the 80's in an attempt to wipe out the nests of rustlers that infested the Badlands country from central Montana to the Dakota border. They were both members of the Montana Stockgrowers' Association, which met at Miles City in the spring of 1884 to discuss measures to curb these rustling gangs, which were costing Montana-Dakota stockmen more than two million dollars a year.

Roosevelt and the Marquis, both fire-eaters with the neophyte's ignorance of the problems involved, urged a dramatic sortie in force against the rustlers' dens hidden in the rugged Badlands. But older heads among the stockgrowers were quick to turn thumbs down on a plan that, aside from warning every rustler for three hundred miles around, might have meant a minor civil war, with perhaps many innocent men killed or injured.

The meeting adjourned without any definite plan being formed —and the rustlers grew bolder than ever. But preparations for action were nevertheless being quietly made. Granville Stuart, pioneer Montana cattleman, had called a secret meeting at his ranch and a vigilance committee of fourteen members was organized to rid the country of the Badlands gangs. Their methods were to be clandestine and direct. Since the law had failed to solve the problem of the rustlers, the ranchers would proceed without its sanction.

Their decision began to produce results almost immediately. Within two weeks after the meeting three rustlers had been caught and disposed of. One was shot dead in an exchange of gunfire; the other two were captured, placed under guard, and later hanged after the guards had been mysteriously overpowered by "unknown men." The bodies were found swinging with the ominous placard "Horse Thief" pinned on them.

After a few more such introductory measures, on July 7, 1884, the Stranglers, as the vigilantes came to be known, moved in force into the Badlands, the very stronghold of the rustling fraternity. They succeeded in surprising the outlaws in their lonely hideout and surrounded their cabin before the alarm was given; but an all-day siege followed before the Stranglers managed to bring the battle to a successful conclusion. Five men died in the cabin when it was set afire, another was shot dead as he tried to flee, and five others escaped in the melee. The Stranglers suffered only minor wounds. And a few days later four of the escaped rustlers were seized some distance downstream on the Missouri as they were fleeing toward safer parts. They were promptly hanged, too, after the guard placed over them was again mysteriously overpowered.

There was a sharp falling-off in the number of horse and cattle thefts after this cleanup, and several others similar to it, were completed. Montana was getting too hot for the few surviving badmen who lived by rustling; and local newspapers reported a hasty exodus eastward of a number of shady-looking characters, most of whom floated away downstream on the lonely Missouri in whatever craft they found available. Montana and Dakota ranchers breathed easier.

PROSPERITY in the cattle business had reached high tide by the middle of the 80's. A series of mild winters, during which cattle on the dangerously overstocked ranges had been able to forage for themselves with little loss, led to the foolhardy speculation that the condition was bound to continue. Only here and there was there a foreboding of catastrophe.

The summer of 1886 was hot and dry. Prairie fires swept over the dry grasslands, blackening the grass that was already parched by an implacable sun. The smaller creeks and rivers vanished to a trickle or dried up completely in late summer, for there were no longer innumerable beaver to dig and dam and conserve the precious water. Their ruthless slaughter at the hands of man was to turn now and aid in destroying the destroyer. The few beaver that were left built heavier lodges than usual that fall, and piled up larger quantities of winter forage. Other fur-bearing animals grew thicker coats, and the wild fowl headed southward earlier than was customary. Nature had posted her signs for him who would read; but mid-November found the cattle barons unprepared for the icy tempest that swept down on them from the north.

From November until February the bitter cold continued, with blizzard following blizzard until the snow lay packed and level to a depth of five feet on the open prairie. Temperatures dropped to 40, 50, and 60 degrees below zero. White snowy owls of the Arctic appeared for the first time in the memory of white men. Coulees where the cattle might have sheltered were choked with drifts, and on the level grasslands the cattle muzzled vainly in an attempt to reach the sparse grass buried below. Herds of antelope, driven by the pangs of hunger to forget their fear of men, came to the very edges of the settlements in search of feed and shelter.

Early in February a Dakota editor wrote: "There is a serious apprehension that there will be an appalling loss of human lives in Montana and western Dakota. Snow began falling early in November and there is more on the ground than for ten years. Most of the stage roads are entirely closed up and trains are running at irregular intervals, some being four or five days apart and the supply of fuel is almost exhausted. The snow is drifted to enormous depths and should another protracted storm occur it is believed that hundreds would succumb to its terrors. As it is, more people have frozen to death this winter than for a quarter of a century. The cold has been intense. Reports are coming in from the ranges of Dakota, Montana and Wyoming of the large losses of cattle owing to the scarcity of feed and insufficient protection from the severe weather. Losses already reach eight to twenty per cent and it is not overdoing it to say that in the event of the snow lying on the ground for four weeks longer the loss will reach from fifty to seventy-five per cent."

His gloomy predictions were fulfilled. The Texas dogies and eastern pilgrims, unused to the rigors of the northern winters, were the first to perish; but as the savage storms continued, even the hardier native stock huddled together in the snow-packed gullies and died by the tens of thousands. The fences illegally erected by the ranchers proved their undoing now; cattle that might have found their way to safe havens piled up against them and perished helplessly. Gaunt, staggering skeletons that had once been sleek range animals gnawed at the tarpaper coverings of isolated ranch houses. Wolves and coyotes grew fat and bold as they pulled down weakened survivors or fed greedily on half-dead cattle imprisoned in the drifts.

The ranchers themselves, barricaded in their homes by the bitter subzero temperatures, could do little to aid their helpless stock. Many of them, attempting to battle the blizzards to save a portion of their herds, lost their lives in the swirling smother within a few paces of their doorsteps. A northern plains blizzard is a fearful enemy: stinging, slashing pellets of icy snow that cut and blind a man; wind that snatches the breath from his lips and nostrils so that he can breathe only in painful gasps; gales of such violence and power that one cannot stand against their buffeting force; and all around, the white darkness that hides a man's mittened hand from his own eyes even at midday.

When the grip of the terrible winter relaxed in early March the cattle ranges of the upper river were a scene of death and desolation. At Medora a rancher noted: "One had only to stand by the river bank for a few minutes and watch the grim procession going downstream to realize in full the depth of the tragedy that had been enacted within the past few months." The grim procession was made up of the bodies of tens of thousands of dead range cattle. It marked the end of the teeming herds of the great cattle barons.

Losses varied throughout the cattle country from 40 to 90 per cent. The Hash Knife outfit lost disastrously; the Home Land & Cattle Company of Montana lost two thirds of six thousand cattle; Nelson Story, who had brought in the first Texas drive in 1866, suffered a two-thirds loss; the Swan Cattle Company of Wyoming and Montana and the Niobrara Cattle Company went into bankruptcy. Smaller ranchers like Theodore Roosevelt were left with a few hundred head, which they promptly sold before departing from the cattle country forever.

And from Helena, Montana, Kaufman and Stadler sent inquiries to the foreman of their outfit in the Judith Basin, wanting to know the extent of their losses. One of the outfit's riders was Charley Russell, then an unknown cowhand. On a postcard young Russell sketched in water colors the painting of the skeleton steer and the grimly waiting coyote that has since become famous as *The Last of Five Thousand*. Sent to the Helena ranchers, it attracted attention to the cowboy artist and started him on the career that was to bring him nationwide fame as a delineator of western scenes.

Many ranchers experienced a sense of revulsion at the terrible death toll among their stock. "I never again want to hear of the open range," said one embittered cattleman who had been an unwilling witness of the suffering of his animals during the disastrous winter.

HALF a million cattle had perished in the upper river valley that winter; but the loss, tremendous as it was, was not without salutary effects. Improved methods were introduced by the ranchers who were able to stick it out. The size of herds was reduced, hay was produced to lessen dependence on grazing as the sole source of feed, and the great ranch spreads of former days were reduced in size and owned by the cattlemen, who were thus able to fence their ranges and provide better care and shelter for their animals. The southern drives were resumed, and six years after the disastrous winter the Northwest's ranges were restocked even more heavily than before. But the era of the huge herds and the open range was gone forever.

And gone with it was the romantic era of the cowboy. In *Sheep*, one of the wisest and wittiest of western books, Archer Gilfillan, a South Dakota theological student turned sheepherder, has pointed out the depths to which the cowboy's once high estate has fallen:

"There is an almost universal belief that a cowboy's work is romantic. . . . He puts up hay for a couple of months during the summer and he feeds it for many a long month during the winter. In fact he puts in six to eight months a year handling hay in one form or another, and then another month or two handling the inevitable results. If this be romance, make the most of it. . . .

"When the ignorant herder sees the cowboy risk his neck in breaking a bronc for five dollars, he comes to the conclusion that either the cowboy's neck is worth only five dollars or that his brains are located in that portion of his anatomy which clings most closely to the saddle. . . . Throughout a large part of the West today, cowboy stuff is merely a phase which boys pass through, like playing Indians or soldiers, only some of them never grow up. There will probably always be in the West a certain type of young fellow who cannot go out and drive in the milk cows without buckling on chaps and spurs. But with the present stringent laws against murder there is probably nothing that can be done about this."

Now that men and the elements together had proved that the open range was impracticable on the northern plains, the cattle lands of the Upper Missouri began filling up with smaller ranches, better adapted to the country and its climate. From the eastern United States and the troubled backwaters of restless Europe settlers were making their way westward to the new land that had been cleared of hostile Indians and opened to the white man's civilization.

But on the reservations of the Sioux, last of the Indian races to submit to the white man's will, there smoldered a final spark of rebellion. A last bloody chapter was still to be written in the Northwest's record of conflict between red man and white.

219

Chapter 14

RED MESSIAH

This happened in the time when the sun died.

It was January 1, 1889, and the old men of the Standing Rock Sioux speak of it even today with a curious, hushed, and nostalgic kind of awe. For on that day, while the sun was blotted out by a total solar eclipse, Wovoka, who lived among the Paiute Indians of Nevada, had a vision.

It was no ordinary vision that came to Wovoka in his dreams while his frightened people cowered in terror of what they believed to be the death of the sun. When he awakened he announced that he had become the Great Spirit's representative on earth to lead his people out of bondage. He was the new Messiah, the Saviour of the Red Man.

Wovoka's doctrine was a remarkable compound of Christian and pagan mythology, seasoned with a liberal dash of medicine-man mumbo jumbo. In his vision Wovoka had seen that a new world was to be created, a world free from the white man's restraining influence, where the spirits of all the Indian dead would be resurrected and the buffalo would return to roam the plains as in the days of old.

Wovoka was quite vague about the time of all this, saying merely, "I do not know when they will be here; maybe this fall or in the spring. Do not refuse to work for the whites and do not make any trouble with them until you leave them. When the earth shakes at the coming of the new world, do not be afraid; it will not hurt you. You must not fight. Do right always. Do not tell lies."

In Wovoka's revelation, too, were instructions for a new ceremonial dance, the ghost dance, to be conducted in anticipation of the new day to come.

The fame and the doctrine of the new messiah spread on the wings of the wind among the unhappy and credulous red men, and in a short time his teachings had laid such a hold upon the Indians of the Northwest that a few timid officials feared a wholesale uprising. Ghost dances were held daily on all the great reservations, and as the movement spread, garbled versions of Wovoka's teachings began to excite the interest of chronic malcontents among the reservation Sioux. In time the new doctrine came to the ears of the embittered Sitting Bull, where he sulked in unwilling subjection among the Sioux of the Standing Rock agency.

"Crafty, avaricious, mendacious and ambitious." This was the way James McLaughlin of Standing Rock, the Indian agent who knew Sitting Bull best, described him. But McLaughlin, of course, was not unprejudiced.

After the Custer battle the old leader had fled to Canada with his followers, but a half dozen winters of hardship and hunger forced him finally to capitulate and return with his people to the Dakota reservations. Many of the Hunkpapa Sioux had lost faith in him; he was disliked by certain of the more important war leaders, the famous Gall among them; but Sitting Bull himself had become more arrogant than ever in later years, largely as a result of the attention he received while traveling with Buffalo Bill's Wild West Circus. A kindly Canadian priest had taught him to scribble his name, and awe-stricken tourists who read flamboyant accounts of him in eastern newspapers or on Buffalo Bill's circus posters were glad to purchase the old medicine man's autograph for a dollar and a half. Now, in the whispers of the new religion which came to his ears, he saw an opportunity to strike a blow at the white men who had deposed him and rendered his leadership impotent.

Sitting Bull was himself too clever to place any faith in the dreams of visionaries. As a medicine man he knew all the priestcraft and fakery of his kind, and there can be little doubt that his only interest in the new religion was the amount of trouble he could create through its dissemination. Be that as it may, in the summer of 1889 Kicking Bear of the Cheyenne agency was dispatched to the West to learn the true inwardness of the new messiah's religion, and he returned bearing a mighty tale that lost no fat in the telling. There was little left of Wovoka's humble teachings in Kicking Bear's flowery version, as recorded by Agent McLaughlin:

"My brothers, I bring you the promise of a day in which there will be no white man to lay his hand on the bridle of an Indian's horse; when the red men of the prairie will rule the world and not be turned from the hunting ground by any man. I bring you word from your fathers the ghosts that they are now marching to join you, led by the Messiah who came once to live on earth with the white men, but was cast out and killed by them. I have seen the wonders of the spiritland and have talked with the ghosts. . . .

"I traveled far on the cars of the white man, until I came to a place where the railroad stopped. There I was met by two men, Indians, whom I had never seen before, but who greeted me as a brother and gave me meat and bread."

Kicking Bear traveled for several suns with the two strangers, escaping only by the skin of his teeth from the temptation of Satan, for, said Kicking Bear, "we saw a strange and fierce-looking black man dressed in skins . . . He would wave his hands and make great heaps of money; another motion, and we saw many spring wagons, already painted and ready to hitch horses to; yet another motion of the hands, and there sprang up before us great herds of buffalo." But he escaped this devilish trap successfully and he and his two companions were met at last by the messiah.

"He led us up a great ladder of small clouds, and we followed him up through an opening in the sky. My brothers, the tongue of Kicking Bear is straight and he cannot tell all he saw, for he is no orator, but the forerunner and herald of the ghosts."

One can readily imagine the effect of Kicking Bear's words on the ignorant and superstitious red men of the plains. Here, face to face with them, was a man who had not only met the messiah, but was now about to make the acquaintance of even higher personages. And sure enough: "He whom we followed took us to the Great Spirit and his wife, and we lay prostrate on the ground, but I saw that they were dressed as Indians!"

The Great Spirit, after seating them on rich skins of animals before the door of His tipi, delivered Himself of this awful and terrifying blast: "I will cover the earth with new soil to the depth of five times the height of a man, and under this new soil will be buried all the whites . . . and the new lands will be covered with sweet grass and running water and trees, and herds of buffalo and ponies will stray over it, that my red children may eat and drink, hunt and rejoice. And the sea to the west will I fill up that no ships may pass over it, and the other seas will I make impassable . . . And while my children are dancing and making ready to join the ghosts, they shall have no fear of the white man, for I will take from the whites the secret of making gunpowder, and the powder they now have will not burn when it is directed against the red people, my children, who know the songs and dances of the ghosts . . . Go then, my children, and tell these things to all the people and make all ready for the coming of the ghosts!"

Kicking Bear and his fellows were then fed rich and exotic foods in the Great Spirit's tipi, after which they descended the ladder of clouds and took their way homeward, the messiah flying along in the air above them to teach them the new songs of the ghost dance and guide them on their journey.

THIS was the brave tale, with many embellishments and variations, that Kicking Bear brought with him to the Pine Ridge agency and to Standing Rock in the north. Its effect upon the Sioux was almost incredible. Not since the great dancing mania which swept Europe at the time of the Black Death in the fourteenth century had anything like it been seen upon the earth.

The new religion could not have come to the Sioux at a more inauspicious moment. The government, in the mistaken notion that a reduction in rations would hasten the Indians toward self-support, had just inaugurated a policy which had large numbers of them in a state of semistarvation. Their way of life was gone forever; they were desperate.

In the decades just ended they had seen their lands seized by the white man; their numbers decimated by alcohol, disease, war, and starvation; their children forced into alien schools where they were treated like reform-school inmates or worse; their religious ceremonies forbidden; and their economy and civilization destroyed forever. The spoils system flourished in the Indian service.

Incompetent or dishonest agents and contractors cheated them of the meager goods allotted them by the government. When they resisted, as some did, they were murdered or flung into prison.

A defeated, frightened people, knowing not which way to turn, they were ready to grasp at anything that promised to alleviate their plight. And here, in the religion of the new messiah, was the promise of a utopia that would bring back once more the glory of their ancient days and departed customs. They flung themselves into the practices of the new faith with the fervor of desperation.

The rigors of the ghost dance were alone sufficient to have rendered them half crazed. Long hours of dancing, steaming in sweat lodges, and fasting reduced many of them to a state where they were quite literally out of their minds. Men and women fell in trances and received messages from departed ancestors while they lay writhing and foaming at the mouth. The medicine men of the tribes, temporarily back at their ancient trade, urged on the deluded victims with every means at their disposal.

Yet, actually, the affected Indians numbered only a small minority of all the reservation Sioux. Many of the Indians had become Christianized; others were simply too intelligent to succumb to the fantastic claims of the native prophets and soothsayers. But even a minority of a nation which still numbered thirty thousand people provided some cause for alarm.

At his camp on Grand River, Sitting Bull was taking full advantage of the frenzy into which his people were thrown. So, too, were the enterprising editors of eastern papers, who had not had a good Indian scare in a decade. Ghost dances were being held daily on all the Dakota reservations, and it was not long before the Northwest was swarming with special correspondents—among them Theodore Roosevelt, representing *Harper's* magazine. One reporter with a sense of humor and perspective—and perhaps a gift for invention—wired what he said was an old warrior's description of the ghost dance.

"It is our church, just like the white man's," the ancient was reported to have said, "except that we don't pass the hat!"

All the correspondents could report, in truth, was a religious ceremony such as may be found among the Shoutin' Baptists, the

Holy Rollers, or the Snake Cultists of the Bible Belt today; but enthusiastic reporters managed nevertheless to send back reams of copy hinting at dark and bloody plots against the white race— which in this year of 1890 outnumbered the red population of the northern plains by about twenty to one.

The government was loath to act, for there had not been a single hostile demonstration; but settlers of the region, perhaps misled by the newspapers, thought they recognized the symptoms of revolt and pleaded for protection. Agent Royer at Pine Ridge, a new and inexperienced appointee, was wild with terror and began calling for troops to avert a second massacre of the innocents.

In November 1889 President Harrison finally ordered the War Department to take steps which would safeguard the settlers of the Indian country. Agent James McLaughlin of the Standing Rock agency advised against it, suggesting that the Sioux be allowed to continue their dancing until the next spring, when, at the failure of the new world to materialize, the ghost-dancing mania would be forgotten. But in the public clamor McLaughlin's wise counsel went unheeded. General Nelson A. Miles, commander of the Department of the Missouri, immediately stationed troops in great numbers at all the areas of threatened trouble, while the Indian agents continued their efforts to halt the dancing by means of persuasion.

Then into the situation came Buffalo Bill, famed slayer of bison, showman extraordinary, and friend of Sitting Bull, whom he had formerly employed in his Wild West Circus. Bill was probably considering only the publicity value of the suggestion when he offered to employ his friendship with the old medicine man to effect Sitting Bull's arrest and end the threatened uprising. Much to everybody's surprise, however, General Miles wrote Cody an order for the chief's arrest, and Bill set out to accomplish his mission of mercy.

This did not please Agent McLaughlin, who had been advocating Sitting Bull's detention for some time, nor did it please the military stationed at the scene. McLaughlin wired Washington to have the order rescinded, while a group of army officers attempted to stay Cody's hand by inviting him to a banquet where the grog flowed freely.

But Bill was as famous a tosspot as he was a buffalo hunter. Instead of winding up under the table, he rose fresh—though a bit unsteady—and set out to arrest Sitting Bull. He was overtaken and turned back from his mission a few minutes later when the awaited order arrived from Washington.

Sitting Bull continued to lead the ghost dancing at Grand River, and on December 12 the government at length issued an order for his arrest. McLaughlin and Colonel Drum moved at once, for they had learned that the old medicine man was about to leave the reservation and lead his followers to join Short Bull and Kicking Bear, who had fled from the presence of the soldiers to the wilds of the Badlands, where they hoped to continue their ceremonies unmolested. Some three thousand religion-crazed Sioux were gathered in the rugged buttes, and with them Sitting Bull hoped to find refuge.

About forty Indian police under Lieutenant Bull Head, supported by the U.S. Cavalry from Fort Yates, were ordered at once to Grand River, where it was decided that the Indian police could probably make the arrest with less friction than the federal troops. The soldiers were to intervene only in case of trouble.

Early in the frosty dawn of December 15 Bull Head and Shave Head led their forty Indian policemen into Sitting Bull's encampment on Grand River. Exhausted from the ritual of the ghost dance, the camp was not yet astir when the police detail entered the old medicine man's cabin and informed him that he was under arrest. His two wives set up a great clamor at the news, but Sitting Bull himself seemed docile enough.

"Very well," he said quietly, "I will go with you."

The camp outside was aroused now and angrily demanding information from the policemen stationed at the door of the crude log hut. Sitting Bull, apparently unperturbed, dressed himself in his best clothing. At his request one of the police was dispatched to saddle his finest horse—a gift from Buffalo Bill—and bring it to the door of the cabin. Bull Head and Shave Head each grasped the medicine man by an arm and, with Red Tomahawk bringing

226

up the rear, stepped out into the white light of morning to face two hundred armed and angry ghost dancers.

Sitting Bull could read in the faces of his followers their devotion to him and their readiness to die for his sake if need be. His son, Crow Foot, seeing the old man hesitate, taunted him openly: "You call yourself a brave man and you have said you would never surrender to a Blue-Coat; and now you give yourself up to Indians in blue uniforms!"

Sitting Bull paused, torn between his hatred for his captors and the certainty of death if he resisted. His black eyes darted nervously from face to face among his people. Suddenly he screamed out a command to his followers: *"Mni kte sni yelo! Hiyupo! Hopo!"* (I am not going! Come on! Let's go!)

It was his last command. Red Tomahawk, immediately behind him, clapped his gun to the medicine man's head and fired, killing him instantly. Shave Head and Bull Head fell with the old chief, pierced by the hail of lead which the maddened ghost dancers loosed at them. The opposing groups fired into each other at point-blank range until the police detail ran short of ammunition and retired into a nearby cabin, while the ghost dancers took refuge in the surrounding timber. Then Captain Fechet and his troops of the Eighth Cavalry, who had been awaiting developments in the background, closed in on the camp and dispersed the Indians.

A supernatural touch that might well have struck fear to the heart of the hardiest savage was added by Sitting Bull's horse, which stood saddled and ready when the fighting broke out. At the sound of the shots the animal began an elaborate routine of bowing, kneeling, and moving its forefeet in strange gestures —a procedure induced, no doubt, by the memory of its days as a trained performer with Cody's Wild West show. But to the Indians who knew nothing of the animal's history it seemed that the spirit of the old medicine man had entered into the horse and was directing them in battle.

With the Sioux resistance broken, Captain Fechet was soon able to persuade most of the remaining dancers to return to the village. They were considerably sobered by the discovery that their sacred ghost shirts were no protection against the bullets of the white man, and that the powder which Kicking Bear had assured them would be harmless propelled the white man's projectiles quite as effectively as usual. Captain Fechet made it clear that they would suffer no harm provided all resistance ceased, and order was soon restored.

But the ghost dancing was not ended. Thirty-eight of Sitting Bull's most fanatical followers had fled the camp at Grand River after the medicine man's death, to carry far and wide the story of the old leader's killing and his reincarnation in the body of his horse. It was not long before the refugees fell in with Big Foot's band of Sioux, who were fleeing from their agency to join the ghost dancers in the Badlands.

The military had thrown heavy forces into action against the thousands of Indians gathered there. Surrounding them with such numbers of troops that resistance was impossible, the officers managed to arrange a parley with the Sioux leaders. And the Indians, after hearing the officers' arguments, wisely agreed to allow the troops to escort them in peace back to the Pine Ridge agency, where they were assured of better treatment in the future.

Big Foot and his band, meanwhile, managing to escape the government forces along the Cheyenne River, arrived at last in the Badlands—to find that their compatriots had just departed. While Big Foot debated his next move, four troops of the Seventh Cavalry arrived on the scene and settled the problem for him: Big Foot promptly surrendered. Escorted by the troops, the Indians were taken to Wounded Knee Creek, where Colonel Forsyth, with five additional troops and four Hotchkiss guns, took charge.

With the exception of the unfortunate affair at Grand River, the Army's excellent handling of the Indians had thus far prevented any serious clashes. At Pine Ridge, twenty miles to the south, some four thousand Sioux were preparing to settle down in peace. Big Foot's band—numbering perhaps four hundred with Sitting Bull's followers—were encamped on the open plain near Wounded Knee Creek. They seemed docile enough, but the army commanders were taking no chances.

To the rear of the Sioux village a dry gulch sloped backward toward the creek. Before the encampment, on a gentle rise of ground, were mounted the four Hotchkiss guns, their ugly muzzles trained directly on the Siouan tipis, and drawn up around the camp were the troops of the Seventh Cavalry.

Colonel Forsyth set about the task of disarming the Indians with a confusing combination of diplomacy and imbecility. Chief Big Foot lay ill in his tent, where the colonel courteously provided the old fellow with a camp stove and the services of an army physician. The women and children of the camp were taken aside so that they might be out of harm's way in case of trouble, while the warriors were called together for a consultation. Around the assembled Sioux were placed the troopers, in such a position that they could not have fired without killing each other—which, as will be seen, is precisely what they did.

Squatting on the ground before the companies of dismounted cavalrymen, the warriors listened with ill-concealed displeasure to the news that they must deliver up their weapons to the soldiers of the Great White Father. Colonel Forsyth, to avoid coercion, first urged the braves themselves to go to their tipis and bring out their guns. When they returned with two old rifles, declaring these to be their entire arsenal, Colonel Forsyth detailed a group of troopers to make a thorough search of the lodges and confiscate all hidden weapons. Others were ordered to search the blanketed braves and disarm them.

None of the officers understood the Siouan tongue, so they were only mildly amused at the antics of the medicine man, Yellow Bird, as he pirouetted up and down the line of sullen braves, blowing shrilly on an eagle-bone whistle and exhorting his comrades to resist.

"The white man's bullets cannot pierce your ghost shirts," old Yellow Bird urged. "Attack them while there is yet time."

He stooped suddenly, seized a handful of dirt, and flung it into the air. It was the ancient summons to battle.

While the warriors still stood hesitant, two troopers twitched aside the blanket of a young brave, baring a cocked rifle, and attempted to disarm him. In the struggle the rifle was discharged, and an instant later the camp was a whirling bedlam of war whoops, rifle fire, and locked, straining bodies. It was battle swift and savage, clubbed rifle against knife and tomahawk, during the first few disordered moments of conflict. As the Indians broke and rushed to their tipis for their hidden weapons, Forsyth's troopers poured a merciless point-blank fire into their ranks—and into each other.

From the slope overlooking the camp the four Hotchkiss guns spat murderous havoc into the crowd of Indian women and children who had been placed to one side for "safety." Two-pound explosive shells, hurled at the rate of fifty a minute, plowed into their huddled ranks. As the surviving Indians fled terror-stricken toward the creek, the soldiers followed at their heels, shooting down men, women, and children indiscriminately. Two hundred Sioux, many of them women and children, most of them unarmed, lay dead or wounded near the camp. Even old Big Foot, ill in his tipi, did not escape; he was slain while he lay defenseless in his blankets.

It was massacre pure and simple. Provoked by the foolish words of an ignorant medicine man and the bungling policies of inexperienced army officers, it became a blood bath from which the soldiers themselves recoiled in horror once they had recovered from their fury. The day was black for the sorrowing remnants of Big Foot's band, but it was equally black in the pages of American military history. There was an investigation, of course, when the full story became known, but it ended with the usual glib decision that "nobody had been to blame."

Here, however, are the reactions of a trooper of the Seventh Cavalry who participated in the battle: "After sitting two hours in the saddle, half frozen, we found out that our business was to disarm the Indians. Of course the whole thing was bungled. About a dozen bucks came forward with two old blunderbusses, and then Colonel Forsyth ordered a detail of five men from each company to search the tipis. I was crawling into one when I got a kick from behind that fairly drove my head through the cover on the opposite side and landed me on a pile of dogs and babies. I got outside, mad as a hatter, and there stood a young squaw, grinning with delight. I made a grab at her bangs, when down both of us went, and this saved my life. Suddenly there was a crash and the air was full of bullets. I heard them racing past. The poor squaw had got on her feet first, and went down, shot through the head. Her blood flew over the cape of my coat. I scrambled up. Everyone was shouting and shooting, and there was no more order than in a barroom scrimmage. In front, a crowd of blanketed forms was making for the coulee, when crash went a rifle volley and they were gone.

"No orders were given, either by voice or bugle, that I heard. I shot one buck running, and when I examined him he had neither gun nor cartridge-belt. The women lay thick. One girl about eighteen was supporting herself on her hand, the blood spurting from her mouth as from a pump. Near her lay two others, and all around, like patches on the snow, were dead squaws, each in a pool of blood. Colonel Forsyth looked very white as he gave orders to see if any of the women who lay thick around were alive. From the blanket of one we took a boy five years old and a baby about as many months—both unhurt, but the mother was dead. She must have been shot with a revolver held not five feet away, as her hair was burned and the skin blackened with powder.

"My captain, Wallace, was dead and eight of my company, and when we mustered in it looked as if half the regiment was gone. From beginning to end I don't think I saw two dozen bucks, and it is a mystery to me where all the bullets came from that killed and wounded one-third of my regiment. My left arm felt sore, and I found that a bullet had grazed the flesh and cut my sleeve. . . . I have no doubt that I was shot by one of my comrades—the rip in my coat showed this. . . . Of course the camp liar was in his glory, but who shot the squaws was not known, at least no one boasted of it."

WHEN the news of the Wounded Knee massacre reached the four thousand Sioux who were gathered at Pine Ridge, all thoughts of peace were abandoned. Appalled by the wanton slaughter of their helpless people, many of the warriors set out at once for Wounded Knee and attacked the soldiers who were still roaming over the battlefield. The result might have been another bloody battle, but

231

a Dakota blizzard had set in and its mounting severity smothered the Sioux attacks.

General Miles literally filled the country with troops, basing his operations at Fort Sully—where, parenthetically, the son of the post bandmaster was a rolypoly, dark-eyed youngster named Fiorello La Guardia. Studiously avoiding any clash with the war-painted braves, Miles sent trusted officers to begin negotiations with the Indian leaders. And among these men was a youthful captain named John J. Pershing.

General Miles pledged his personal word that the Indians would be well treated if they returned to their agencies; that their food allowances would be increased; and that the civilian subagents on the reservations would be replaced with army officers whom the Indians knew and trusted. "Bear Coat," as the Sioux called Miles, was held in great esteem by many Indian leaders, and the blasts of winter, combined with the pinch of hunger, aided his plea. Within a few days the ghost dancers had surrendered and returned to their reservations, and the last important Indian war in the history of the West was ended.

IN THE half century that followed the Messiah War the old pattern of Indian life disintegrated completely. The family unit which had been the basis of tribal life no longer existed. Shacks and crude cabins replaced the tipis of ancient days, and a halfhearted and inept attempt was made by the men of the tribes to practice farming or stock-raising. Treaty payments, sale of lands, or leasing gave them a sufficient income to eke out an existence for some years, while their children were taken care of in mission schools.

But with the coming of hard times and drought after World War I, when government payments and leasing fees largely disappeared, the reservation Sioux began a bitter and wretched fight for existence. Horse meat and dog meat were common items of their diet, supplemented by berries and roots gathered by their womenfolk as in the days of old. Trachoma, syphilis, and tuberculosis took a terrible toll of them in health and life.

They were literally a dying race when in 1934, under a new governmental policy, work projects brought back to them a sense of the old communal and social life and gave them new interest and awakened pleasure in their daily tasks. With a re-establishment of the basic family unit of Indian life—brought about by the return of children to the home and the inauguration of communal projects—they are once again making progress toward self-reliance and survival as a people. Even the cumbersome weight of bureaucratic tradition and the dead hand of the U.S. Indian Bureau have not crushed them completely.

But the romantic day of the red man has not entirely vanished. There are old men on the reservations in the land of the Dacotahs who still recall the ancient glories of their race. They are distrustful of the white man even yet; but if they can be persuaded to speak, you may still hear true tales of Gall and Crow King and Crazy Horse, of old battles and dead loves, and of the Gods of the Elder Days.

And here is one of those stories.

Chapter 15

THE REVENGE OF *CROW KING*

∧∧∧

Gray Wolf the one-armed told me this as we sat before his lodge one evening in the Moon-When-the-Wild-Plums-Ripen. Beyond the murky shadow of the river the northern lights raced and shimmered along the autumn horizon, and we crouched close to the campfire for warmth. Gray Wolf flung out a gnarled hand and pointed.

"Among the Chippewas there is a tale that the marching lights are the ghost dance of the spirits, with the women dressed in gay colors and the warriors brandishing their shining war clubs. But the Chippewas have many such foolish fables. My people the Sioux no longer believe in the ghosts or the lying tales of the medicine men. What do the wise men of my brother's people say of the marching lights?" Gray Wolf spoke in the Siouan vernacular and I answered him in that tongue.

"The white men are not certain what makes the lights. Some say the thing one way and some another, until their talk is as the bickering of the little wild dogs of the prairie."

Gray Wolf bared his toothless gums in a grin. "Are there things the whites do not know?" he chuckled. "Yet"—his old eyes looked far past me—"why should it not be thus? If my brother will listen, Gray Wolf will tell him the tale of Crow King, speaking with a straight tongue, that my brother may know of Crow King's deeds, many winters ago, in the lodges of my people."

Gray Wolf paused. A green knot in the fireplace exploded with a tiny report, sending up a miniature fountain of brilliant sparks, and the old man waited till the last firefly ember had hissed into the crisp prairie grass.

"In the time when Crow King was a young man, my people roamed the great plains country from the banks of the Greasy Grass where Yellow Hair fell, to the land far beneath us on the Smoky Water." Gray Wolf swung his withered arm and pointed to the dim shadow below us, where, in the twilight, the broad yellow band of the Missouri stretched darkly southward toward the sea.

"Of all the Hunkpapa Sioux, Crow King was mightiest in battle and wisest in the councils of the lodge. Fleet as the deer, brave as the lion of the mountains and with the strength of Pte the buffalo, Crow King found much favor in the soft eyes of the Sioux maidens. But Crow King's heart was bad. Of all the young women of the tribe he loved only Red Bird, and Red Bird would not share his lodge until she knew that she alone was in his heart.

"In those times a great chief might have many wives, and her love for Crow King was such that she would not share his tipi or his heart with another woman. And Crow King sorrowed, for Red Bird was the fairest of the Sioux maidens, tall as a tree and straight as a warrior's lance, with black braids that hung thick as a man's wrist to her waist.

"So Crow King, to prove his love for the maiden, offered himself in sacrifice at the sun dance, that Onk-te-gi, the spirit which abides in the bodies of all earth animals, might be appeased and send good fortune to the tribe. And while the sun made a three days' journey the medicine men of the tribe prayed and made offerings to the Great Spirit, and the ears of the little children were pierced, and on the fourth day Crow King was made ready for the sun dance.

"With sharp sacrificial knives the medicine men made great slashes in the breast and shoulders of Crow King, until the naked red muscles lay bare and the blood ran like the rains of spring down his breast and back. Then, beneath the naked muscles, the medicine men thrust pointed skewers of polished bone, thick as a warrior's thumb, so that the skewers stood out on either side of Crow King's muscles—thus; and to the tips of the polished skewers they fastened strong ropes of rawhide, which they drew over the lodgepole of the medicine tipi until Crow King's moccasin toes touched but lightly on the ground and he hung in the air by the great muscles of his breast and back.

"Then Crow King stared into the burning eye of the sun and danced the sun dance of the Hunkpapa Sioux. While the sun made a day's journey Crow King danced and whistled, that my people

235

might know his heart was great and his courage like that of the lion of the mountains. And as he hung in the rawhide thongs the medicine men circled about him blowing upon whistles of eagle bone and calling to the spirits to witness the suffering of Crow King and be appeased.

"With the coming of dusk the medicine men drew Crow King high into the air and tied buffalo skulls to his feet, for so mighty were his sinews that they would not break and give him release. And the old men of the tribe marveled, saying, 'Hou! there is a man! Cut him down and end his suffering, for he has hung longer in the sun dance than any warrior of the Hunkpapa Sioux.'

"But Crow King mocked them in a parched and croaking voice —it was forbidden that food or drink should pass his lips during the dance—and terrible was the gaze he turned upon the old men with his swollen and inflamed eyeballs. 'Crow King is not a babe,' he croaked, 'to die of a scratch in his skin. Let the rawhide thongs be!' And he spun in the air and whistled to show that his heart was great."

Somewhere up the river valley a coyote yapped shrilly in the crisp silence, and Gray Wolf's tethered ponies flung up their heads with a collective snort of surprise. The old man called soothingly to them and they resumed their cropping.

"At last even the mighty sinews of Crow King parted under the burden of his weight and he fell backward upon the floor of the medicine lodge. Into the gaping wounds of his breast and back the medicine men rubbed handfuls of earth; and Red Bird came swiftly from her father's tipi, where she had been weeping for his suffering and praying that he might be soon released. And from her hands he received the food and drink for which his throat was parched, while the people of the tribe prepared a feast in honor of his bravery.

"It was three moons before the wounds in Crow King's back and breast were healed. Red Bird nursed him through the long nights of pain, and when he was mended he took his finest ponies and tethered them before the lodge of her father as a marriage offering.

"So Crow King and Red Bird were wed and shared his lodge

together; and Red Bird was the envy of all the young women of the tribe. Such was their love that it became after many seasons a legend of beauty among my people, for Crow King would take no other woman into his tipi, though his lodge was barren for a full five winters. And while Crow King sorrowed that he had no sons, he hid his grief from Red Bird, lest he should destroy her happiness. Such was his love for his woman.

"It was five summers after the marriage of Crow King and Red Bird when my people went forth to war against our enemies the Crows. The Crow warriors went down before our young men like maize before the hail, and many Crow braves were sent that season to join their fathers among the ghosts. Far into the Crow country to the north, near the land of the redcoats, Crow King and the Sioux warriors pursued our enemies, and my people took many scalps and ponies, until at last the Crows were beaten and scattered, with their dead fallen as the leaves when they turn yellow.

"But the hearts of my people were bad. They found Crow King among their wounded, with a heavy Crow war arrow through his breast, and they sorrowed, for they saw that Crow King must die.

" 'Leave me, my brothers,' Crow King said. 'I cannot travel, for my time has come to journey to the land of the ghosts. And Crow King will not be a burden to his people.' And the Sioux warriors did as Crow King said, for it was the custom among my people to respect the wishes of a dying chief; and it was likewise necessary for them to retreat quickly from the land of their enemies the Crows.

"They placed Crow King in a deep gully, where he would be hidden from the sight of his enemies—for they wished no Sioux scalp lock to dangle at the lodgepole of a Crow—and beside him they placed food and water, and tethered his pony nearby, that Crow King's shade might ride in the land of the ghosts and not suffer from thirst or hunger.

" 'Farewell, my brothers,' Crow King said. 'Tell Red Bird that Crow King died like a chief.' And he drew his blanket about him and made ready for the coming of the ghosts.

"While the sun made a three days' journey Crow King lay and

waited for the coming of the spirits; but they did not come. At last he ate of the food and drank of the water, and crept to where his pony was tethered. And Crow King mounted, with much pain and labor, and rode slowly like a drunken man upon the trail of my people the Sioux.

"For many suns he journeyed, until a sickness entered into his body so that he sang and laughed and shouted and saw strange visions; and many times he fell from his pony's back. But always before him he saw the beckoning figure of Red Bird, dressed in the beaded dress she had worn on their wedding day, and Red Bird called softly to him and pleaded with him to be of stout heart. So Crow King came at last to the flickering campfires of my people.

"The people of the village fled shrieking when Crow King, pale and gaunt from hunger and his wound, rode into their midst and fell senseless from his pony's back, for they believed it was the ghost of Crow King, and none dared approach him. But Red Bird came forth from her darkened lodge of mourning and carried him in her arms to a tipi, and summoned to his side the medicine men of the tribe.

"And the medicine men came swiftly, each bearing his secret charm or amulet, for Crow King was rich in horses and a mighty chief in the councils of the Sioux. But he lay senseless in his lodge and babbled like a babe, for the sickness was still in his body; while the medicine men practiced their charms and incantations upon him, each hoping that he might cure Crow King and thus obtain his gratitude and many horses."

"It is even so among the medicine men of the whites,' I said, "when a man has great wealth and falls ill. In the Holy Book of the Black Robes there is a saying: 'Wheresoever the carcass is, there will the eagles be gathered together.'"

"The Book of the Black Robes speaks true words," chuckled the old man, huddling under his blanket. "It was even so with Crow King. Blue Dog, the greatest of all the medicine men, came at last to Red Bird, saying, 'The evil spirits have sent bad medicine to Crow King. They have placed in his stomach an eagle's claw; but I, Blue Dog, will save Crow King by taking into my own body the wicked medicine of the spirits.' And Red Bird wept for joy to know that Crow King would be mended, and gave Blue Dog many horses.

"But Blue Dog was not content, and his cunning was as the cunning of Iktomi, the spider. He envied Crow King his power and place among my people, and he made secretly a cunning plan to shame Crow King before the village. Blue Dog danced many prayer dances and made incantations as he prepared to save Crow King from the evil spirits; and when all was ready he came to the lodge of Crow King, saying, 'The spirits have spoken; they will leave the body of Crow King; but first Crow King and Red Bird must promise, in gratitude, that they will for the space of one sun's journey be as village dogs, going about on all fours and eating with the curs of the camp.' Blue Dog knew this would put a great shame on Crow King and destroy his power among my people.

"But Crow King's heart was turned away from Blue Dog and he answered him, saying, 'Crow King is a chief and no village cur. He will go to join his fathers the ghosts before he will put this shame upon himself and Red Bird.' But Red Bird, loving him and fearing for his death, pleaded with him until, for her sake, he gave his promise.

"Then Blue Dog danced the dances of his medicine while my people watched from outside the tipi; and the evil spirits left Crow King's body and entered into the body of Blue Dog, so that he writhed upon the ground and his mouth foamed like that of a dog with the madness. At last Blue Dog rose and spat forth a great eagle's claw, which he showed to the people of the village; and he was hailed as a great medicine man; and the hearts of my people were good, for they knew that Crow King would recover to lead them once more against their enemies the Crows.

"When Crow King was mended, the thought of his promise was heavy in his breast, and Red Bird, after the manner of woman, sought to beguile him from his word; but Crow King stilled her tongue, saying, 'Crow King is a chief. He has given his word and he will not take back his word. We shall fulfill our vow.'

"When the sun rose from his bed in the dark, Crow King and Red Bird went forth among the streets of the village and became as curs of the camp, going about on all fours and eating of the offal that was thrown to the pack. While the sun made his long day's journey they fulfilled the promise made to the evil spirits. And Red Bird wept bitter tears of shame when my people mocked them, but Crow King was proud and silent.

"When the sun dropped below the hills Crow King and Red Bird arose and returned to their tipi; but, womanlike, Red Bird's heart was turned away from Crow King and she spoke no word to him; and from that day hence her love for her husband was ended. And though they shared their lodge together they were no longer as man and woman.

"The women of the camp who had envied Red Bird spoke now with crooked tongues and made mock of her while Crow King was absent in the hunt, until she came to hate the name of Crow King; but of this he knew nothing, for he was quick and terrible in anger, and none dared mock at him for what he had done. But his heart was bad, for he knew that Red Bird had ceased to love him, and he sorrowed for their love that was ended.

"As Crow King sat one day in the council lodge, Red Bird rose and dressed herself in her best finery and left their tipi, and rode away with a young brave of another tribe who had been visiting in the village. When Crow King returned from the council fire and found his lodge empty, my people feared for the lives of Red Bird and her young lover; for Crow King mounted swiftly, taking with him his two remaining horses—all the medicine men had left him —and rode hard on the trail of Red Bird and her young man.

"When Crow King overtook them in the Place-Where-the-Hills-Look-at-Each-Other—which the whites call Badlands—Red Bird cried out in fear; but Crow King stilled her tongue, saying, 'Crow King comes a friend and not an enemy. Here are these, his last horses, as a gift for Red Bird and her young man. And Crow King hopes that Red Bird will be happy.' Then Crow King placed the halters of the ponies in the hands of the young man and rode slowly back toward the village of my people, with his heart heavy in his breast. And Red Bird wept to see him go, for she was a woman, knowing not her own mind.

"So Crow King returned alone to the village, and in his heart there smoldered a blaze like the fire that sweeps through the grasslands in summer. But he hid his grief and was gay before the village, saying, 'Crow King will make a great feast and all the mighty ones of the Hunkpapa Sioux shall be his guests, that they may see his heart is good.'

"And he sent through the village a Dog Soldier, bearing the painted invitation-sticks of my people, to summon all the warriors of the tribe to his feast. And to the medicine men he likewise sent the painted invitation-sticks asking them to his feast, and requesting that each bring his secret charm or amulet, that the people might witness the powerful medicine which had saved the life of Crow King.

"In the center of the village Crow King caused a great lodge to be built, made of many tipis sewn together, and the women were set to work preparing the Indian maize and sugar and the toothsome buffalo tongues and antelope meat with which Crow King was to regale his guests. And on the evening of the feast all the great men of the Hunkpapa Sioux were assembled in the lodge to partake of the banquet, while outside the lesser men of the tribe watched with envy, for never had such a feast been seen among my people.

"As is the custom among the Sioux, Crow King rose before the feasting began, to make oration to his guests. And he bowed low before the medicine men, saying, 'The medicine men are mighty and their medicine is strong, for it saved the life of Crow King. I have asked my brothers the medicine men to bring with them their charms and fetishes, that they may be shown to the people, and thus bring honor to the medicine men, who are great in the councils of the tribe.'

"And the medicine men vied with each other, each striving to be first in handing his medicine bag with its charm to Crow King, that the people might see it and learn the power of his medicine. When Crow King had collected all the charms and amulets he spoke further, saying, 'All his life Crow King has followed the ways of his people. Is that not true, my brothers?' And the medicine men answered, saying, 'Hou! Crow King speaks true words.'

"Then Crow King wheeled in the leaping firelight and ripped

off his doeskin hunting shirt, so that the flames gleamed on the great scars of his breast and back. 'At the wish of the medicine men,' he said, 'Crow King hung in the sun dance and made no outcry though the blood coursed in rivers down his body. Look! You may see on Crow King's body the marks of the skewer sticks, deep as the blow of a brave's war club.' And he turned slowly before the circle of his guests, that each might see that Crow King's words were straight. 'When Crow King lay ill he promised the medicine men that he would be for the space of one sun as a cur of the village; and to the medicine men he promised all his horses if they would but drive out the evil spirits. Has Crow King kept his word?' And the medicine men nodded, saying, 'Hou! Hou! Crow King's talk is straight.'

"Then Crow King stood tall in the light of the leaping flames, while his eyes flashed like the lightnings of summer, and his voice was as the thunder of the hooves of Pte the buffalo. 'I, Crow King, say that the medicine men are liars!' he cried, and my people quaked with fear at his words. 'They speak with crooked tongues, performing no service in war or in the hunt, and they steal the horses of our warriors. They have lied to Crow King and brought him grief; they have left Crow King in poverty. With their false charms and crooked tongues they have driven Red Bird from my lodge, and left Crow King so that his heart will never sing again at the coming of a woman!' And Crow King turned, lifting his arms high in the firelight, and hurled the medicine bags full into the blazing lodgefire, while the people outside the tipi fled screaming with fear into the darkness.

"The medicine men and the warriors within the lodge would have fled likewise, but Crow King commanded them to sit still. 'For,' said he, 'I have not done with my oration yet.' And he smiled sweetly upon Blue Dog. Then Crow King finished his talk, while the medicine men sat quaking with fear.

" 'From this day hence,' said Crow King, 'no medicine man shall lay his hand upon the bridle of a warrior's horse; and my people need no longer fear their charms, for they are burned and gone forever. The medicine men may work their incantations upon Crow King all they will—for they are lies, anyway—but if they are wise they will not let Crow King hear of it. Now eat!' said Crow King. 'And may the medicine men enjoy their feast, for it is the last they shall get in the lodges of Crow King's people!'"

Gray Wolf paused and looked out over the darkening shadow of the river. "And in that fashion," he said, "Crow King defied the medicine men and their false gods; and from that day hence they were scorned and driven from the lodges of the Sioux. It is a straight tale, my brother."

"But did not Red Bird return to Crow King's lodge when she learned of the mighty deed he had done?" I asked. "In the tales of my people, a man and a woman, loving one another, come together at the end of the tale, living happily from thence onward. It is always thus in the books of the white man."

"Then the books of the white man are lies. No; Red Bird was a woman. She lived with her young brave for many winters and grew very fat and was happy, though her lover beat her frequently. But Red Bird loved him and remained in his lodge, for that is the way of Sioux women."

"It is even so with the women of my people," I said. "But what of Crow King? Did he not sicken and mourn for love of Red Bird?"

"That is the way of a white man," said Gray Wolf scornfully. "I know, for I have seen it often. When the whites are crossed in love their eyes are turned away from all women and their hearts remain bad forever. But Crow King was no white man. He married again and his lodge was filled with laughing children, and he lived many winters in great honor among my people of the Standing Rock Sioux."

Gray Wolf turned his seamed old face and looked away across the river, where the northern lights still wheeled against the velvet sky. Above the horizon, the maize-yellow rim of the full moon was just pushing into view.

"The whites are wise in many ways," Gray Wolf said. "But among my people the Sioux we know that it is not good for a man, even if he be a great chief like Crow King, to live alone in a womanless lodge."

Chapter 16

THE EMPIRE BUILDER

It is an ironic truth that the man who believed himself to be the Northwest's savior and prophet, and altogether its best friend and well-wisher, should actually have been the land's worst enemy.

Men called him the Empire Builder, this unwitting wrecker of the empire of the northern plains. His name was James J. Hill—Jim Hill, the big railroad multimillionaire—and lesser mortals were eager to listen to his voice. Jim was no knocker like that government fellow, John Wesley Powell. Jim had made his pile; hence his views were to be respected and his opinions unquestioned on all matters—even those concerning which he knew less than his gardener. One upstart scientist from Montana State College who ventured to differ with Jim's views on agriculture was told "not to contradict Mr. Hill." What business did long-haired college professors and government bureaucrats, who never met a payroll in their lives, have to contradict a sound man like Jim?

Criticisms would have been wasted anyway. For Jim Hill was truly a man with a vision. He was intoxicated by his idea, and no man could have swayed him from his purpose short of exterminating him. Sincere as are all obsessed men, he labored with indefatigable energy to bring his monstrous brain-child to parturition; unfortunately, he was only too successful. The northern plains and its people have suffered more, perhaps, through his misguided efforts than through the work of any other single agency. They are still suffering from them.

Jim Hill died before he was able to witness the disastrous results of the policies he urged and fought for throughout most of the years of his life. Nobody begrudges him that merciful oblivion. He meant well. He thought his dream would bring hope and prosperity and happiness to thousands of people in the Northwest. That his dream was a tragic error did not, unhappily, lessen the vigor with which he worked for its fulfillment.

244

THE EMPIRE BUILDER

Jim Hill's vision began with the conception of a great network of railways extending from the Great Lakes to the Pacific Coast. With the famous frontier guide Pierre Bottineau, he walked from Winnipeg southeastward through Dakota to St. Paul, mapping out the routes his steel highways were to follow. And during the frosty prairie nights when he lay awake under the winking stars, Jim Hill was stirred by the thought of a mighty agricultural empire springing up on the rich, rolling grasslands of the Northwest.

When his Great Northern Railway first began pushing its way westward into the valley of the Upper Missouri, the report of John Wesley Powell, setting forth the disasters that would follow the breaking of the northern plains, was already gathering dust in Washington's congressional library. In our tragic afterknowledge of the validity of Powell's warning, it seems particularly unfortunate that Hill did not see and heed its foreboding of disaster.

Instead, Jim Hill flung all the tremendous resources of his energy, ability, and riches into the building up of a northwest economy based on large numbers of small, extensively cultivated farms—the very practice which, as Powell had predicted, could end in nothing but poverty, heartbreak, and disaster for tens of thousands of unfortunate people.

Hill employed only those "scientists" who would agree with him in his propaganda extolling the virtues of the upper river valley. He found willing aides, too, in the newspapers and boomers of the day, who naturally wished their territories to grow and prosper. "Behold, I show you a delightsome land!" said a Dakota publicity pamphlet of 1885; and in Dakota Territory the acreage sown to wheat increased from 720,000 acres in 1882 to 8,413,000 in 1907.

Pamphlets praising the Northwest as a second Garden of Eden were distributed over all the eastern states and shipped in huge bundles to the Scandinavian countries and other northern European nations. Steamship companies, eager for the immigrant trade, abetted this cruel folly, with the result that scores of thousands of unhappy people, ill-fitted for the life they were to encounter in the new paradise, were induced to leave their homes and embark for America. The acres to which they came were not

245

the passably good farming lands settled by the immigrants of the 70's and 80's; they were the dryland benches west of the Missouri, for which John Wesley Powell had reserved his gravest warnings.

Montana, where the average annual rainfall is even less than that of the central and western Dakotas, plunged recklessly into intensive wheat farming, heedless of the consequences that must follow destruction of the land's natural cover. Homesteaders who broke the land in the hope that it would prove a wheat bonanza, in the single decade of 1909–19 skyrocketed Montana's cultivated acreage from 258,000 to 3,417,000. North Dakota's population, which was 320,000 in 1900, leaped to 577,000 in 1910—and virtually the entire increase was made up of wheat farmers who had come to Jim Hill's promised land to share in the benefits described in his flamboyant publicity campaign.

As in all booms, the people of the country, most of whom should have known better, came to believe in the fairy tale themselves. Rudyard Kipling, traveling through the Northwest in the 80's, stopped briefly at Livingston, Montana, and noted a phenomenon which has since served novelist Sinclair Lewis well:

"In every bar-room lay a copy of the local paper, and every story impressed it upon the inhabitants of Livingstone that they were the best, finest, bravest, richest, and most progressive town of the most progressive nation under heaven; even as the Tacoma and Portland papers had belauded their readers. And yet, all my purblind eyes could see was a grubby hamlet full of men without clean collars and perfectly unable to get through one sentence unadorned by three oaths. They raise horses and minerals round and about Livingstone, but they behave as though they raised cherubim with diamonds in their wings."

James Bryce had observed before him that "the confidence of these Westerns is superb." Now, when no less an authority than Jim Hill told them that the time had come for every 160-acre plot in the Northwest to support a farm family, they were ready to believe the thing could be done. Some of them, that is; there were many who knew better. But even the skeptics who were pessimistic about the outcome of Hill's program were little inclined to oppose him strongly. The name of Hill was a magic one in the northern plains country, and Jim was a man of strong persuasive powers.

All through the Middle West, Hill's Great Northern and Northern Pacific trains carried exhibits of the bumper crops grown on the dryland prairies of Montana and Dakota. Illustrated pamphlets, bristling with "scientific" proof that the northern plains could support an agriculture and a population hitherto undreamed of, were scattered with a lavish hand among the crowds that gathered to inspect the exhibition trains. Expositions in far-off cities were always treated to a display of the rich produce of the northern plains. Under Jim Hill's vigorous hand the Upper Missouri country was beginning to acquire a reputation that would bring thousands swarming into the dryland plains to wage a hopeless fight against drought and dust storms and crop failures.

In the first two decades of the twentieth century such circulars as the following described the wealth to be found on Montana's fertile plains:

More Free Homesteads; Another Big Land Opening; 1,400,000 Acres Comprising Rocky Boy Indian Lands Open to Settlers . . .

Professor Thomas Shaw, the well-known agricultural expert, after making a thorough examination of the soil and crop conditions of this land, writes as follows:

"The soil of this entire area is essentially a clay loam, very rich in mineral matter . . . The native grasses are more than ordinarily abundant and in this fact is evidence of producing power that can be relied on. The water supply is relatively good. In much of this area it is possible to secure a quarter section without a single foot of broken land on it . . . A portion of this region has been homesteaded for the past two or three years by persons who have prospered since they came."

John Wesley Powell thirty years before had prophesied that for a series of years there would be abundant rainfall and good crops, but that these would be followed by lean years when little moisture would fall and disaster would come to thousands of people; yet here was the eminent Professor Shaw urging that Montana's plains be plowed and settled because part of the region had been farmed successfully "for the past two or three years."

LAND OF THE DACOTAHS

At the Seattle Exposition a year earlier, in 1909, a placard extolling the virtues of North Dakota was placed above an exhibit of the state's grain produce: "North Dakota has more wealth per capita than any other state in the Union; it has no millionaires and no paupers." A quarter of a century later almost one half of its population was receiving government relief in one form or another.

The Montana brochure's optimistic forecasts continued:

The winter climate . . . is less cold than that of eastern Dakota. The snowfall is also usually considerably less than that of the Red River Valley. There have been no records kept of the rainfall for any lengthened period, but it is safe to conclude that it is not far different from the rainfall at Williston, North Dakota. This would mean that the average rainfall is about 15 to 16 inches a year, sometimes running higher than 18, sometimes, but rarely, as low as 11 to 12. This is not high rainfall . . . but is sufficient to grow crops fair to excellent on summer fallow land any season . . .

As stated previously, these lands comprise 1,400,000 acres. Giving each man who files 160 acres, this area will furnish 8,750 farms. At first thought it might seem to be many months before all these farms would be taken. If any cherish such a view they will be greatly disappointed. It is questionable if a single farm will be left unfiled upon one month after the opening of the lands for entry.

One-way settlers' fares, $12.50 from St. Paul and Minneapolis to Bainville, Culbertson, and other points in eastern Montana.

FREE land for the taking, in this demiparadise of the West, beguiled struggling farmers in other states, who sold their wornout holdings and eagerly departed to share in the new prosperity. As it turned out, one-way fares were not what these hopefuls needed. Round-trip tickets would have been far more appropriate, for it was not many years before thousands of the settlers on the dryland benches left the country beaten and embittered. Others, unable even to scrape together the scant sum necessary for departure, remained as a kind of submarginal agricultural population.

But they did not foresee this outcome at the time—any more than Jim Hill the Empire Builder did. They flocked into the western Dakotas and eastern Montana in hopeful caravans that often brought hundreds into the new lands in a single day. Rickety old Model-T Fords, laden like the jalopies of the Joads in a later day, brought some of them; others came in tourist sleepers or in immigrant trains. The latter, despite the name, were made up of freight cars in which the settler could place his household goods, machinery, vehicles, twenty head of small stock, and ten head of horses or cattle. Other items he might include in his boxcar, which rented for fifty dollars from St. Paul to eastern Montana, were fifty bushels of grain, twenty-five hundred feet of lumber, five hundred fence posts, a small portable house, and trees and shrubbery. If there was room for the immigrant after this Noah's Ark had been loaded, he might ride along also.

For three or four days and nights the settler rolled westward in his twentieth-century argosy toward the golden fleece Jim Hill's circulars had told him of. Then, at some western Dakota or eastern Montana village, he found himself unceremoniously dumped on the station platform, along with forty or fifty more of his kind, with the immeasurable loneliness of the prairie all around him.

The natives of the villages were invariably helpful, for there were locators' fees, usually of twenty dollars, to be gouged out of these tenderfeet—many of whom had been salesmen, bootblacks, schoolteachers, clerks, small businessmen, or barbers, with no experience of the plains country or, in many cases, of farming. These bewildered strangers could not know where the best land lay, or where those tracts were that had not yet been filed upon. They were ripe for the plucking, and the racket flourished until a large part of the native population had entered into the filing and locating business. Nobody troubled, of course, to inform the fledgling farmers that from 25 to 75 per cent of the land on which they settled was unfit for agricultural purposes. That unpleasant fact they were left to learn for themselves—later.

It was as if nature herself were also conspiring against the settlers, for during the few years immediately following their arrival rainfall was relatively abundant and prices abnormally high. A year or two of drought might have driven many of them away and saved them incalculable tragedy and bitterness and wasted years; instead, the weather was unusually good and the shadow of war, followed by actual war, in Europe kept prices of wheat advancing. Inept as many of the newcomers were in the business of farming, they were nevertheless able to make a living. The boom psychology was in full tide, and as the years passed, land values increased out of all proportion to their true worth. It actually began to look as if Jim Hill had been right. The land was productive; the rainfall and crop yields were adequate.

But northwest farmers, temporarily spared the ravages of drought and black rust and dust storm, began gradually to realize that they had enemies other than nature to contend with. Railroad freight rates were discriminatory; the great milling terminals at Minneapolis, Duluth, and Chicago controlled almost at will the prices offered on the market for the farmers' produce; the growers of the Northwest, unorganized and inexperienced in corporate tactics, were helpless to alleviate their own plight. Time and again, through collective action and political pressure, they tried to bring about some measure of control over the abuses they suffered; time and again they found themselves defeated by the powerful forces which controlled their legislatures, their officials, and their avenues of credit. The stage was set for agrarian revolt.

Chapter 17

THE REVOLT OF THE FARMERS

During the 1880's a young Englishman traveling in the American Northwest boarded a train which was to take him through Montana to Yellowstone Park. He was dowered with a quick eye and a gift of vigorous expression that have preserved for us a revealing glimpse of the western scene of that day. But let the youthful Rudyard Kipling tell it in his own words:

"We were a merry crew. One gentleman announced his intention of paying no fare and grappled the conductor, who neatly cross-buttocked him through a double plate-glass window. His head was cut open in four or five places. A doctor on the train hastily stitched up the biggest gash, and he was dropped at a wayside station, spurting blood at every hair—a scarlet-headed and ghastly sight. The conductor guessed that he would die, and volunteered the information that there was no profit in monkeying with the Northern Pacific Railway."

Had Kipling known it, he was witnessing an allegorical illustration of the railroads' treatment of all the citizens of the Upper Missouri Valley in the days when the railroads were kings. Protest as they might against discriminatory freight rates, threaten as they might not to pay, the men of the Northwest usually learned in the end what Kipling's gentleman learned: that it didn't pay to monkey with the Northern Pacific Railway or any of its colleagues.

But while their heads were often bloodied, they remained unbowed. And they found, in time, a means of curbing to some extent the arrogant dominance of their corporate masters: the railroads, the chain elevator companies, and the grain trust. It is a story with undertones of tragedy and overtones of comedy; and it should perhaps begin with some account of the problems northwest farmers found themselves facing as a result of the growth in their number and the rich increase in their harvests.

LAND OF THE DACOTAHS

As EARLY as the 1870's, Ignatius Donnelly of Minnesota, first of a distinguished succession of middlewestern liberals, was pointing out the inequities of the grain exchange: "When a thousand men are found at work producing results for the common good, there will be found a score of fellows sitting on the fence devising schemes to steal the reward of their efforts, and they generally succeed. . . . In Minnesota the wheat ring has got the market monopolized in this way. Twenty-five years ago when a farmer took his load of wheat to market he was beset by a dozen buyers competing for it. Now he will generally find one and sometimes two elevators at each station. The price is the same at both places, and if you inquire they will tell you that they have received a telegram from the Minneapolis fellows telling them what to pay."

Concluding with a rural illustration shrewdly aimed at his farmer listeners, Donnelly likened the practices of the grain exchange to that of a farmer who, when gathering eggs, leaves one in the nest to encourage the hen to lay again. The parallel was not entirely accurate. Northwest farmers often found that the market manipulators did not leave them even enough profit to enable them to plant again the following year.

It was in North Dakota that the hand of the railroad and milling interests lay heaviest, for it is more completely dependent upon agriculture than any other state in the Union. It was only natural that the farmers of that state should be among the first to organize in the fight against exploitation; it was there the fight was most successful; and it was there the Nonpartisan League arose, to spread to fourteen surrounding states before World War I broke the back of the organization.

From earliest days North Dakota, like neighboring Montana and South Dakota, had been governed from the East. With the coming of statehood in 1889 conditions were scarcely altered, for the state's legislatures and its executive machinery continued to be dominated by eastern interests. Peopled as the state was by large numbers of foreign-born immigrants who were not yet familiar with American political ways, it was ripe for outside domination of the boss type.

THE REVOLT OF THE FARMERS

Without capital for the most part, North Dakota's farmers were dependent on the cities of St. Paul, Minneapolis, Duluth, and Chicago for markets for their grain. They were dependent on the railroads for the transportation of their products to the distant terminals. And in the matter of fair treatment they were at the mercy of both. Prices for North Dakota wheat were arbitrarily fixed by the chambers of commerce or boards of trade of the big milling centers; and the farmer, faced with the necessity of selling his grain if he was to exist, had to learn to take it—even if he never learned to like it.

The actual seat of North Dakota's government was for many years among a little group of industrialists and political bosses who met at the Merchants Hotel in St. Paul. True, a set of state officials and a legislature existed in North Dakota, but they took their orders from their bosses, chief of whom was Alexander McKenzie of Bismarck, New York, Seattle, and a number of other places—the Boss of North Dakota, of whose activities we have heard before.

McKenzie, since his capital-city intrigues in the 80's, had grown in power and political influence. He represented not only the railroads, but the banking and insurance companies, the milling and elevator companies, and the large lumber firms which conducted business in the state. It was his job to see that legislation curbing the exploitative activities of these companies was defeated in the North Dakota legislatures—and he performed the task with consummate skill for a quarter of a century.

For decades the farmers of North Dakota were powerless in the grip of the McKenzie Ring and the invisible government behind it. Even such enemies of the Nonpartisan League movement as Andrew Bruce admitted freely that the farmers of the upper river valley were pitilessly exploited. The League had ousted Bruce from his position as chief justice of North Dakota's supreme court, so he could hardly be considered biased in its favor; yet he testified in his book, *Non-Partisan League*, that not even a postmaster could be named in North Dakota without the approval of the powers in St. Paul.

The economic injustices the farmers suffered were numerous

and unbearable. From the early days of the valley's settlement farmers had been aware that the market prices for their grains were arbitrarily fixed by the elevators in their communities. It was not long before they learned too that the elevators were members of great chain systems, owned and controlled by interests in the cities to the east. The solution seemed simple. A group of farmers would band together and construct their own cooperative elevator, store their grain, and later sell it in the terminal markets where reasonably fair prices might be assured. The scheme was partly successful. Under the stress of competition, the company elevators were forced to raise their local prices and to discontinue the more flagrant of their thefts.

But the "old line" companies were more than a match for farmers unused to the cutthroat game of high finance. In those towns where a farmers' elevator existed, the companies offered prices well above the market. Farmers living from hand to mouth were naturally tempted away from their own cooperatives to the companies' elevators, where they could get several cents a bushel more for their grain. They did not realize, of course, that their good fortune was being paid for by their neighbors in those towns where no cooperatives existed. In those places the chain companies made up their deficits by paying prices ruinously below actual market values. And the farmers were helpless, for they were unorganized and without capital to combat the ruthless practices which were impoverishing them.

The human element was a factor, too. Many of the cooperatives which started out with high hopes soon fell into the hands of a few individuals or a single individual—as a result of hard times, lack of interest, or dissatisfaction with the firm's management. Often the cooperative came finally into the possession of one of the chain companies, which blithely continued using the name "Farmers' Cooperative Elevator."

Aside from the local price problem, it was not long before the grain growers of the Northwest began to observe that the great terminal markets were not open marts in which the law of supply and demand produced a price equitable alike to seller and buyer. Instead, the markets were in the hands of chambers of commerce or boards of trade which were in effect close corporations. The price of grain was willfully and efficiently depressed during the period of harvest when the farmer must sell, and was skyrocketed upward once the harvest was in the terminal elevators of the big grain buyers.

THE tide of liberalism that swept the Northwest from the time of Ignatius Donnelly to that of Arthur C. Townley in the second decade of this century, cast up a multitude of liberal leaders and an equal multitude of agrarian panaceas. From Bryan to La Follette, from Weaver to Loftus, men who were helping the common man and the farmer and the laborer in the fight for social betterment proselytized vigorously, each for his own particular form of utopia, as if only it could usher in the new day.

The Grange, one of the earliest of the great farm movements, failed because it did not believe in political action; Greenbackism, with all its odd variations, proved a will-o'-the-wisp; the Farmers' Alliance, which preceded the wave of Populism, proved no more effective than its predecessors. But northwest farmers climbed eagerly aboard all these band wagons. They had nothing to lose but their red flannels, and they had the frontiersman's love of adventure and change and new horizons. One of the Populist national conventions was held at Sioux Falls, South Dakota, and in North Dakota the year 1892 ushered in a Populist administration, with Eli C. Shortridge for governor.

Shortridge's single term produced much progressive legislation. As early as 1892 these Populists were toying with the idea of establishing a terminal elevator of their own, where farmers might receive fair prices for their grain. Maximum freight rates on coal mined within the state were fixed despite the protests of the railroads. Public scales were ordered established by county commissioners at convenient locations, and farmers no longer had to depend on the dubious integrity of the chain elevators' own weighing system. Laws fixing the responsibility of railroads for prairie and grain fires caused by their locomotives were passed, usury was outlawed, and an extension of time for the payment of personal property taxes was granted in certain cases. But the

255

Populists' reign was brief; the panic of '93 toppled them from power after a single two-year term, and opened the way for another twenty years of rule by the McKenzie forces.

The Populist idea of a state-owned grain terminal did not die. But the McKenzie Ring effectively blocked any legislation toward that end, and the farmers were defeated in their attempt to obtain a seat on the Minneapolis grain exchange.

The Minneapolis chamber, which had been authorized by the Minnesota legislature to make its own rules and regulations with the force of law, had set up some almost insurmountable obstacles to be hurdled before a seat could be obtained "on the chamber." A fee which might be as high as twenty-five thousand dollars was required, the applicant's credit rating must be approved by the board, and he must charge the regular commissions as well as abide by all the rules and regulations of the chamber.

In the face of this ironclad means of keeping out any member who might be inclined to give the farmer a square deal, the growers of North Dakota naturally found themselves unable to obtain a seat. They were thus prevented from offering their samples on the floor of the exchange. Only one course remained open to them: the establishment of their own terminal elevator. And in 1911 the Equity Cooperative Exchange was formed for that purpose.

Although the farmers did not yet have sufficient capital to achieve this major end, the work of the Equity Exchange in educating the northwest grain growers to the abuses of the grain trust was not without a salutary effect. They learned, for example, of the infamous "switching fee"—a fee of a dollar and a half for each car of grain that was switched on the tracks. Equity members discovered that while the fee was real the switching was nonexistent.

The huge spread between the price which the grower received for his grain and the price of finished flour or bread was sufficient to open the eyes of northwest farmers to the fact that middlemen and speculators were extorting huge profits from both producer and consumer. As men who toiled on the farms throughout the upper river states perceived these things, there gradually arose among them a belief that state-owned terminal elevators where their produce would be fairly graded and priced would solve their problems.

Largely responsible for the growth of this belief in North Dakota was the work of a little group of college professors at the North Dakota Agricultural College in Fargo. President J. H. Worst of the college and Edwin F. Ladd, head of its chemistry department, were two of the leading men in making North Dakota farmers aware that they were the victims of a vicious and costly system of grain grading and dockage. An interesting table was circulated among grain growers showing the amounts of various grades of wheat received and shipped out during a single season by one Duluth elevator:

GRADE OF WHEAT	BUSHELS RECEIVED	BUSHELS SHIPPED
No. 1 Northern..................	99,711	196,288
No. 2	141,455	467,764
No. 3	272,047	213,549
No. 4	201,267	None
No Grade	116,021	None
Rejected	59,742	None
Total	890,245	877,512
On hand, estimated		12,733
		890,245

That which was rejected had become the cornerstone of the temple, so to speak. Hundreds of thousands of bushels which the elevator had graded as No. 4, No Grade, and Rejected and bought for ruinously low prices had miraculously become No. 1, No. 2, and No. 3—top grades of the finest wheat produced in America. It did not take an overly intelligent farmer to see that the company was shamelessly robbing him of his just grades and the higher prices he should have been paid for those grades.

Experiments at the agricultural college had also revealed that the low prices paid for lightweight wheat were not often justified. Loaves baked from the lighter weights often made just as high quality bread, and the high protein content of the lighter weight grain was sometimes as great as that of heavier wheat.

This work of the Fargo professors furnished the grain growers of the state with some of their more cogent arguments for reform in the methods of grain grading and price fixing, but it was primarily the work of George S. Loftus of the Equity Exchange which brought about a practical program aimed at correcting the abuses.

Loftus was a forceful and dynamic individual, an effective platform speaker who could talk to his farmer-stockmen audiences in their own language. His experience at Minneapolis in the grain and commission businesses had given him a shrewd insight into the methods of the grain trust. His forceful, pithy addresses before enthusiastic North Dakota audiences soon earned him the hatred of the established operators, who at once put pressure on their North Dakota underlings—the bankers, merchants, and elevator operators—to oppose Loftus' dangerous doctrines. He was denounced as a radical and an agitator who would set class against class, and halls were closed to him in many towns; but the farmers of the state knew what they wanted and they listened to George Loftus.

At last the growers had a program. And in 1912 an amendment to the North Dakota constitution was adopted by the people of the state—an amendment empowering the state to purchase its own terminal elevator in one of the eastern cities where the grain exchanges were located. A McKenzie-dominated legislature did nothing to put the measure into effect. Two years later a second amendment, empowering North Dakota to construct its own terminal elevator within the state boundaries, was adopted, and a legislative committee was named to investigate the best method of carrying the mandate into effect.

The will of the people apparently meant nothing to the committee, for it committed a breach of duty unparalleled in the state's history. Instead of reporting on ways and means of accomplishing the project as it had been ordered to do, the committee after long procrastination brought in a report *opposing* the entire scheme— which had just been overwhelmingly adopted by the people of the state. It developed that the committee had talked to such men as

THE REVOLT OF THE FARMERS

James J. Hill, E. P. Wells of the Russell-Miller Milling Company, and Julius Barnes, a large exporter, before coming to their astounding conclusion. This was all the people of the state needed to convince them that the project was a good one!

North Dakotans were angry and embittered. The Equity Exchange shortly afterward called a convention in Bismarck while the legislature was in session there. The timing was deliberate. It was hoped that delegations from the convention might put pressure on the legislature to enact the people's will. Instead, the farmers met with a rebuff that has become famous in North Dakota's political history.

Treadwell Twichell, a member of the legislature from Cass County, politely inquired of a delegation by what right "a bunch of farmers come down here to browbeat the legislature?" Then he advised them contemptuously: "Go home and slop the hogs!"

Twichell ever after denied having said any such thing, but the farmers were convinced that he did say it, and the phrase became a potent rallying cry on the lonely prairie farms and ranches, where hard-working men and women who felt they were being cheated did not relish the suggestion that they were fit only to "slop the hogs" while their betters ran the affairs of the state. The farmers were ready for action.

In the crowd that witnessed the farmers' rebuff at Bismarck early in 1915 was a lean, intense young man of thirty-five. Arthur C. Townley was born on a farm in northwestern Minnesota in 1880. Like other farm lads he attended country school and later enrolled in the high school at the little town of Alexandria. There was nothing about his youthful career to indicate that he was one day to become the leader of the most controversial political movement in the history of the Northwest. "I was a Sunday-school boy," he said later.

His only trait that might have pointed the way he was later to follow was an interest in debating and forensics, an interest encouraged by an elderly friend he had made in the town. This was a tailor young Townley had met when he went to have a suit pressed for an oratorical contest in which he was to appear. The old man

259

took an interest in the quiet lad and introduced him to two of his cronies, a carpenter and a jeweler of the town, who shared the tailor's interest in philosophy, religion, and mysticism.

Young Townley spent fascinating evenings listening to these three humble philosophers discuss the works of Herbert Spencer and the essays of Ralph Waldo Emerson. In their company he learned to think and question, and to discuss the meanings of life and the foundations of society. Almost without realizing it the young high school student was becoming a rebel against the conventional and accepted forms of social and economic thought. Spurred by the ambition these teachers had awakened in him, he began to read omnivorously during the two years following his graduation from high school—years spent in teaching a country school near his farm home.

"Finally I grew sick of books," he said later. "I had read until I felt I never wanted to see another book. I was tired of writing and theory. I wanted action. I was then as impractical as a man could be. I didn't know anything about business. I didn't know anything about dealing with men. I was a hopeless bookworm."

Dissatisfied with his sedentary life, Townley determined to go out into the world and make a place for himself. Westward he went into North Dakota and took up farming in Golden Valley near the Montana-Dakota border. His unorthodox and progressive ideas began to assert themselves almost at once, and it was not long before he had talked a number of his neighbors into pooling their resources and forming a farming syndicate. With the capital acquired by this merger, the group purchased steam tractors and plows and began extensive operations.

But the weather, the unpredictable factor in their rosy dream, upset the whole plan. When it began to appear that there would be little or no crop, the group agreed to break up and go their individual ways, each man trying to salvage what he could. Bitterly disappointed, Townley returned to Minnesota. It was an untimely departure, as it turned out, for after he had gone the long-awaited rains came, and the other members of the syndicate had a fairly successful season.

The next year young Townley became an itinerant plasterer's

helper, traveling throughout the entire West, but the call of the soil was too strong for him and he came back again to Golden Valley, afire with plans for a new venture. A new wilt-resistant flax had been developed at the agricultural college and the linseed-oil industry was calling for all it could get. With characteristic energy Townley plunged into the business of flax-growing, and within two years had vastly increased his holdings. He did things in a large way, acquiring the most modern machinery and constantly expanding his operations by the purchase or the rental of additional acreage.

In 1912 the empire of the young farmer, who had become known as the "Flax King," disintegrated under a series of misfortunes. Rainfall was scant, his yield was small, and most important of all, the price of flax fell off disastrously as a result of market manipulations by speculators. Townley, under contract to pay for expensive machinery and heavy land purchases, found himself bankrupt and facing liabilities of nearly one hundred thousand dollars. It was at this time, judging from his later remarks, that his hatred for the market manipulators and speculators crystallized.

"A few months before I had been a good fellow and an able farmer," he said, "but after the failure nobody in town wanted to speak to me or see me. I was a fool, a dub and a crook, and everybody had always known that I was going to blow sooner or later. All because somebody in Chicago or Minneapolis sought to break somebody else who was buying flax."

The next few years were difficult ones. Townley toyed for a time with North Dakota's minuscule Socialist party, making speeches and doing organization work, but he soon became impatient with the debating-society methods of the timid liberals who made up the party. "In method they were as conservative as the old parties," he declared afterward. "Offer them a plan by which they could really accomplish something instead of merely talking, and they were afraid of it." He broke with the Socialists and went to Bismarck, where he witnessed, early in 1915, the rebuff of the farmers of the Equity Exchange by the state legislature. He saw that the grain growers were ripe for revolt. And in February of that year he conceived the idea of the farmers' organization that later became known as the Nonpartisan League.

I⊤ was a bold conception. Coming as it did from a man who had nothing but the clothes on his back, it might have seemed laughable. But Arthur Townley had something else too: he had a vision, and the force of speech and conviction to awaken other men to that vision. He began by sounding out leading men at the Equity convention on their reactions to his hastily sketched plan. From several he got an enthusiastic response. One of them was Fred B. Wood, a prosperous farmer who was able to offer the bankrupt Townley the financial assistance he would need. In a speech years later, describing the beginnings of the League, Wood said: "I had told Townley that he could come to our farm when spring broke and I would help him get started. But the snow wasn't off the ground when one day he showed up. He told me he couldn't wait."

Townley's organizational plans were perfected in a series of talks with Wood and his sons. The program of the organization was written out in five brief planks by Townley himself. Simple and terse, they struck at the very heart of the farmers' grievances: state ownership of terminal elevators, flour mills, packing houses, and cold-storage plants; state inspection of grain and grain dockage; exemption of farm improvements from taxation; state hail insurance on the acreage tax basis; and rural credit banks operated at cost.

In his book *The Nonpartisan League,* Herbert Gaston has shrewdly pointed out wherein Townley's program differed from other plans which had preceded it. It was not that Townley's ideas were new; it was that his approach was different. "Practical salesmanship, a program of immediate and forceful action and the use of the Ford automobile," wrote Gaston, "are the factors principally explaining the rise of the Nonpartisan League."

It remained only to begin the actual work of organization, and Townley and Wood set about the task at once. Wood took Townley to meet several neighbors of his in the community, introduced him to the farmers, and then sat back while Townley did the talking. Results were gratifying during the first few days of their trial work; farmers were eager to join a group which promised them the things they had been fighting for for a quarter of a century. On the spot they paid their dues of two and a half dollars each into the "treasury"—which was nothing more than Townley's pocket at the time—and hoped for the best. Things went so well, indeed, that several of the first members, meeting at Wood's home a few days later, signed notes that enabled Townley to purchase an automobile and set up state headquarters at Minot, North Dakota.

With the success of the organization seemingly assured, Townley set about developing his staff of organizers, which was to cover the entire state and spread the Nonpartisan program throughout the grass roots. The technique to be followed was essentially the one Townley had already worked out with Wood. A prominent farmer would be approached, "sold" on the League idea, and would then act as an introductory wedge in the organizer's visits to surrounding neighbors.

The League's first organizers were recruited from the ranks of farmers who showed unusual ability in speaking and organizing, and from Townley's old friends of the Socialist party. These latter were especially able advocates of the League's cause, for they had at their fingertips the economic and social abuses of the day, and many of them had been burning with a desire to do something practical, instead of merely holding weekly meetings.

As the organizers spread the gospel of the League over the state and the group began to grow by leaps and bounds, Townley found that he had achieved a success beyond his wildest expectations. By summer's end he had enrolled twenty-six thousand North Dakota farmers in his mushrooming organization. Dues had been increased to six dollars a year to support the huge headquarters staff necessary to keep up with correspondence, the training of new organizers, and the direction of the large force already in the field.

But looming dark on the horizon were the first faint clouds of opposition to the new militant farmers' organization. Townley had carried on his work with a minimum of publicity. The approach had been direct and personal; organizers had even been instructed to avoid towns and cities. But inevitably the word got about, and soon the press of the state was commenting on the new organization.

North Dakotans were warned against "slick young outsiders" who were swindling farmers with promises of better days to come. Several papers commented on the fact that no persons living in towns had been approached—a sure sign, according to these journals, that the scheme was a swindle. Here is a fair sample of these editorial comments in the country weeklies:

Recently the *Ozone* referred to the presence in the state of a number of solicitors for membership in some kind of "party" which was to be of special advantage to farmers, and who also offered a year's subscription to some paper or magazine as material inducement for joining. A fee of $6 was collected from each subscriber . . . It is more than ever evident that the farmers who took stock in the smooth strangers were too easy victims of a confidence game. In no case have the strangers sought to interest anybody in towns where they have stopped, and it has been noticed that in making even a trifling purchase they always tender $6 checks, cashing them in that way. They never go to a bank . . . As before stated, the *Ozone* believes, with the Fargo newspapers, that this is only a scheme for fleecing the unwary . . . Our belief is that they are operating a questionable scheme, as there is no public knowledge of such a farmers' protective party as they affect to represent, and their avoidance of association or contact with townspeople, and advance dating of checks are suspicious.

The implication that townsmen were not approached because they were sharp enough to see through such a crooked affair was not a particularly fortunate one. Indeed, the real reason was that the farmers were often forced to operate on credit advanced by the local banker—who in turn was controlled by his eastern creditors—and cases had arisen where local bankers had refused to honor checks made out to the League. This pressure was something Townley wanted to avoid. If possible, dues were paid in cash; in other cases they were made out by check in the name of the individual organizer, instead of the League, so that the local banker could not recognize what the check was for and consequently apply pressure to his farm debtors. Even postdated checks were accepted, and the amount of defaults was surprisingly small—about 12 per cent.

The subscriptions referred to in the editorial quoted were for *Pearson's* magazine, and were offered with each membership the first year, during which the magazine published several favorable articles by Charles Edward Russell, the well-known Socialist. But by the fall of 1915 the League had successfully founded its own newspaper, the *Non-Partisan Leader*, and *Pearson's* was no longer offered, although Russell and Walter Thomas Mills, another Socialist leader, continued to aid the movement and did much work on early editions of the new *Leader*.

"You have launched in a just and honest way a just and honest cause," wrote Russell. "Do not believe anything you read about it unless you read it in your own journal or in journals that you know are absolutely with you."

That policy has been quite faithfully followed by Nonpartisan Leaguers ever since, and at various periods in North Dakota history the *Leader* has reduced the opposition press of the state to virtual impotence. More than once League candidates have been elected to office despite the bitter and united opposition of almost the entire North Dakota press—a direct result of the *Leader's* constant campaign against the "kept" and "venal" newspapers that opposed it.

As the League's membership grew toward the fifty thousand mark, the daily papers of the larger cities began to take alarm and attack the organization and its methods. J. D. Bacon of the Grand Forks *Herald* and L. T. Guild of the Fargo *Courier-News* were particularly venomous foes, charging that the whole plan was a swindle and that Townley was a dictator who had never been elected to head the party. Later the newspapers of the state made such ridiculous charges as that the leaders of the League were "Socialists," "atheists," "freelovers," "pro-Germans" (during World War I), and "Reds."

"Who elected Townley president?" queried the Grand Forks *Herald*. Townley had his answer ready, and in a 1917 address he replied to his critics in typical fashion:

"I want to be very frank with you this afternoon. The Grand

Forks *Herald* . . . and all the fellows that oppose this organization, say that I was not elected president of the League.

"They want to know by what right I call myself president of the Nonpartisan League. I am going to be very frank with you and explain what right I have. When Howard Wood and his father and two or three more of us found that this thing would go . . . we saw that it would be necessary to have some kind of committee to take care of it.

"We didn't have automobiles and gasoline enough to go to all the farmers in the state, and to Jerry Bacon and the Grand Forks *Herald,* to ask them who this committee should be.

"So we got busy and picked out a committee. The old gentleman [Mr. Wood] named five men that we knew, and asked this little group of farmers if they thought these men would be all right. . . . Mr. Wood was suggested as treasurer and vice-president. So we took a piece of paper and wrote the League program on it; and wrote the names of this committee up at the top; and because I had the idea, they named me chairman of the committee and wrote my name on there as president . . .

"And this fellow and that fellow [pointing] and every one who joined the League read the program and those names and signed up and paid his money. And I have got a kind of a foolish idea that all of those men who signed that paper voted for me at that time. I don't know of anyone that voted against me.

"And we have got the names of 40,000 farmers, in their own handwriting, on this paper, subscribing to this program and to these men to carry out this program. I think that was a pretty fair election.

"About as good as we could accomplish at that time, with the machinery we had. Of course it might have been better to have got 4000 or 5000 farmers to come down to Grand Forks and hold a convention; but we could not have convinced them at that time that they ought to come.

"I will tell you who would have been there if we had tried to do that. There would have been about half a dozen politicians and corporation lawyers, and a newspaperman or two. But you farmers would not have come. We had to show you first that something could be done, before you would come. Now that is how I came to be president of the committee and how these other men came to be members of the committee."

Townley's position on this point was doubtless well taken. True, he was vulnerable to the charge of dictatorship, but he well knew that an election would disrupt the League before it was fairly begun. It would have been easy for League opponents to find a defaulter in the ranks of the organization, and then sponsor an election to defeat Townley—and this development would have split the party hopelessly.

IT WAS inevitable that the growth of a movement like the League should attract innumerable quacks, crackpots, and opportunists as well as sincere liberals and honest farmers. Opponents of the organization charged that it was socialism in disguise, and the charge was not without a certain credibility, since many of the party's early speakers and organizers were Socialists or had been affiliated with that group in the past. Full-page advertisements appeared in the opposition newspapers asserting that the League meant to make "occupancy and use" the only standard of land ownership in North Dakota.

The state-owned mill and elevator plank in the party's program was certainly socialistic, but the League was far from espousing any program that a real Socialist would recognize as similar to his own. Many Leaguers were restless reformers or progressives who welcomed the chance to throw their energies into a fight which promised real results, but the great mass of the membership was made up of ordinary hard-working farmers and ranchers.

As the movement grew, though, there came into being a sort of lunatic fringe recruited from all over the nation. From New York, from Washington, from every state in the Union, men of varying degrees of chicanery, liberalism, honesty, and dishonesty came to plague or assist the new revolt against the old order. North Dakota herself furnished numerous examples of many kinds. But in the beginning their influence was little felt; it was only later that such remarkable schemes as fish hatcheries in the Bering Sea, sisal plants in Florida, real estate ventures in Mexico, and other equally fantastic enterprises began to be advanced as League programs. The party was founded on a strong and sensible basis; its aims were the aims of the great mass of North Dakota's farmers, most of whom had nothing to do with the hodgepodge of crackpot schemes which later made the League a temporary laughingstock in the eyes of the voters and caused its partial eclipse for a number of years.

The League organization, in the beginning, brought for the first time the processes of actual democracy to the voters. It advanced a plan that was admirably devised to strip of their opportunity for control the politicians and others who dominate the machinery of conventions and elections. Even today the principle that "the office must seek the man and not the man the office" is a cardinal tenet of League political philosophy. Ways have been found to circumvent this principle in the past, but on the whole its effect has been salutary.

At the time the idea was first advanced, it was a revolutionary step in political methods. Politicians who incautiously announced their candidacy for office found themselves repudiated by the party, and usually turned in anger to the opposition. The system was simple. In each of the state's eighteen hundred precincts a local caucus of League members was held to elect delegates to the forty-nine district conventions. And Townley advised his followers:

"Avoid the politician who seeks office, for he usually, though he may not admit it, seeks it for himself and not for the good that he may do for all the people. Avoid also the men who may be too friendly with bankers, middlemen and big business, for they may betray you."

This was demagoguery and an appeal to class hatred, but Townley knew what he wanted: the solidarity of North Dakota's farmers. And he was shrewd enough to see that one means of achieving that solidarity was to give the farmers a personalized enemy against which to fight. This vague opponent of human rights and justice became widely known as "Big Biz" during the early days of the League. If Townley angered a few bankers, businessmen, politicians, and lawyers, he cared little. More than three fifths of

North Dakota's voters were farmers; they were the men Townley wished to reach, and he knew precisely how best to reach them.

Hear him: "If you put a lawyer, a banker and an industrialist in a barrel and roll it down hill, there'll always be a son-of-a-bitch on top!" The average farmer was delighted at this attack upon bankers, businessmen, and lawyers—for he was usually indebted to all three of them. The quip expressed in a striking way something he had always felt vaguely to be true but had never quite known how to say.

I talked to Arthur Townley in 1946. He is aging now, in his late sixties, and the aims of his movement have long since been achieved, while his organization has fallen into other hands. But he is not bitter, nor has he lost his sense of humor. When I asked him about his famous barrel statement, which had been repeated to me by an old North Dakotan, he mused for a while. "It's hard to remember everything you said thirty years ago," he told me finally. Then, with a sudden smile: "But put it in your book anyway; if I didn't say it, I wish I had!"

Such statements were scarcely calculated to endear Townley to the gentlemen named in his indictment. Opposition to the League was fanned to an even higher pitch. But the results of the farmers' caucuses were at once apparent. In virtually every precinct in the 1916 election delegates were selected from the rank and file of the working farmers. Many had never before attended a political meeting or held any public position. The same condition prevailed at the district meetings. The professional politicians were not only terrified, they were helpless; and their yelps of anguish could be heard even in the throne room at St. Paul.

It was not Townley's intention originally to sponsor a third party. He welcomed members from all established political parties and from the ranks of independents. The League leaders chose, rather, to operate within the framework of the Republican organization and attempt to capture the party by nominating their candidates in the primary elections.

It was a shrewd political device, and as the League district and state conventions began to arouse tremendous enthusiasm the opposition became thoroughly frightened. They charged Townley with "Bossism" (this from the McKenzie Ring!), with "hand-picking" the candidates, and with attempting to foist a socialist regime upon the unsuspecting voters of North Dakota.

The first charge was undoubtedly well founded, for Townley did exercise a considerable measure of influence and control over the party tactics and program; but the two latter accusations were completely without foundation. Indeed, it is doubtful whether a less controlled selection of delegates had ever before occurred in the state. As for the charge of Socialism, not a single member of the League ticket endorsed at the state convention belonged to that party.

The ticket was headed by a Pembina County farmer named Lynn J. Frazier, who later served for many years as United States senator from North Dakota and achieved some measure of national fame for his cosponsorship of the Frazier-Lemke farm moratorium bill. Frazier was a graduate of the University of North Dakota and was forty-one years old at the time of his nomination. He was almost unknown outside his own immediate community, had never held a public office of other than local significance, and was completely unversed in political tactics.

His farming interests had absorbed his life since his graduation from college. He was plain, blunt, honest—all in all, a quite average substantial and solid citizen. Despite the fact that he was chosen almost unanimously at the state convention—which he did not even attend—he was loath to serve; he had not made a public address since his debating-team days as an undergraduate.

Among the other League candidates—of whom only four had been active in politics before—William Langer, the candidate for attorney general, was by far the most colorful. He was just twenty-eight years old. Recently elected state's attorney of Morton County, he had dedicated his first day in office with such a burst of energy as the county had never seen. One hundred and sixty-seven warrants for the arrest of vice operators and bootleggers were issued from his office before his job was twenty-four hours old. Then, with the petty racketeers out of the way, Langer turned toward bigger game.

He brought suit against the Standard Oil Company, the Northern Pacific Railway, the Occident Elevator Company, and several large lumber firms in an attempt to put on the tax rolls some thirty million dollars' worth of property which those companies had placed on railroad right-of-way lands in order to escape state and county taxes.

Arrayed against the "Boy Prosecutor" was some of the finest legal talent in the land, but Langer was successful in his suits. The property went on the tax rolls and the supreme court ordered the companies to pay back taxes to the extent of one and a quarter million dollars. His sensational victory over the enemies the farmers had been fighting unsuccessfully for years assured him a place at once on the League ticket.

League candidates campaigned that spring of 1916 to enthusiastic audiences of farmers at rallies, picnics, and crossroads gatherings of every description. Toward the close of the campaign a special train was chartered to carry the candidates and the League program into every corner of the state. But the day of the primary election proved to be scarcely an auspicious one for the League's hopes.

Heavy rains fell throughout the day, turning the dirt roads of the countryside into rivers of mud. It seemed scarcely possible that rural voters would be able to get to the polling places in country schoolhouses and farm homes scattered over the storm-lashed prairies. Faces grew long at Townley's campaign headquarters when the first returns, principally from the cities, indicated heavy majorities for the opposition candidates. But broader returns the next day swept away all doubts. The entire League slate had been nominated.

In North Dakota, Republican endorsement is tantamount to election, and the primary returns were sufficient to guarantee a victory at the general elections in the fall. It was a smashing victory for the new, militant farmers' group of amateur politicians. Their opponents, temporarily confounded, were unable to make a convincing summer campaign, and in the fall the entire slate of candidates, with one exception, were elected by substantial majorities.

THE League's rejoicing did not last long. They had a majority in the house of representatives, but in the senate, where the terms were staggered, the opposition still held control. They found their program effectively blocked, despite a clear mandate from the electorate, by this opposition majority in the senate, as well as by several recent decisions of the outgoing supreme court concerning the method of amending the constitution. The initiative process for amending the document, which had been adopted by the people, was held to be inoperative until made otherwise by the legislature. Other methods of amendment meant a delay of at least three years. It began to appear that the party's program would be successfully blocked by the minority for so long a time that there was danger of the organization's falling apart for lack of interest and achievement.

League leaders then came forward with a daring proposal—that the legislature draft a new constitution for the state and present it to the people for immediate popular approval. The screams of their opponents rose to a new high pitch at this "anarchistic" suggestion. Competent legal opinion was not lacking, however, that the process suggested by the League was quite proper, if a bit unusual, and the new constitution was accordingly introduced as House Bill 44.

Actually, the new constitution was not dissimilar to the old one except for changes which would enable the legislature to finance the program just approved by the people. It provided that the state could engage in business for public purposes and that it could issue bonds to finance the proposed state-owned industries. It made provision for a tax to support the state hail-insurance program. Means of amending the constitution were simplified, the terms of state officials were increased from two to four years, and all state offices aside from governor and lieutenant governor were made appointive instead of elective—just as they are in the federal system.

The attacks on the proposed constitution in the legislature were of a peculiarly vitriolic nature, despite the fact that they often dealt with trivialities. Not wishing to attack openly the important changes in the constitution which the people had approved, opponents of the bill had to limit themselves, often with amusing results, to scarifying certain minor changes that had little to do with the matter in hand.

A change in a paragraph concerning education evoked an especially bitter attack from Representative A. G. Divet of Wahpeton. The text of the original constitution read: "A high degree of intelligence, patriotism, integrity and morality on the part of every voter in a government by the people being necessary to insure the continuance of that government and the prosperity and happiness of the people, the legislative assembly shall make provision for the establishment and maintenance of a system of public schools which shall be open to all the people of North Dakota and free from sectarian control. This legislative requirement shall be irrevocable without the consent of the United States and the people of North Dakota."

Under the new constitution this article had been amended to read: "The legislative assembly shall make provision for the establishment and maintenance of a system of public schools which shall be open to all the children of North Dakota and free from sectarian control."

The Honorable Mr. Divet was horrified at this underhanded attack upon "intelligence, patriotism, integrity and morality"— and obscurity. Or perhaps it was because Mr. Divet was fond of excess verbiage that he objected to this simplification. His speech might lead one to believe so:

"I say this change in this section was made designedly, and I cannot pass it by without making the statement that to my mind these changes represent the malicious cut of a poisoned dagger of treason and licentiousness held in the secret hand of disloyalty and hate; that the hand that penned these lines and deliberately made that change would put poison in the wells in front of the country's armies, or would lead a little sister to the brothel."

Such outbursts came not only from enchanted orators in the legislature; they were repeated by soberer and more authoritative observers. Andrew Bruce, former chief justice of the supreme court of North Dakota and professor of law at the University of Minnesota, made the same charge in somewhat more restrained language in his book *Non-Partisan League*. Mr. Bruce gave it as his considered opinion that the "Socialist" leaders of the League had deliberately changed this passage because they did not believe in "patriotism." Mr. Bruce was doubtless smarting under his recent defeat for chief justice by the League forces, but his legal training should have made it clear to him that the reduction of a clumsy and involved paragraph to a simple statement of law scarcely constituted an attack on American institutions.

Despite the violent opposition encountered in the legislature by the proposed constitution, an overwhelming majority of the lower house voted for the bill. The count was eighty-one to twenty-eight. Some of those favoring it were opponents of the League. But in the senate, where the hold-over members had the whip hand, the measure was beaten by nine votes. Under the existing constitution it was impossible to carry the party program into effect. The terminal elevator project was feasible, since the people had approved that by a previous amendment, but the constitution prevented the issuance of bonds to provide for its construction. The League was temporarily baffled.

Yet there were many progressive measures enacted under the party's sponsorship. An amendment providing for woman suffrage was passed; rural school appropriations were increased by 300 per cent; a law guaranteeing bank deposits was enacted; a Torrens title registration act was passed; laws aimed at reducing freight rates were made; a state highway commission was created; and most important of all, a state grain-grading law was enacted. This law produced immediate beneficial effects, not only in the more honest grading which resulted, but in the prices paid for the farmers' produce.

William Langer, the youthful attorney general, was meanwhile continuing his attacks on the McKenzie gang and the chain elevators that operated in the state. The capital city of Bismarck had been suffering periodic outbreaks of typhoid fever, and the source of the infection was traced to the privately owned waterworks controlled by McKenzie. Langer promptly brought suit to force McKenzie to install a filtering system; McKenzie protested that the cost of such an improvement would amount to virtual con-

274

fiscation of his plant. Too bad, said the attorney general, and went ahead with the suit until the condition was remedied.

To combat the chain elevators' system of offering prices below market value in towns where there was no cooperative elevator and prices above the market where there was such a cooperative, Langer one day sent out twenty trucks loaded with wheat of the same weight and grade. Sale of the grain to various chain elevators scattered throughout the state proved that the companies' prices varied by as much as twenty cents a bushel—depending upon the amount of local competition. Langer immediately brought suits against the companies, which were still pending when he went out of office in 1920.

That was the extent of the reforms achieved by the League. Hamstrung by the old guard minority, the legislative session of 1917 ended in an impasse. But the League was not beaten. On the contrary, its leaders were more determined than ever to carry the fight into the enemy's territory. They set their eyes on the elections and the legislative session two years hence.

Early in 1917 the League announced that it had opened a national headquarters in St. Paul and that organizers were already at work in the neighboring states of Montana, South Dakota, and Minnesota. By the end of the year the movement had spread also to Washington, Idaho, Nebraska, Kansas, Texas, Oklahoma, Iowa, Wisconsin, and Colorado. Without the peculiar conditions that had made the farmers of North Dakota ripe for the League movement, the party organization progressed more slowly in those states.

In Montana, particularly, the League found strong influences at work against it. The Anaconda Copper Mining Company, which dominated the state, fought with every weapon at its command to prevent the dissemination of the League's propaganda. Burton K. Wheeler, long a United States senator from Montana, and Jeanette Rankin, first woman member elected to the national house, were supported by the League in their early races for office. Senator Wheeler, indeed, was dubbed "Bolshevik Burt" and was smeared so freely and unfairly by the copper company's kept press that he has had a hatred of trusts and corporate power ever since—despite the fact that his natural bent is toward the conservative side.

Another avenue of attack against the League was opened with the rapid growth of the party's membership. When more than one hundred thousand members were paying eight dollars a year each in dues, the opponents of the organization began to circulate charges that Townley and other League leaders were lining their pockets at the expense of gullible farmers. Actually, there was never a surplus in the League treasury. The staff of organizers and other necessary employees made the financing of the party a source of continual worry. Townley, in petitioning the courts for a discharge from the bankruptcy into which he had been forced by his failure as a flax king some years before, was given a clean bill financially by federal Judge Amidon:

"The trustee has been permitted to go through the record of all these concerns as with a lighted candle. He has found no trace of any grant of any of the funds or property of the Nonpartisan League or its subordinate agencies to Mr. Townley, except a salary of $300 per month. On the contrary, the record shows clearly and affirmatively that the Nonpartisan League and its subordinate agencies have never granted to Mr. Townley any part of their funds or property as his personal estate and that he has never used them for any purpose except that of a political leader, devoting them honestly to the achievement of the objects of his party. The record is full and has been honestly kept and it shows an honest purpose to give an account of an honest stewardship."

As THE year 1917 moved toward the day in April when the United States would enter World War I, the League in North Dakota had endorsed its first candidate for a national office. Thirty-year-old John Baer, cartoonist for the *Leader*, was chosen to run as a congressional candidate for the unexpired term of W. T. Helgesen, who had died in office. Baer made the race successfully, and the League had its first representative in Washington. But opponents of the farmers' movement saw now, in the emotional tension produced by America's entry into the war, an opportunity to strike a lethal blow at the organization that was threatening their established dominance. They began, first guardedly, then openly, to attack the League as an anti-American movement.

Their tactics were simple and unscrupulous. The League had seen that the war was providing opportunities for certain interests to make unconscionable profits, and it had come out forthrightly for heavy taxes on war profits and for government control of railroads and federal fixing of prices. This was, in simple terms, a suggestion for an office of price administration such as experience has since taught the nation is necessary, but to opponents of the League it offered a heaven-sent opportunity. The League opposed the government's current program. Hence, said the League's enemies, the League must be a friend of Germany's.

This was illogic at its worst, but it had serious effects in the states where the League was not yet well known. Townley's speeches calling for the national government to take the profits out of war were not only misquoted by the daily press, but served as a peg on which to hang charges that the League was "disloyal and pro-German." League members were referred to as "Kaiserites" and "the Hun in our midst." That they were also called Bolshevists and Reds did not seem illogical to the gentlemen making the charges. A quotation from the Fargo *Forum*, referring to a contemporary speech of Townley's, will serve to illustrate the sort of incitement to riot engaged in by the press:

The *Forum* hopes that when Mr. Townley comes to Fargo the members of the Home Defense League, 100 or 150 strong, will march into the hall, stand at attention during his address, and give him a chance to repeat those remarks or others in the same vein. If there isn't a public officer in the state with backbone enough to put the speaker behind the bars, there is enough spirit in the Home Defense League to prevent him from repeating the offense.

Not even Townley's worst enemies ever accused him of lack of courage, however, and the Fargo speech was duly delivered despite the presence of the Home Defense League. It was simply too difficult to convince North Dakotans that fifty thousand of their friends and neighbors—men whom they knew personally and whose lives were as open to scrutiny as are all rural lives—were "traitors and pro-Germans."

But in other states, where the movement was not as well established or as well known, the "patrioteers"of the day committed acts of almost unbelievable ferocity and unparalleled ignorance. In North Dakota the sniping was confined to such petty acts as refusing contributions to the Red Cross from League groups, or refusing League speakers the right of access to halls and other forums. Elsewhere it was a different story.

In Winlock, Washington, two League organizers, Alfred Knutson and M. L. Edwards, were dragged from their rooms, severely beaten, and tarred and feathered. They recognized and identified their captors, but could get no action from the local authorities. In Glencoe, Minnesota, N. S. Randall, another League speaker, was mobbed and beaten, as was Nels Hokstad, near Hinckley. Hokstad was afterward tarred and feathered.

J. A. McGlynn, a Montana organizer who attempted to speak at Miles City, was abducted and forcibly held in the Commercial Club, then forced to take the next train out of town. Other Montana speakers were attacked by mobs armed with shotguns and forbidden to carry out their meeting plans. In South Dakota, League meetings were broken up by armed hoodlums concealed behind the famous last refuge of a scoundrel—patriotism.

And in Texas, where League speakers were attempting to organize the farmers against the brutal exploitation of the Ginners' Association, H. L. Higdon, A. A. Cother, and H. F. Hoover were kidnapped near Quitman and after being stripped naked, were horsewhipped. Salt was then applied to their bleeding backs and they were driven out onto the prairie while the mob fired over their heads. Two of these men were native Texans; the third was an elderly minister. Yet the Greenville, Texas, *Banner* gloated: "The three organizers learned by bitter experience and to an extremely painful degree that pro-German propaganda will not go in Texas."

The Montana *Loyalist*, a newspaper sponsored by anti-League elements in the state, explained in a brilliant flash of economic inspiration why the League movement promised a false utopia.

278

"There will always be riches—there will always be poverty," declared this organ of the copper trust magnates—as if a multimillionaire were somehow an elemental force of nature, rather than a taxable individual, subject to whatever laws society may see fit to pass.

League organizers in virtually every state where the party was operating were arrested, indicted, and otherwise harried by local authorities, who charged them with everything from vagrancy to draft-dodging and spying for Germany. Townley himself was indicted and convicted in Minnesota for "discouraging enlistments" in a pamphlet setting forth the party's aims. He was later acquitted by the supreme court of the state in a decision overruling the action of the lower court.

Said the high court, in part: "The resolutions taken as a whole appear to be nothing more serious than a rhetorical and somewhat flamboyant platform upon which a certain class of citizens are solicited to join an organization whose avowed purpose is the amelioration of the alleged evils of present economic conditions, and to bring about a more equitable distribution of the wealth of the world among all classes of mankind. The pursuit of this object does not violate the statute in question . . ."

Local groups who wished to use the war as a club with which to crush the League appealed to national authorities to scotch the serpent in their midst. George Creel, chairman of the federal Committee on Public Information, brought down the wrath of League opponents on his head when he made a public statement on the question. Said Creel, in a letter to a national farm group:

"It is not true that the federal government is pressing the Nonpartisan League in any manner, or that the federal government considers it an act of disloyalty to be a member of the League.

"The federal government is not concerned with the political, economic or industrial beliefs of any organization at a time like this, insisting only that every individual stand behind this war, believing absolutely in the justice of America's position.

"The Nonpartisan League, by resolution and organized effort, has given this pledge of loyalty. North Dakota, controlled by this organization politically, has as fine a record of war support as any other commonwealth in the union. Mr. Baer, its representative in the lower house, has never even been criticized for a single utterance that might be termed disloyal.

"Mr. Townley is under indictment in Minnesota, and there is a very bitter fight being made on the League in that state by certain groups. With this the government has nothing to do, refusing absolutely to take part in these local differences."

THE wartime speeches of League leaders, castigating the huge profits that were being made by certain groups, at length awakened eastern corporations to the fact that the spreading philosophy of the League might be dangerous to them. They began to take action by bringing pressure to bear on their smaller allies in the Northwest.

In the state of Montana a special group known as the Loyalty League was organized by a representative of the Anaconda Copper Mining Company to combat the farmers' party. Chambers of commerce and employers' groups were urged to destroy the League before its "Socialism" destroyed the nation. Townley's speeches, it is true, were sufficient to scare the britches off conservatives. When he began to urge the confiscation of war profits and advocate government control of food distribution and transportation, the howls of the industrialists could be heard even above the jingle of their wartime cash registers.

It is noteworthy that the federal government later adopted several of Townley's suggestions during World War I: federal control of prices and of the railroads, for example. History has borne out, in a large measure, certain other views expressed in his speeches.

Townley pulled no punches. He was a master of sarcasm and of the "homey" platform manner. His tall, thin, angular figure, hunched over as if he were peering into the face of each individual member of the audience—with perhaps a thumb thrust through one suspender—might seem amusing at first, but he was a master of crowd psychology and a shrewd judge of farmer nature in particular.

His methods and phrases were sometimes demagoguery at its

most flagrant, but the speeches were only too often fundamentally true, and his enemies winced under his attacks. Here are a few extracts from one of the "seditious" addresses which he delivered throughout the Northwest in the year 1917. After citing figures showing the huge increases in profits made by Swift & Company, United States Steel, Du Pont, and other large corporations, he proceeded to the attack:

"I want to say to you that this nation can never succeed in war unless this, your government, instead of serving the interests of the United States Steel Corporation and the sugar trust and the beef trust—this nation can never succeed in war until it governs the business of transporting your products and wipes off the face of the earth the gamblers in food products and the necessaries of life . . .

"Now here is the seditious and treasonable and unpatriotic part of my discussion. We respectfully suggest, and then we demand, that this nation, instead of serving the interests of the gentlemen it must be serving now—or it would not permit these gigantic corporations to rob you of so many millions a year—I am afraid it must be serving them, because I can't figure out from these reports how they are serving us—and so as a war measure we respectfully suggest and demand that the United States government shall do the one thing first of all necessary, and take over, before they send one single boy to Europe, take over the railroads and the distribution of food into their hands, and kick the gamblers into the sea or send them to war.

"Last Tuesday about ten million young men—I see them in the crowd here, and here, and here—about ten million young men went to the registration booths and there pledged their lives in the defense of their country's honor, went to the registration booths and there said in effect: 'I will serve my country in any capacity that she may demand. I pledge you here my life. Take it and use it as you will . . .' That is what these young men said in effect.

"This is the acme of patriotism . . . And it is right that they should have done it. I believe in the conscription of life in time of war, because it is not right that the burden should be shouldered upon those few who have the courage in their blood to go and fight . . .

"But the steel trust makes two or three hundred million dollars of profit; the sugar trust makes profits; the harvester trust makes profits; the railroad trust makes profits; the lumber trust makes profits; the shoe trust—the whiskey trust—the grain trust—the beef trust—every trust makes an enormous war profit . . .

"And I say to you that the first thing this government should do is take the profits that they are making today to pay the expense of the war.

"Is this treason?

"Is this anarchy?

"More than that, if by the duration of this war, those war profits are not enough to pay the cost of the war—if we must go so far as to exhaust these profits, and need more money, there is still another reservoir; and that is the millions that they piled up before the war. We will take that, too."

One can readily conceive the effect these words had upon the farmer-worker groups to which they were addressed—to say nothing of their effect upon the corporations named in Townley's indictment. But Townley's words here were not idle demagoguery. In 1916, in Minneapolis alone, the grain trust which Townley excoriated had made a profit of $7.19 a barrel on the staggering total of eighteen million barrels of flour. Herbert Hoover has never been charged with being a radical, yet in a 1917 address, while he was secretary of commerce, he delivered an attack against the grain trust that amply backed up Townley's assertions:

"With righteous manufacturers' and distributors' prices, the price of flour should not have been over $9.00 a barrel, yet it averages $14.00. In the last five months, on the item of flour alone, $250,000,000 has been extracted from the American consumer in excess of normal profits."

But despite the words of Hoover, Creel, and others, the campaign of vilification and abuse triumphed, and almost before the war was ended, the back of the movement was broken in every state except North Dakota and Minnesota. No charge was too vicious or fantastic for the League's enemies to make against the party leaders. But even charges that they were "free lovers" who were about to corrupt the morals of the nation and debauch its womanhood could not break the party's power in North Dakota. In the elections of 1918 the League candidates again swept the state ticket and elected at last a majority of the members in both houses of the legislature. Now the last barrier to the enactment of their program was removed.

Nor was the organization entirely powerless in other states. During the years of its greatest strength, the League endorsed and helped to elect such officials as the late famous Senator Borah of Idaho; Congresswoman Jeanette Rankin of Montana, foe of the Anaconda Copper Company; Senator Wheeler of Montana; Senator Nugent of Idaho; and many other men who have since become well known nationally. Congressman Lemke of North Dakota as well as Senators Frazier, Langer, and Nye were all originally elected with League endorsement, although Nye was later repudiated by the party. Congressman Lindbergh of Minnesota, father of the famous flyer, also benefited from League support.

When the 1919 legislature met in Bismarck to enact the League program into law, national attention was focused upon the farmers' revolutionary party, and newspapers and magazines of the day were filled with comment and prophecy—much of it dark and gloomy. The files of such magazines as the *Literary Digest*, the *Nation*, and the *World's Work* contain numerous articles about the mysterious A. C. Townley—the *Digest* was unable even to obtain a photograph of him—and his new radical movement in the agricultural Northwest.

Townley himself was in great demand as a speaker all over the United States. He visited the President in Washington and addressed a large crowd in famous Cooper Union in New York, where he was apparently something of an enigma to the citizens of the state that was even then the home of Franklin Roosevelt. They did not seem to understand what Townley was talking about, although they understood well enough when Roosevelt addressed them on the same general subject a few years later.

Townley's program, as amended by the League throughout the years, was, in simple terms, a New Deal two decades before Roosevelt. It advocated, in 1919, such dangerous innovations as a work-men's compensation law, regulation of working conditions and hours of employment for women, a state-hail insurance law, a plan of distance tariffs to eliminate railroad rate discrimination, a home-building program, a graduated income tax, a mine inspection law to provide safe working conditions for miners, exemption of farm improvements from taxation (designed to penalize speculators who allowed land to lie idle), and most important of all, its three cardinal points: the creation of a state bank, the establishment of a state-owned elevator and flour mill, and the creation of an industrial commission made up of the governor, the attorney general, and the secretary of agriculture to administer the state-owned institutions.

In North Dakota a bond issue of five million dollars was provided to establish working capital for these enterprises. The farmers' program was on its way. The funds, at long last, were provided. But now, with the party firmly in the saddle, the gentlemen who were to bring about the organization's downfall and temporary eclipse began to creep from their hiding places, each with his own particular bag of tricks. Some were political mountebanks, some were plain crooks, others were cranks. But they all seemed to have one thing in common: they wanted to use the League's name and power and prestige to develop their utopian schemes.

The League was to suffer now from a weakness inherent in all revolutionary parties: liberals, farmers, workingmen, and intellectuals are not always good businessmen or administrators. Most of the League officials had had little or no experience either in politics or business; they were easy marks for every glib-tongued promoter with a plausible scheme to offer.

For a time it was a three-ring circus whose fantastic performances tended to overshadow the party's real accomplishments. Besides sisal enterprises in Florida and fish hatcheries in the Bering Sea, North Dakota farmers were persuaded to invest their money (a postdated check was usually good) in Mexican lands, consumers' cooperative stores, League banks and exchanges, and almost every other activity that offered an opportunity of separating a farmer from his money.

The League leaders and the promoters were not entirely to blame. The farmers had the bit in their teeth; they were ready to try anything. It was partly their own attitude which made it easy for shrewd and fast talkers, masquerading under the name of the League, or through some vague League affiliation, to bring about a period of buffoonery and high comedy such as North Dakota and the nation had not seen for many a day. But there was a less amusing side to the matter: The frenzied financing infected even the regular League projects and brought about a financial debacle that discredited the farmers' movement and forced it temporarily out of power under particularly humiliating conditions.

Banks crammed to the eaves with postdated checks and similarly inert paper were commonplace. North Dakota farmers who owned stock in any of the dubious corporations which mushroomed overnight were resentful of any suggestion that some of these crackpot enterprises might be unsound. They were only too ready to characterize as a villain anyone who tried to warn them, suspecting, perhaps, that he was an agent of Wall Street or the ogre Big Biz, against whom they had been repeatedly warned.

And then entered the villain, in the person of William Langer, young attorney general for the League and later United States senator from North Dakota. Not that Langer was actually a villain in the matter. He merely suggested that some of the so-called farmers' banks, notably the Scandinavian-American Bank of Fargo, were tottering institutions in which no farmer who wanted to save his red flannels should place his money. Langer was bitterly attacked by League leaders and officials of the bank, who were using the institution as a reservoir from which to finance many of their doubtful enterprises.

Governor Frazier, a member of the state banking board, refused to believe the charges, and Langer was unable to have a satisfactory audit of the bank taken. But Langer was a resourceful character. He arranged that the chief auditor of the state should be called out of North Dakota on business; then, with two deputy auditors, armed with the proper credentials, he descended on the bank to examine its books and assets.

"Mr. Langer emerged," wrote Walter Davenport in *Collier's,* "crying at the top of his voice that the bank was so crammed with such collateral as postdated checks and uncollectible notes that the doors of the vaults could scarcely be shut."

There was little if any exaggeration in Langer's charges. Officials of the League and the bank attempted to reorganize the institution, but their efforts were futile. The bank collapsed; shortages of $216,378.09 were discovered before the investigation was completed; Townley and Lemke, along with several officials of the bank, were charged with embezzlement and indicted. Says Mr. Davenport: "The indictments seemed to include everybody of importance and everything that can happen to a bank short of arson—indictments for false reports to the bank examiners, for receiving deposits while insolvent, for false statements to the depositors and false entries, for perjury . . ."

A number of the bank's officials were sent to prison, but the indictments against Townley and Lemke were later dismissed on the ground that they were improperly executed. "Anyway," as Mr. Davenport concludes, "there was no evidence that Messrs. Townley and Lemke had the $216,378.09."

The unsound financing which marked some of the League's projects—such as the Scandinavian-American Bank, for example—was not a result of improper practices in all cases. If the League was sometimes forced to embark upon dubious financial schemes, it was in large part because regular loaning and credit agencies boycotted the League projects in the hope of wrecking the organization. Said the *Nation* on October 19, 1921: "The pith of the whole contest in North Dakota is financial. The carrying-out of the Non-Partisan League industrial program has depended upon money, which for the past two years it has been impossible to obtain."

North Dakota's state bonds were being rejected by investment firms and banking circles in the hope of smashing the "socialist" regime which was threatening their dominance of the Northwest. The program of the League's opposition in smearing its leaders

From shanty to skyscraper. Bismarck, Dakota Territory, in 1873, and the state capitol in Bismarck today.

Night song in the Badlands

Sheep on the range in Montana

Cattle on a South Dakota ranch

Carved by the wind and the waters of countless centuries. "The Needles" in the Black Hills of South Dakota.

John Wesley Powell   **James J. Hill**

Their plans for the Northwest differed

Arthur C. Townley   **Alexander McKenzie**

W. P. SEBENS, FARGO, N.D.

Mining lignite coal in North Dakota. The state has 600,000,000,000 (yes, billion) tons of this coal.

"The richest hill on earth." Copper mines at Butte, Montana.

MONTANANS, INC.

Before and after in the Dust Bowl. A Dakota farm in 1935, taken over by sand drifts and Russian thistle, and the same farm in 1943, restored to productivity by soil conservation measures.

Promises of better times to come. Irrigation in the Yellowstone Valley, and strip cropping in North Dakota.

BELL PHOTO, RAPID CITY, S.D.

"Hell with the fires out." The South Dakota Badlands.

**The great stone faces by Gutzon Borglum on Mt. Rushmore
in the Black Hills of South Dakota**

H. E. LARSEN PHOTO, STATE PUBLICITY DEPT., PIERRE, S.D.

never abated. William Lemke, the League's attorney, became known as Commissar Lemke. New York newspapers sent reporters to the fastnesses of North Dakota to report on the activities of the "freelovers" who desired to divide up all the women of America among themselves and establish seraglios on the plains.

When League legislatures met, breathless reporters were present to flash to the nation the breakdown of the American way of life and the triumph of Bolshevism. Needless to say, they went home disgusted upon discovering that the legislatures were made up for the most part of stanch Lutherans and Roman Catholics who would as soon have thought of founding a harem as of cursing Martin Luther or the Pope.

While native North Dakotans did not believe the more extreme charges made against the League, there nevertheless arose in time a storm of such bitter feeling that the thunder of it echoes in the state to this day. There was no longer a question of political parties; there was only the question whether one was "League" or "anti-League."

"It is doubtful," wrote the North Dakota historian Lewis Crawford, "whether any society has experienced a more bitter partisan strife since the days of slavery than North Dakota passed through in the period of about ten years following the legislative session of 1917. Almost our whole social and business life was influenced by the continuous turmoil into which all were drawn. The League and its doings formed the chief topic of conversation wherever men gathered: on the street corner, in the cross roads, in the barber shop, or business office. We had League picnics, women's auxiliaries, public debates, newspaper controversies, independent voters' associations, special legislative sessions, House Bill 44, farmer-owned banks, newspapers, stores, and whatnots, injunctions, initiatives, referendums and recalls that consumed the energy and disturbed the peace and quiet of every citizen from the mere voter to the Supreme Court. This controversy was not confined to officials, candidates for office, or professional politicians. The daily life of even the common citizen was a round of bitter political acrimony in which each freely backed up his beliefs, however ill-founded many of them were, with his time and money."

The bitterness and political acrimony extended to even lower levels than the mere voter. Children barely able to talk—but quite able to hear—knew which side of the fence they were on in North Dakota's political revolution. In 1920, when Townley traveled over the state by airplane, he attracted great crowds, not only because of the intense interest in League affairs, but because of the then novel means of transportation he employed. Says Walter Davenport: "From roundup to roundup he flew, swooping from the skies upon startled audiences, who, properly coached by livelier imaginations, hailed Mr. Townley as a winged messenger from heaven. Gabriel over the wheat fields. Michael putting Wall Street to the sword."

Even children of six or seven, despite the awe and admiration they felt for these daring aviators, spat fiercely on the wings of the plane when they learned that it carried A. C. Townley, of whom they had heard so much. I can verify this, for I was one of those children. It is not to be wondered at, either; there is an old story that North Dakota mothers sometimes frightened their errant offspring into decorous behavior with a paraphrase of the old bogeyman story: "Townley will get you if you don't watch out!"

POSTWAR deflation struck devastating blows at the northwest farming country just at the period when the League was getting its start. In the 1920 elections the opposition had a strong, if invalid, talking point in the increase of the cost of government, which had risen to twenty million dollars during the 1918–20 biennium. The increase was a direct result of wartime inflation, rather than of League squandering; in the single year 1918–19 property valuations in North Dakota had leaped from four hundred million dollars to one and a half billion dollars!

The League was nevertheless successful once more in its campaign to return its candidates to office. But as the first months of its third consecutive term passed, drought, deflation, and mismanagement of League affairs provided potent ammunition for its enemies. Legislative committees appointed to investigate the party's state-sponsored projects—as well as opposition auditors—brought charges that the affairs of the state were hopelessly muddled and mismanaged. Huge deficits were alleged to exist in the affairs of several state enterprises.

The leaders of the League were ousted from state office under most humiliating conditions, and under the terms of a law which they themselves had initiated. Liberals all over the nation had praised their enactment of a Recall Act which provided that any elective official could be removed from office by vote of the people in a special election. Now, by a curious quirk of fate, League leaders were the first officials against whom the law was directed. It was, indeed, the first time in the history of the United States that a recall election had been successfully brought against a governor of a state.

It is almost impossible, even today, to estimate how much of the people's antipathy was founded on actual fact, how much on distorted propaganda of the opposition, and how much on unavoidable economic conditions for which nobody could properly be held responsible. The disastrous deflation of the postwar years was bringing hard times to the northern plains; and it is a political truism that the party in power invariably suffers—or benefits—from current economic conditions, regardless of what influence it may have had in bringing about those conditions.

It is beyond doubt, however, that the political inexperience and confused administration of the League's leaders had a great deal to do with their own downfall. The projects of the party, however laudable they might have been in theory, were badly administered; but this was not always the fault of the League officials. They were hamstrung and opposed at every turn by a particularly violent opposition whose only interest was to smash the League—even if it had to smash the state's economy and credit at the same time.

In the special election called to attempt the ouster of the Industrial Commission, the opposition sought also to repeal the entire League program of state-owned industries. But the people of the state indicated that they still knew what they wanted. Two hundred thousand voters expressed their will in this bitter contest, which ended with the peculiar result of the people voting to continue the League program, while ousting the League officials and placing opposition officials in their places to conduct that program. The results were quite naturally not notable for their success.

That the people of the state later felt they had erred in this action is indicated by their subsequent treatment of the men they had ousted. Governor Frazier was later nominated by the party for United States senator and elected for three successive terms; William Lemke, the ousted attorney general, has been repeatedly returned to the United States Congress by the people of the state; and John Hagan, the ousted commissioner of agriculture and labor, was later given a League endorsement for governor of the state.

But at the time, the issues were so clouded and the feeling so bitter that the Independent Voters' Association, as the League opposition was called, was able to re-elect its gubernatorial candidate, R. A. Nestos, in 1922. In 1924 the League made a partial return to power with the election of Governor Sorlie; but from the session of 1919, when the League completely dominated the government and began its program, to the 1930 session, when the I.V.A. forces completely dominated the legislature and the state offices, there ensued a seesaw for power between the two forces.

As the decade of the 1920's progressed, political differences began to seem less threatening and political activity less important. Men discovered more frightening enemies than their political opponents, as the prophetic words of John Wesley Powell began to come true on the northern plains. The thousands of settlers whom Jim Hill had induced to come into the northwest prairies found themselves embroiled in a desperate fight for existence that left them little time or energy for political struggles. The battle of the farmers against economic spoliation resolved itself now into a war against the implacable forces of nature.

Chapter 18

THE GRAPES OF WRATH

wwwwwwwwwwwwwwwwwwwwwwwwwwwwwwwwwwwwwwwwwwwwwwwwwww

In the days following World War I, when crops were so hard hit by drought and black stem rust that they were scarcely worth harvesting, a Dakota farmer was visiting friends in Minneapolis in the hope of finding a city job to tide him over the winter. One day he received a telegram from his wife announcing the birth of a child—a prematurely born infant who weighed only three pounds and was being kept alive in an incubator.

Since it was his first-born, the farmer was very proud and passed out the cigars as expansively as his meager means permitted. A couple of his friends, however, kidded him a bit for being so thrilled over the birth of this tiny mite of humanity.

"Listen, fellows," the farmer told them, with a weariness born of grim experience. "Out in Dakota these days we're thankful if we even get our seed back!"

There is scarcely less of truth than earthiness in this Dust Bowl tale which gave northwest farmers one of the few chuckles of an otherwise humorless period. There actually were times when the harvest was less than the grain they had seeded; in other cases, where the yield was moderately high, prices in the eastern markets were so ruinously low that the check the farmer received for a grain shipment was less than the freight charges he had paid to the terminal market.

During the early years of World War I the men who had come west on Jim Hill's trains in the decade of the 1900's saw bumper crops come up on the trans-Missouri prairies. In 1915 North Dakota raised the staggering total of 151,000,000 bushels of wheat—a record that was not to be attained again until the wet and successful years of the middle 1940's.

Then disaster struck. In 1916 the yield dropped to 37,000,000 bushels; in 1917 it was 50,000,000 bushels, only a third of the 1915 crop. Drought such as had never before been seen by most of the homesteaders, coupled with a disastrous black rust epidemic, found the state's farmers losing money even at the price-pegged figure of $2.20 a bushel, as the average per acre yield dropped from 18.2 bushels to less than 5 bushels.

South Dakota farmers who had settled on the west-river benches suffered in like measure with their northern neighbors, while in Montana conditions were even worse than in the Dakotas. Montana's dryland farms, which had produced an average yield of 25 bushels to the acre in the early years of the century, dropped in 1919 to a low of 2.4 bushels. All over the upper river valley there was a series of disastrous failures as the drought persisted through 1918–19–20.

But despite all this, northwest farmers continued to expand their holdings under the war-inspired program of increased acreage and greater food production. Much submarginal land that should never have been broken was torn up and planted to wheat in answer to the government's plea for more wheat production. Credit was easy to obtain, because men remembered the bumper yields of the preceding decade, and speculative capital was flowing into the country. A few wet years with big yields and high prices could make a man moderately wealthy if he had sufficiently large holdings. Land values soared to inflationary heights as northern plains farmers reached out to purchase additional acres and began to mechanize their farms for extensive operations. Like the new lands they bought, most of the new machinery was purchased on credit at war-inflated prices, while they waited for the rains to come.

And instead of the rains came the first of the dust storms. The wind lifted the loose, powdery topsoil and blew it in choking clouds over the parched fields. Northwest homesteaders gaped at the unprecedented phenomenon. This year they would not even need to harvest their crops, for the wind scoured deep into the soil and blew away the very seed they had sown.

Land that they had summer-fallowed and plowed deeply, as Jim Hill's scientists had advised them to do, drifted away now before the ceaseless urging of the wind, leaving gaping holes in the sun-dried fields; the exposed edges of the holes wore outward under the constant erosion until entire quarter sections were stripped of inches of precious and irreplaceable topsoil. Land fertility that had been created through countless centuries of growth and slow building was being ripped away by the fist of the wind in minutes and hours. Exhausted lands where reckless soil mining had been practiced were among the first to wear away under the continual drilling of the wind. Then neighboring fields exposed to the wind's abrasive action began to suffer. Once begun, the terrible denuding continued despite everything the desperate farmers were able to contrive.

Out on the range lands of the cattle country years of drought brought destructive prairie fires, and what growth the fires did not destroy, the fierce rays of the sun parched and stunted until western cattlemen were forced to sell their herds or ship them eastward where feed was available. Special freight rates to enable them to import hay were finally inaugurated, but speculators who saw an opportunity to profit from their desperation sent the price of hay to fifty dollars a ton. Boxcars loaded with moldy grass were shipped as "hay" at these prohibitive prices. The cattle industry, like the wheat industry, was rapidly disintegrating.

In 1920 railroad rates went up 17 per cent throughout the Northwest; the price of farm machinery doubled between 1916 and the early 20's; and the cost of clothing and other necessaries which stockmen and farmers must buy increased sharply. But the prices of wheat and livestock slid steadily downward after the war years, until by 1921 wheat had reached a low of ninety-two cents a bushel, instead of the two dollars and a quarter of the war period. The farmer, who had bought on credit more land and machinery to produce the war abundance which the government asked of him, found himself heavily in debt, with the cost of living rising and his market steadily falling.

In effect, the farmer's debt had doubled as a result of the changed conditions: at current prices it took two bushels of wheat to pay the debt that one bushel would have paid a year or two before. And his credit, which had been advanced so liberally during the war years, was now to be taken from him.

The large banks of the Northwest, pursuing the stated policy of the Federal Reserve system, commenced a program intended to deflate the wartime boom in land values—a boom that had been caused largely by their own previous program of reckless extension of credit. This was supplemented by a policy whose purpose was to drive down the "too high" prices of northwest agricultural commodities. Northern plains farmers, scourged by drought and crop failure, who were actually losing money even at war-inflated prices, could only shake their heads at this curious reasoning.

The government's banking policies, which during the war years had encouraged northwest bankers to advance credit beyond normal limits in an effort to induce farmers to buy more land, produce more food, and, incidentally, buy more Liberty Bonds, were turned now toward curbing "inflationary borrowing" by forcing the Liberty Bonds out of the banks. This the Federal Reserve system achieved in masterly fashion by a drastic curtailment of credit throughout the farming country. The Liberty Bonds came out of the banks all right—at eighty cents on the dollar. Not only had the government broken faith with the purchasers of war bonds; it had, by this same gesture, deprived the Northwest of its only remaining liquid assets.

Northern plains farmers, many of them with unpaid notes for one, two, and three years in arrears as a result of drought and crop failure, were utterly unable to meet their obligations. Thousands of them, despairing of ever being able to pay their debts, gave up and let their farms and homes revert to the mortgagees. In the decade from 1920 to 1930 there was an exodus from the Upper Missouri states of seventy-two thousand persons from North Dakota, seventy-one thousand from Montana, and forty-two thousand from South Dakota. One half of Montana's farmers lost their homes through mortgage foreclosure before 1925, and one fifth of the state's farm acreage, which had been settled so hopefully by Jim Hill's drylanders, was left lying idle. The price of farm lands throughout the Northwest dropped 50 per cent.

But the Federal Reserve system had not done yet with the Northwest's tottering economic structure. The rediscount rate of its banks was raised from 4½ per cent to as high as 7 per cent in some cases. Agricultural paper was forced out of the country's

THE GRAPES OF WRATH

banks until the institutions ceased to be of service to the communities in which they had been designed to function. And next came the "additional collateral" policy, under which northwest bankers were arbitrarily driven to put up additional security for previous loans.

The system sought to justify this astonishing plan with the statement that the value of agricultural paper was rapidly dropping under current market conditions. Northwest bankers were well aware of this fact themselves, but they also knew that a farmer's note which may be worth little in a drought year will be perfectly good a short time later. Bankers who sent in notes for rediscount to the Twin City banks found, in certain cases, that the notes were being held as "additional collateral" for previously discounted notes. At last the Reserve banks refused altogether to rediscount individual notes, and the banker was forced to make a direct loan—submitting a number of notes as security, of which the Reserve bank coolly took its pick in an amount sometimes equaling three times the amount of the banker's loan.

Now, with the sources of credit dried up, the farmer and the livestock producer were forced to sell their grain and cattle to keep alive and to pay up notes which the Reserve banks were calling in. The smashing of "high commodity prices" which the Federal Reserve system had set out to achieve in the Northwest was accomplished. But in the process it had smashed, too, the economy and the banking system of the states on the northern plains.

By the middle 20's banks were bursting like popcorn throughout the Northwest. Montana lost one third of her banks by 1924; in 1926 North Dakota lost fifty-nine national banks and South Dakota one hundred and fifteen, wiping out millions of dollars of the meager savings of stockmen, farmers, and small businessmen.

There is a considerable body of evidence to indicate that the brutal policies of the Federal Reserve system in the Northwest were not entirely the result of shortsightedness or stupidity. Congressman Usher L. Burdick of North Dakota charged in the national House of Representatives that the "Twin City bank gang" had controlled the administration of the War Finance

Corporation in violation of the purposes and intent of the laws under which the corporation was established. Under the management of the "Twin City crowd," Burdick asserted, "not a cent of the money lent went to aid agriculture as the act intended." The loans, he said, were made "to country banks holding farmers' paper, but which paper the First National Bank of Minneapolis and the First National of St. Paul were holding as collateral to loans secured by the country banks to which this money was loaned."

The loans, in short, were made only to those country banks which could be forced to endorse the check and return it to the correspondent bank in the East. "When it became apparent that the Twin City bankers were milking the government and that the losses of this corporation would be amazing," Burdick continued, "this same group secured a set-up known as the Agricultural Credit Corporation, established in February 1924, to rediscount paper of the War Finance Corporation, and it worked overtime . . . but was soon taken over by the Federal Reserve Bank of Minneapolis. It was not intended that any cash should be sent to small banks to keep them from closing."

In the tragic case of one North Dakota banker, Burdick's assertions proved to be quite accurate. This man was able to obtain from the War Finance Corporation a loan of twenty-five thousand dollars, which would have tided his bank over the depression period. But the Minneapolis bankers who held the man's collateral learned of the loan and brought pressure upon him to turn the check over to them. If he refused, they would crack down and close his bank. The banker had to accede to their wishes. Later, when his bank was forced to close, he was given the appointment of deputy receiver and managed to support his family for several years, until some 60 per cent of the bank's losses had been repaid. Then the receivership was terminated. Unable to rebuild his life, with a wife and six children to support, his only assets being the insurance he had kept through the years, he took his own life in order to provide for the future of his family.

So, under the cold and ruthless treatment meted out to the smaller banks and the men who depended on those banks for credit, the economy of the northern plains states crumpled in bankruptcy and disaster, while the rest of the nation was busily engaged in an economic joyride.

MOST Americans—unless they happened to live in the Northwest during the years following World War I—will scarcely recognize the foregoing as a picture of the postwar years. Montana and the Dakotas have had little time or leisure to develop writers who make an impact on the national consciousness. The Northwest and its affairs do not loom large on the national horizon. And newspapers and magazines of the day had stories a-plenty that were better circulation builders than the dreary affairs of poverty-stricken farmers and ranchers.

For this was the decade of the Roaring Twenties. The decade of Al Capone and Insull, of sheiks and flappers and bathtub gin and jazz; of bulls and bears and "normalcy" and the Big Money. When New York City brokers were gleefully hailing Andrew Mellon as "the greatest secretary of the treasury since Alexander Hamilton" and were extolling the virtues of capitalism triumphant, nobody troubled to look at the Northwest, where a miniature preview of the coming national debacle was being enacted.

In the Upper Missouri Valley men had another name for the greatest secretary of the treasury since Alexander Hamilton, as they saw their farms and the fruits of lifetimes of toil stripped from them for want of a little sound financial foresight on the part of national leaders. Elsewhere in America it was still a time of Coolidge and Hoover prosperity, of well-filled pockets and miniature golf, of mahjong and gang murders and millionaire bootleggers; in the Northwest—although one can find scant mention of it in the newspapers of the day—it was a time of exodus and desperation, of broken banks and broken hopes and broken lives.

Then, as the Roaring Twenties merged into the Threadbare Thirties, something more than a credit drought struck at the northern plains. There began in 1930 a cycle of dry years that were the worst in the experience of the oldest residents. Blinding dust storms that made those of the early 20's seem trifles by comparison swept over the Upper Missouri states. Automobiles drove with headlights turned on even at midday to pierce the darkened atmosphere. Dust sifted through the frames of tight-shut windows until it lay drifted a half-inch deep on the sills. Whole farms were carried bodily eastward and dumped into the streets of far-off cities. It is estimated that twelve million tons of rich topsoil fell on the city of Chicago alone in one of the great storms. Soil from the distant farms of Montana and the Dakotas enveloped cities of the Atlantic seaboard with great dark clouds, and ships far out at sea found a dust film settling on their decks. It began to look as if the warnings of John Wesley Powell had not been grave enough; it seemed, to red-eyed farmers who scanned the skies in vain for rain clouds, that their land was in danger of becoming a second Sahara—for wind erosion carries away only the precious and fertile humus, leaving the sand to lie in heaped and furrowed desert windrows.

And it was not only the drought the farmers had to contend with. Even where they were able to produce scanty yields, it bene-fited them little, for the price of wheat dropped to forty cents a bushel and lower. Once again the stage was set for agrarian re-volt. And once again the revolt came about most effectively in North Dakota, where a resurgent Nonpartisan League returned to power in 1933, during the most trying period in the North-west's history.

Governor William Langer, who had taken Arthur Townley's place as the League's recognized head, was largely responsible for the organization's new dominance. For the first time since the famous 1919 legislature the League had complete control of the executive and legislative branches of the state government. Its officials had, too, a decade and a half of political experience to draw upon. But even so, the party's task was no simple one.

The outgoing administration of Governor Shafer had left a bonded indebtedness of $40,000,000. (It is perhaps pertinent to add that only $10,000,000 of this amount had been incurred under League administrations; the remaining legacy of $30,000,000 had been left by anti-League governors.) The Bank of North Dakota was carrying $2,225,000 in interest coupons on these bonds which the state could not meet. The state's bonds were selling at eighty-four cents on the dollar, and its people were suffering, in many cases, from actual hunger and want. Thousands were leaving for other parts of the nation in hopes of finding employment. There were $25,000,000 in unpaid taxes outstanding; schoolteachers were being paid by warrant; insurance companies and other mortgagees were gathering in North Dakota farms by the score as a result of foreclosures; banks were closing right and left as they had closed in the middle 20's; there had been three successive years of drought and crop failure. And into this seemingly hopeless situation came the League and its new governor on January 1, 1933.

Governor Langer—later elected to the United States Senate—was soon to occupy a unique position in North Dakota political affairs. In the early days of the League, men were classified as Leaguers or anti-Leaguers; under Governor Langer's regime they came to be known as pro-Langer or anti-Langer; there was scarcely any other political designation of importance. That situation obtains even today.

Langer has been called every known variety of scoundrel by his enemies, who number roughly one half of North Dakota's six hundred and forty thousand people. But this situation has its compensations, for his followers are as fanatical in their devotion to him as his enemies are in their opposition.

For a clear understanding of William Langer and his career, it is necessary to go back to his early associations and personal history. Born on a farm in North Dakota, he learned early the problems of an agricultural state from firsthand observation and experience. His flair for politics was perhaps acquired from his father, Frank Langer, who was a member of the state's first legislature.

Young Langer whizzed through high school and the University of North Dakota's law school at such a dizzy pace that he found himself a full-fledged lawyer at eighteen—three years too young to practice legally. So the gangling farmer boy packed his bag, dusted off his yellow shoes, and set out for Columbia University in New York City. His political talents were beginning to show themselves even then. Before he was through at Columbia he was elected class president, won the Roelker award for outstanding scholarship, and—for the third time in his life—was graduated as valedictorian of his class. Incidentally, he was chosen by his classmates as "the man most likely to succeed."

His brilliant work as the youthful state's attorney of Morton County and his subsequent affiliation with the League as its attorney general have already been told. During the desperate days of the late 20's and early 30's, it was chiefly his work in reorganizing the party that brought him into the governor's chair in January of 1933.

"We must balance the state budget," declared Governor Langer in his inaugural address. "North Dakota goes into the coming year with unpaid borrowings of $2,500,000. We have arrived at a point where expenditures of taxpayers' money consume approximately fifty per cent of the cash farm income of the state. Continuation of these policies can mean only one thing: bankruptcy. Unless some immediate drastic remedy is adopted to equalize taxation with income, complete ruin faces the farmers of North Dakota."

Such words are often heard from politicians in times of stress, particularly just before an election, but the governor and the League legislature soon demonstrated that they were not engaging in mere campaign oratory. The biennial budget of the previous administration had been approximately $10,000,000. Under the League's economy program this was slashed to less than $5,000,000—and as a result North Dakota led every state in the Union in reduction of the cost of state government in 1933.

With the exception of the elementary schools, every department received such a paring and pruning as had not been seen since statehood. The squawks of jobholding politicians were loud and prolonged, but they were not the only ones to suffer. The state's underpaid college professors suffered further reductions of pay as well; yet there were few complaints from them. The spectacle of an administration which was really balancing the budget —after an election—was too refreshing to cause much criticism except among professional politicians who were being nudged away from the public trough.

When the legislature failed to pare appropriations sufficiently, Governor Langer seized his red pencil and vetoed an additional $500,000. This was, very likely, an illegal use of the veto power, for North Dakota law prohibits the vetoing of appropriations bills in part; but Langer had always been an advocate of the direct approach. Constitutional limitations did not mean much to him or to the desperate people of the state at the time, as will be seen. At any rate, nobody objected to the further reduction, whether it was legal or not.

Before the 1933 administration the state had been paying from five to nine cents a kilowatt hour for power furnished its public buildings by private companies. Governor Langer called in rate experts and had them do a bit of figuring. Their report was illuminating, and a few days later the League legislature approved an expenditure of $350,000 for the construction of a state-owned power plant. The mere threat was enough. The power companies capitulated and signed a ten-year contract to furnish the state power at one cent per kilowatt hour—a saving of some $400,000.

Next, with a fine disregard for the United States Constitution, which specifically prohibits any embargo, the legislature enacted into law a bill empowering the governor to declare an embargo on the state's produce whenever, in the governor's opinion, prices became "confiscatory." This astonishing measure was a result of the fact that the grain trust had reverted to its old ways in the years of the League's impotence. Arrogant and powerful, it again depressed prices at will, and poverty-stricken farmers, forced to sell their grain if they were to exist, had to dispose of it at any price the syndicate saw fit to offer. But the new administration had a trick or two up its sleeve.

North Dakota produces some 85 per cent of all the durum wheat grown in the United States—a fact which gives it a practical monopoly on the product. But an uncontrolled monopoly is as ineffective as none at all. It was this situation that Langer set about remedying under his embargo powers. The milling and grain interests, which had chuckled at the farmers' unconstitutional law and predicted that it would never be invoked, were startled when Langer abruptly ordered the cessation of all wheat shipments from the state. Aside from the effect on the supply of durum wheat, which could be obtained nowhere else, the milling terminals found that the withholding of North Dakota's huge hard spring wheat crop—largest of any state in the nation—had completely upset their plans and schedules.

The price of wheat on the Minneapolis exchange jumped five cents the day the embargo was announced and another five cents the following day—while the grain trust howled bloody murder and brought legal proceedings against the state. Langer, however, had foreseen what would happen: the processes of the law were slow but the rules of supply and demand were quick and constant. While the case dragged through the federal courts the price of wheat continued to rise until it had reached a point where Canadian growers could afford to pay the high duty and still ship to the United States at a profit. At this point the governor lifted the embargo. He would have had to do so soon anyway, for the millers shortly afterward obtained a permanent injunction preventing the state from engaging in any such unconstitutional shenanigans in the future.

"What if it was unconstitutional?" said Governor Langer. "It worked, didn't it?"

And North Dakota's farmers, who had themselves been trimmed frequently by the grain trade, were more than glad to see the tables turned for once. A hundred Sargent County farmers telegraphed the governor: "Your action in placing an embargo on wheat is the best thing that has been done in this state in forty years. We are with you until hell freezes over."

Two days before the embargo took effect, No. 1 dark northern spring wheat was selling at forty-nine cents a bushel; five weeks later the price had gone to seventy-two cents—a rise that put millions of dollars into the pockets, not only of North Dakota farmers, but of the growers of the entire Northwest. Durum wheat, because of North Dakota's near monopoly, rose to ninety-two cents a bushel.

There were indirect benefits, too. The League administration's courageous and unprecedented action, even though it was unconstitutional, dramatized for the whole nation the desperate plight of the farmer and hastened the passage of national legislation for agrarian reform. The governors of Minnesota, Montana, South Dakota, Iowa, Nebraska, and Kansas wired their commendation of Langer's stand—though none of them found the courage to emulate his action.

The League turned its attention next to the problem of mortgage foreclosures and evictions, and in April 1933 Governor Langer issued his famous moratorium edicts. Despite bitter criticism and heavy pressure from certain groups the governor called a halt to farm foreclosures and evictions, thus keeping thousands of honest but unlucky farmers from being dispossessed for the crime of poverty. His action, labeled by many a travesty of the sacred rights of property, was supplemented by the calling out of the National Guard to enforce the edicts.

"The big business interests know," declared Langer, "that as long as I am Governor, until we have good crops and fair prices, the moratoria are going to remain in effect, even though I have to keep on calling out National Guardsmen three times a day, as I did last Saturday. As Governor I am not going to permit eviction or oppression of debtors, whether they be farmers or small businessmen; and if the only way the big business interests figure they can get rid of the moratoria is to remove me, they are right. I knew the penalty that would be inflicted when I declared the moratoria and I am fully prepared to pay it."

North Dakota farmers breathed easier now. Had some such moratorium on debts been given them in the 20's, it would have saved thousands of them from losing their homes and farms—for good years always come sooner or later on the northern plains. As a result of the moratorium measures hundreds of farm families were able to keep their homes and farms and pay off their indebtedness soon afterward; there were no savage mortgage riots such as occurred in other states when harried and desperate farmers blasted away at sheriffs with shotguns in a vain effort to stave off eviction; and, largely because of the moratoriums, North Dakota produced but few of that miserable clan that was to become known as Okies.

With the success of their suits to restrain North Dakota from declaring an embargo on wheat, the milling interests had again grown confident. During Langer's second term they attempted to return once more to their old methods, but this time they found the League men ready. They now had powerful weapons with which to fight for their rights. The work of the 1919 legislature, with its program of state-owned credit facilities and a state mill and elevator, bore rich fruit in the hard years of the middle 1930's.

Black stem rust ravaged North Dakota's wheat crops in the year 1937. While the scourge did not always ruin the grain it attacked, it invariably resulted in a harvest of lightweight wheat. The work of Doctor Ladd of the state agricultural college twenty years before had shown northwest farmers that lightweight wheat often had a high protein content and was of excellent quality for milling purposes.

Farmers had forgotten these lessons in the years that had passed, and they were totally unprepared for the action of the grain trust when, on the evening of July 22, 1937, the price of 37-pound wheat was suddenly reduced from eighty-nine to thirty-seven cents a bushel—a drop of fifty-two cents in a single night! Millions of bushels of the state's crop were of lightweight quality that year, and the action of the grain trade meant a loss of millions of dollars to farmers of North Dakota and the whole upper river valley.

But the men of the Nonpartisan League had not forgotten the early days of the party's organization. Governor Langer at once called a meeting of prominent state and farm leaders at Fargo, and men were dispatched throughout the state to secure two-pound samples of wheat, which were rushed to the State Mill & Elevator at Grand Forks, where the grain was threshed, milled, and baked into bread. Three days after the trust's reduction of the price of lightweight wheat, the governor had his answer: the wheat was ideal for the making of high quality flour.

Through the Industrial Commission, which the League had originally established to conduct the state-owned enterprises, the State Mill & Elevator at once offered thirty-seven cents a bushel above market price for the lightweight wheat. A day later the price on the Minneapolis market zoomed upward to meet the mill's offer and in some cases went even higher, a tacit admission that the milling interests had been planning a gigantic robbery.

Now if ever the League's long and bitter fight for a state-owned grain elevator and mill was justifying itself. For sixty days the price was kept up, with the grain trade meeting the state's prices, and this brought to the farmers of North Dakota alone an estimated ten million dollars which would otherwise have found its way into the pockets of market speculators. The total amount invested by the state was twelve thousand dollars, the sum expended in buying wheat before the grain trade raised its price to correspond with that of the State Mill & Elevator.

In 1938 the state's leaders, recalling the attempt of the previous year, watched carefully for a repetition of the grain trade's tactics. But the syndicate cagily refrained from quoting any price at all on 37-pound wheat. Instead, it drove the price of durum wheat down to forty-eight cents in a minor variation of its former procedure. Governor Langer, recalling the federal court injunction of several years before, again turned to the State Mill & Elevator to rescue the price from these unprofitable depths. The mill announced that it would pay sixty-five cents a bushel instead of the quoted market price of forty-eight cents.

"I am not going to monkey with any embargo," Langer declared. "We will buy the wheat outright. We have the money and the credit, and the wheat is worth twice what we will pay for it." It was worth at least sixty-five cents a bushel, at any rate, for the Minneapolis market at once rose to meet the mill's offer, and again northwest farmers benefited to the extent of millions of dollars.

Good times were coming back to the northern plains as Governor Langer and the League administration went out of office on January 1, 1939. Eighteen million dollars of the bonded indebtedness of forty million which Langer had inherited was paid off by the close of his second term. North Dakota bonds, which had been selling at eighty-four cents on the dollar when the League administration took over in the bleak days of 1933, were selling at a dollar and a quarter on the dollar when the League went out of power in 1939.

AN UNBIASED observer will discern a curious paradox here. He will be inclined to wonder why an administration with such an excellent record as the League established during the 30's should be voted out of office to be replaced by its opponents. The question is puzzling even to North Dakotans.

It is axiomatic in the state's politics that the League prospers in times of agrarian adversity and invariably loses ground in times of prosperity. Beginning in 1940, North Dakota had an unbroken cycle of wet years with high prices which brought to the state the greatest prosperity it had ever known. The years 1940 to 1946 yielded the longest straight succession of bumper crops since the white man first sank his plow into the earth's cover. The average gross income per farm in North Dakota in 1945 was almost eight thousand dollars. And since the League thrives on adversity and agrarian discontent, there was little fertile ground for it to exploit.

But John Wesley Powell's "years of disaster" will come again. When they do, if history is a true teacher, the farmers of the state will turn again to the Nonpartisan League as they have done in the past. Whether or not this condition is a healthy one politically, it would be idle to debate. The state's administrations are usually about equally divided between Leaguers and non-Leaguers, and the government suffers from the factional pulling and hauling that results. This is unfortunate, of course, but the benefits the League has brought to North Dakota in the way of progressive legislation far outweigh any inconveniences which have resulted from a divided political system.

Today in North Dakota the League is just another party. The extreme bitterness and violence of early days is gone, although the state's political fights are still heated and strongly contested. Farmers no longer look upon every businessman, lawyer, and banker as a tool of Wall Street and a greedy agent of Big Biz. Nor do reactionary businessmen, bankers, and lawyers any longer refer to Leaguers as free lovers, Bolshevists, anarchists, and Reds. Not even an archconservative would dare advocate today the abolition of the state-owned mill and elevator or the Bank of North Dakota. The men who fought these projects as socialism twenty years ago are today forced to approve of them publicly if they wish to be elected.

Antipathy between Leaguers and non-Leaguers is today largely based upon force of habit. There is no longer anything radical about the Nonpartisan League—for with the passage of the years the radicalism of yesterday has become the accepted governmental philosophy of today. Nonetheless League opponents maintain their opposition, which is no longer without valid foundation, while on the other hand, the League continues to arrogate to itself a liberalism which it is no longer alone in possessing. There are many men in the League today who could be classified as conservatives, although they were progressives when they became Leaguers thirty years ago. They have not moved forward since that time, while the world has—but they are unaware of this fact and still think of themselves as progressives.

The Bank of North Dakota has been a consistent success, despite gloomy predictions that it would fail; it turns over a neat half million dollars a year in profits. The State Mill & Elevator was for many years, under both League and anti-League administrations, mismanaged and packed with faithful payrollers. But since it has been taken out of politics and efficiently managed, it too has been steadily profitable; it likewise made a profit of half a million dollars in 1945. And its intangible savings to the state's farmers have been inestimably greater than that.

The most important work, perhaps, that is being done by the League today is its attempt to maintain the family-sized and self-owned farm against the rising threat of huge estates operated by hired hands. The Farmers' Union, the most powerful farm group in the Upper Missouri Valley, is a leader in the fight for the family-sized farm unit. Upon the efforts of these twin groups in North Dakota rests the social and agricultural future of the state. Vast mechanized farms run by skilled personnel are admittedly more efficient; whether they are socially more desirable is the question at issue. Until recent years tenant farming had increased alarmingly in the Northwest; today, with good crops and high prices, it is again on the wane.

But the issue must be met in the near future. Whether the

northern plains will be a land of self-owned farms operated by independent and free men, or whether it will be, in Sinclair Lewis's phrase, a land of "placid châteaux ringed by sullen huts" —that is the question. The League and the Farmers' Union are willing to sacrifice a modicum of efficiency for an economy of free and independent growers. *Tenant farmer* is only the northern term for sharecropper, and the lot of the northern serf is little better than that of his Dixie counterpart.

Strong and practical steps have been taken under the Non-partisan League and the Farmers' Union to see that it does not happen in North Dakota. An anti-corporation-farming law, which prohibits any corporation of any kind from engaging in farming activities in the state, has been passed and upheld by the Supreme Court of the United States. A graduated land tax measure, which would discourage the accumulation of huge holdings by wealthy exploiters, has been sponsored by both organizations. It will be interesting to see where the struggle ends: whether, as in unluckier industries than agriculture, "efficiency" triumphs over "independence."

NOT only in political matters did the Northwest wake up to the threats it was facing during the terrible 20's and early 30's. Out of the struggle of man against the elements during the drought and the dust storms grew a hard-won and specialized body of knowledge that will make future periods of agricultural depression infinitely less difficult to bear.

The policies of the U.S. Soil Conservation Service and the work of the Reclamation Bureau, which were considered revolutionary fifteen years ago, are eagerly accepted today by farmers who "didn't want anybody telling them how to farm" in the days before the agrarian tragedy of the 30's. Conservation of rainfall and the control of wind and water erosion, measures urgently needed in the upper river valley, are now being carried out on an extensive scale. The methods are many and varied: the replenishing of organic matter in the soil; balanced livestock and farming operations; the use of protective vegetation in the form of grass, legumes, stubble mulch, and windbreaks; stock-water ponds;

proper distribution, rotation, and deferment of grazing; and adjustment of the animal population to the capacity of the land.

Strip and contour farming—two inestimable boons to the Great Plains—also grew out of the desperation of the drought days. Contour farming, the process by which the natural formation of the land is followed in cultivation, not only has proved easier on men and machinery in working the soil, but has had valuable effects in conserving moisture and arresting erosion. It is strip farming, though, an agricultural device as old as agricultural man, that has provided at least a partial answer to the problem of wind erosion on the dryland plains of the Northwest.

In strip cropping the land is plowed in narrow strips, with a band of unbroken soil left between each two cultivated strips to bind down the earth. Set broadside to the wind, the breaks serve as an effective check to its insistent gnawing. As the ancient terraces of China's rice fields serve to prevent water erosion, so do the protective bands of strip cropping prevent erosion by the wind through offering a series of successive checks as it sweeps westward over the plains.

Never again, even in case of a drought as severe and protracted as that of the 30's, can the disaster to the economy of the northern plains be as appalling as was that of the Dust Bowl days. New methods, intelligent planning, and bitter experience have left the farmers of the Northwest in a far better position to meet any future dry and barren periods which may come—as they surely will come sooner or later. And most important of all, the harnessing of the mighty Missouri which is even now taking place in the upper river valley will transform the land and mold its future as nothing has done since Thomas Jefferson purchased it from Napoleon almost a century and a half ago.

Chapter 19

MISSOURI COMPROMISE

The Missouri is a giant among rivers. From its remotest sources in Red Rock Lake and Hell Roaring Creek to where its waters mingle at last with those of the Mexican Gulf, it is the longest continuous watercourse in the world.

In most seasons it is like a sluggish yellow serpent, coiling and heaving slowly in the prison cage of its sandy bends; but in times of flood, when the rushing mountain rivers pour themselves into its upper reaches, it becomes an angry, unleashed monster that lashes from side to side for miles beyond its banks, gulping whole farms and cities in its voracious jaws.

One hundred million tons of fertile earth are annually carried by it to the sea, or spread over the lower reaches of the river bottoms to cover the crops of downstream farmers with a smothering blanket of silt. In the upper valley the precious water that means life to the northern plains has slipped for decades past the dryland farmsteads; in the lower valley, where the great floods caused damage amounting to $150,000,000 between 1942 and 1944, the water is a menace and a perpetual enemy. Ever since the coming of the white man, visionaries have dreamed of the day when the titan of the plains would be tamed and the waters that devastate the lower valley would be conserved to irrigate the upper reaches where they are so desperately needed.

"The waters you need are flowing past you to the sea," John Wesley Powell told the upriver men as early as 1883. Hiram Chittenden, the army engineer who made the Missouri his life's study, told them a few years later: "Turn out the waters upon the land."

But nothing was done to chain down the wild Missouri. In the drought years the precious waters flowed on past the parched fields, while three hundred thousand persons left the Missouri Valley to seek homes elsewhere and more than a billion and a quarter dollars were poured into the depressed areas in govern-

318

ment relief to offset the ravages of the Dust Bowl period. Such a vast sum, had it been expended for flood control, irrigation, and soil conservation, would have made the valley almost immune to the ills which today beset it—and in addition would have provided a source of cheap hydroelectric power to attract industry to the basin states and stabilize their unbalanced economies.

In the time when the first keelboatmen and voyageurs set poles in the river's yellow current, with the song "We Are Bound for the Wild Missouri" on their lips, the waterway was the most significant factor in the life and trade of the region. It was the Missouri which built the great American cities of Omaha, Kansas City, and St. Louis—and it is the Missouri which today periodically inundates and partially destroys those cities and their hinterlands.

But as the days of the keelboats and the river steamers vanished into the past, the upper and lower rivers tended to lose their community of interest. Trade routes developed east and west instead of north and south; no longer does the great stream of traffic pour its way up and down the river to unite the people of the two great Missouri Valley areas as they were united in bygone years. Instead, the coming of the railroads has tended to drive them farther and farther apart in their interests and their points of view.

But nobody, seemingly, has told the Missouri River that the stream of trade is now east and west; and the Big Muddy would hardly condescend to change the direction of its course anyway. Once it did run north into Hudson Bay, it is true, but that was twenty or thirty thousand years ago; and today the people of neither upper nor lower valley feel like waiting an entire geological epoch for a second miracle. No, the Missouri continues to pour its great yellow tide southward, whether there is river trade or not, and the people of both north and south are at last agreed that something ought to be done about it. They know that the days of drought in the north and the days of flood in the south will come again, and that it is only good business to spend a billion and a half dollars—the sum the proposed Missouri Basin development will cost—for permanent works that will make unnecessary any huge government disbursements for relief costs in the future.

ALL of the nation will benefit from the great projects now under construction or proposed on the Missouri and its tributaries—and it is only right that all of the nation should, for the river belongs to the American people and it is the American people as a whole who will pay the cost of the development program. There has been much misguided talk of states' rights in the discussions of the river and its problems. Such talk is meaningless, for the Missouri is a navigable stream and as such is subject to federal control.

The famous New River decision of the federal Supreme Court in 1940 has settled that question, although it has not stilled the cry of certain groups that the "rights" of their states are being trampled underfoot. Other groups resent what they term "outside interference" in the affairs of the Missouri Valley by the citizens of other states. This complaint is equally meaningless; under the Constitution of the United States all navigable streams are in the control of the federal government. The Missouri is the people's river, and it is for the whole people to decide how its development shall be carried out.

Powerful interests are affected under all the various plans proposed for taming the wild Missouri, and high-power propaganda campaigns are being carried on through press, radio, and pressure groups to swing the people's decision one way or another. The final decision has not yet been made, and may not be for years. It will take a quarter of a century to carry out the huge Missouri Basin program, and its benefits or drawbacks will only then begin to show themselves—aside from the flood control projects, that is, which will immediately harness the river upon their completion within a few years.

The fight for control of the policies under which the Missouri is to be developed has been going on behind the scenes for years. But it was only recently, when it began to appear that the funds for the work were at last to be made available, that the warfare became open and bitter.

MISSOURI COMPROMISE

In 1934 the late Senator George Norris of Nebraska, father of the TVA development, introduced the first measure for control of the river: a bill setting up a Missouri Valley Authority under the management of the Bureau of Reclamation. His measure got no farther than the Senate committee on irrigation. The drought years of the 30's did not produce the terrible floods which periodically overflow the lower valley, and little progress was made until the disastrous spring of 1943.

That year the Missouri came rushing down out of the Northwest, glutted with mountain torrents, swollen from heavy snowfalls and early thaws, and spread disaster over the river valley from Bismarck to St. Louis. Thirty-five million dollars in flood damage was the result of its spilling over its banks, rampaging over the countryside, and sweeping away homes, farm buildings, cornfields, and towns. It paused for a moment to demolish two million dollars worth of army flood control structures before hurrying on to the sea, leaving the Engineers' Corps with a million dollars worth of rescue work on its hands. Again in 1944 the river leaped its banks and spread devastation over the valley, flooding four and a half million acres of fertile bottomland and bringing the loss for the two flood years to more than a hundred million dollars.

This was too much for the people of the valley. Their calls for action moved Congress to request the army engineers to set up some plan for flood control, and Colonel Lewis A. Pick, the Missouri River Division engineer at Omaha, was given the job. Pick, later to become famous as General Pick, builder of the Ledo Road in China, wasted no time. Within three months he had his plan completed. It was basically designed for purposes of flood control and promised to save one billion dollars in property from future flood damage; but it carried the added provision that the construction projects were to be multiple-purpose structures to produce power as well as to aid navigation and irrigation. The Army was to build and operate all facilities under the program—although the concession was made that functions other than flood control were to be carried out in collaboration with other departments of government involved.

This was the Pick Plan—the first comprehensive over-all program for flood control on the unruly Missouri. It proposed a chain of levees on the lower river from Sioux City to St. Louis, five multiple-purpose dams and reservoirs on the Missouri proper, five on tributaries of the Upper Republican River, one on the Yellowstone in Montana, and another on the Big Horn in Wyoming. Eleven other projects already approved by Congress but not yet constructed were also to be included in the system. The total cost was estimated at six hundred and sixty-one million dollars.

Although the major proportion of the work was not to be undertaken until the end of the war, the Pick Plan nevertheless evoked a veritable blizzard of controversial writing and speechmaking when it was made public.

The Bureau of Reclamation had been working for years on a comprehensive plan for the river, and W. G. Sloan, assistant regional director of the Bureau at Billings, had planned to file his report by May 1, 1944. Now, however, the Pick Plan suddenly turned up in Congress for hearings before the House committee on flood control, and the Reclamation Bureau and its friends were caught unaware.

Strong objections to the Pick Plan came from the upper river people, for, while it did not appear to slight any facet of river development, it was primarily a plan for flood control and navigation, and these two interests were largely confined to the lower river population. The governors of North Dakota, Montana, and Wyoming at once went to Washington to protest against its adoption. Then tempers flared in the lower river states, which protested against anything that might delay control of the disastrous floods that were wrecking the lower valley and causing millions of dollars in damage every year.

In Washington the three upper river governors learned a new and startling fact: A separate army plan was under consideration before the House rivers and harbors committee—a bill proposing the creation of a nine-foot navigation channel from Sioux City to the river's mouth. To deepen the river from six feet to nine and broaden the channel from two hundred to three hundred feet would mean, said the upper river governors, that there would be no water available on the upper river for purposes of irrigation. The Army said that there would too, according to their calculations! The Reclamation Bureau replied that there would not, so there!

Protesting that it was "the policy of the Congress to recognize the interests and rights of the states in determining the development of the watersheds within their borders," Senators O'Mahoney of Wyoming and Millikin of Colorado sought to protect the welfare of the upper river states by amending the Pick Plan and the channel-deepening bill in the Senate commerce committee. A bloc of twenty senators supported their efforts, and amendments were drawn up placing navigation in a subordinate position and specifying that it should not adversely affect irrigation west of the ninety-seventh meridian.

The lower valley states at once protested that this was a dangerous revival of the old states' rights question, and that such amendments might result ultimately in recognizing the "water rights" of state utility companies. As a result the amendments were voted down.

But it soon became apparent that neither the bill to deepen the channel nor the Pick Plan could possibly be passed until the upper river states were assured that their own irrigation and reclamation needs were to be adequately met. The amendments were revived in slightly different form and added to the pending bills.

The two bills as approved required the Congress to submit to the states for consideration any proposed legislation concerning their interests, and to take under advisement any protests entered by the states in question. Water from the river could be used west of the ninety-eighth meridian for navigation purposes only when such use did not conflict with the use of the water for "domestic, municipal, stock water, irrigation, mining or industrial purposes." This definitely placed irrigation ahead of navigation in the law.

BY THIS time the Bureau of Reclamation had completed its own comprehensive river plan. This Sloan Plan, as it became popularly known, was based on years of research and offered a much broader and more far-reaching program than that of Colonel Pick. Bulging with detail and calling for an expenditure of a billion and a quarter dollars, it proposed the construction of ninety dams and reservoirs as compared to the Army's twenty-two. It proposed, further, to provide new irrigation for almost five million acres and increased irrigation for half a million more. The Bureau stated flatly that returns from power, irrigation, and other sources would amount to a hundred and sixty-eight million dollars each year, while the annual costs would be only sixty-five million. The whole program would be amortized in a period of fifty years at 3 per cent interest—whereas under the Pick Plan flood control and navigation development would not return a cent, but would instead be charged up to the American people.

Not only would the Sloan Plan provide flood control to rival that proposed by the army engineers, but it would produce nearly four billion kilowatt hours of power annually for commercial, industrial, and domestic use. And the structures to be built under the Sloan Plan would aid navigation on the lower river as well as provide an ample source of water for municipal and domestic needs.

The great Fort Peck reservoir in Montana, which had been constructed for navigation and flood control purposes, was to have an entirely new function under the Sloan Plan: it would be employed principally for irrigation, with flood control and navigation subordinated. The proposed army dam at Garrison, North Dakota, intended to control flood waters and restore the shrinking water level in Devils Lake, was declared unnecessary in the Bureau's plan. The Bureau, instead, proposed a staggering water diversion project that would pump water from the Missouri near Fort Peck into the Souris River Valley of North Dakota—which is not a part of the Missouri Basin—and irrigate more than a million acres of land there. There were numerous other points of disagreement, both major and minor.

But there was nothing minor about the gale of disapproval that blew out of the lower river states when the Sloan Plan was made public. "The purpose of the irrigationists and the land development companies upriver to control the waters of the Missouri for their own local developments has been brought into plain view," wrote the Kansas City *Star*. "Why add four million acres?" it asked, charging that upriver plans were "parasitism" which sought to seize prior control of all the waters of the river, "even when the rights to the use of them downriver have been stabilized by many decades of use far antedating the claims of the dry land development companies." The *Star* protested that there was already plenty of farm land available for the next several generations, and expressed fear that the millions of added acres would compete with Missouri and Kansas farmers and produce surpluses that would have serious effects on farm prices.

Newspapers in the upper river states pointed out that irrigation was no new thing in their part of the valley; it had been established there for three quarters of a century, and therefore had quite as good a claim on the ground of historical precedent as navigation interests. As to the *Star*'s reference to "dry land development companies," the upper river people could easily establish that there were no such companies. The whole Sloan Plan was based on the idea of small family farms and a diversified system of agriculture which would serve to stabilize the upper river farm economy. The number of acres that could be acquired by any individual under the plan was, in fact, limited to one hundred and sixty.

More important, perhaps, was the consideration that under an irrigation program all costs of the projects would be repaid by the irrigators, while under the flood control and navigation laws the work would be done at public expense. In view of this fact, just who are the "parasites"? the upper river folk asked pointedly.

So THE bickering continued until, on May 14, 1944, the St. Louis *Post-Dispatch*, in a full-page editorial, called for an over-all Missouri Valley Authority in such eloquent terms that it attracted attention throughout the entire nation. The *Post-Dispatch* was not the first newspaper to advocate a valley authority, but its stirring appeal, coming at the crucial moment, brought the question into sharper focus than before. The *Post-Dispatch* had previously been a supporter of the Pick Plan, but it minced no words in reversing its stand and stating the reasons for its editorial conversion:

"This newspaper confesses an error of the past—a preoccupation with the interests of its own section to the exclusion of those of Montana, Kansas, Nebraska and the Dakotas. All along the valley, from the mountains at 13,000 feet to the low plains of the river's mouth, men have given a similar loyalty to the interests of their sections.

"Yet is this not our common problem? Will not all our interests be better served—be multiplied—by working together toward a common solution . . .

"There must be men up and down our valley who have a vision that transcends the futile rivalries of the past. The editors from Montana to St. Louis have it within their power to preach the gospel that the Missouri is one big river with one big problem . . .

"We urge the editors of the Missouri Valley to lift up their eyes, to make stout their purpose. With unity we can conquer the one big problem that the one big river challenges us to solve."

Despite the ringing appeal of the *Post-Dispatch*'s editorial and its evident common sense, the editors of the Missouri Valley did not at once drop their shears and their paste pots and break into hosannas of welcome for a Missouri Valley Authority. In Montana particularly, where the necks of many editors are heavy with the "copper collars" they wear, most newspapermen were, apparently, unable to "lift up their eyes" any higher than the interests of the Montana Power Company and the Anaconda Copper Company. Throughout the valley newspaper opinion was variegated; less than half of the valley's papers—and these for the most part the smaller ones—welcomed the *Post-Dispatch*'s clarion call for a new approach to the vexing problem.

Elsewhere, however, there were more explosive effects. Proponents of the Pick and Sloan plans, hitherto at each other's throats, now leaped into one another's arms with almost lecherous cries of mutual affection. The National Reclamation Association, an organization sympathetic to the Bureau's work, pleaded with the two federal agencies to devise some workable compromise, lest an MVA should receive serious consideration. The National Water Conservation Conference urged a like procedure, as did a meeting of the governors of the Missouri Valley states, who turned thumbs down on an MVA.

But the work of the Farmers' Union, organized labor, a few members of Congress, and a number of crusading newspapers had lent weight to the *Post-Dispatch*'s plea, and on August 18, before the Pick and Sloan plans could be reconciled, Senator James Murray of Montana introduced a bill calling for the creation of a Missouri Valley Authority. Representative Cochran of Missouri introduced the Murray Bill in the House of Representatives, and Senator Gillette of Iowa offered a similar, but somewhat revised, MVA measure in the Senate. Then, to thoroughly frighten the Army and Reclamation Bureau forces, President Roosevelt in a special message to the Congress called for a Missouri Valley Authority.

But Congress itself was not at all sold on the idea of an MVA. It passed a joint resolution asking the two federal agencies to see if they could not agree on a plan. The Army and the Bureau, with the MVA breathing hot on their necks, were now most obliging, and a few weeks later, on November 8, their joint Pick-Sloan Plan was issued.

Opponents of MVA were enthusiastic, hailing the plan as a solution of all previous difficulties, but not all observers were so sanguine. "It's a shameless, loveless shotgun wedding," said James S. Patton, president of the National Farmers' Union.

This was an apt phrase. The "agreement"—far from being an expression of mutual accord—was that each agency would confine its activities to a particular portion of the proposed installations, and that each would accept certain parts of the other's plan which it had previously disapproved. The Army, for example, had declared the Bureau's plan for diversion of Missouri water into the Souris Valley unsound and unneeded, but in the Pick-Sloan "shotgun wedding" it meekly accepted this $122,000,000 project.

The Bureau, on the other hand, had attacked the Garrison and Gavin's Point dams of the army plan as "unnecessary and not worth the expenditure." This was no small matter if the charge was true, for the two projects would cost $176,000,000; yet the Bureau politely accepted them in the Pick-Sloan merger. Responsibility for determining reservoir capacities in the case of irrigation structures would fall to the Bureau under the plan; the Army would have control over navigation and flood installations. Many important details were barely mentioned. Installations for the production of power and how the power should be employed were left for future decision. The size and height of some of the dams were not specified.

This was no new plan, MVA enthusiasts protested. It was merely a loose joining of two already imperfect plans—with all the imperfections of both embraced under a single title. There was not a single addition to the two original plans under the Pick-Sloan compromise; only a hasty marriage of convenience had given them a semblance of unity at all. It looked to some MVA supporters as if the American people were to be charged for a quarter billion dollars worth of possibly worthless projects merely to allow the Army and the Bureau to have their bureaucratic ways.

To iron out anticipated difficulties, the plan set up an organization known as the Inter-Agency River Basin Committee, representing the Bureau of Reclamation, the Army Engineers, the Department of Agriculture, and the Federal Power Commission, but the functions of the Department of Agriculture and the Power Commission are purely advisory. Notably, nothing was said in the plan about soil conservation, the building up of industrial resources through cheap power, timber conservation and control, research, or community and regional planning such as have been carried out so successfully under TVA.

The nine-foot channel authorized by Congress from Sioux City to St. Louis was not mentioned in the Pick-Sloan Plan. It is to be created, however, for the law is specific; but what its future usefulness will be remains to be seen. "The Army Engineers," says General Crawford, "believe it to be possible, but some years there will probably have to be give and take; we'll have to ask the downstream people to shorten their navigation season and the upstream man to cooperate by yielding some irrigated acreage." There will be trouble about this when the drought years come again to the northern plains, for the O'Mahoney-Millikin amendments certainly give irrigation the preference; and it will prove difficult to convince an upriver farmer whose very life depends upon his crops that he should "yield some acreage" in order that barges may operate on the lower river. With the law on the side of the upriver men, the lower river barge-owners may presumably look for some cheerless times in years to come.

The Pick-Sloan Plan, attached to the flood control bill, was passed by Congress in 1944, but this did not mean an end of MVA. President Roosevelt signed the bill, but he added a few pertinent words: "My approval of the bill is given with the distinct understanding that it is not to be interpreted as jeopardizing in any way the creation of a Missouri Valley Authority, the establishment of which should receive the early consideration of the next Congress." The bill provided for the commencement of several projects on the river, but these would not, as the President pointed out, in any way interfere with a later MVA bill, if one should be desired.

In February of 1945 Senator Murray introduced a new MVA measure, which, despite Murray's request that it be sent to the committee on agriculture and forestry, was sent by Vice-President Truman to the Senate commerce committee, a group dominated by senators who were notoriously hostile to the idea of river valley authorities. This was a most unusual procedure, for a bill is usually sent where its author wishes it to go. So the sponsors of the bill objected and the matter was brought to a vote in the Senate, where it was finally arranged that the bill should be sent to three committees—commerce, irrigation, and agriculture. This procedure in effect put the whole question in a parliamentary strait jacket. Each committee was to consider the bill for sixty days. The commerce committee disposed of it in short order with an unfavorable report and it went next to the committee on irrigation, where it received additional rough handling at the hands of hostile senators. In late 1946 it had yet to be considered by the committee on agriculture and forestry.

LAND OF THE DACOTAHS

AN ILLUMINATING exchange that took place between Senator Overton of Louisiana and Senator Murray of Montana during a Senate hearing on the MVA bill expresses in succinct fashion the fundamental divergence of views between the supporters and the opponents of an MVA.

SENATOR OVERTON: I am taking all ten states of the Missouri Basin. Their legislatures have, for the most part, resolved against the MVA?

SENATOR MURRAY: Yes. Take my state, for example. The power interests, of course, are against it.

SENATOR OVERTON: Off the record, more power to them.

This colloquy between the two senators was not intended by one of them, at least, to be as illuminating as it actually was. The phrase *off the record* is a common device employed at committee hearings when the speaker does not wish to have his views set down by the stenographers. But a slip occurred here, and Senator Overton's sympathies were inadvertently placed upon the record—where they should please the private power interests, if not the supporters of MVA.

Essentially, the whole struggle for and against MVA is based upon whether America is to socialize its power industry or whether the American people are to expend billions of dollars in public projects whose vast production of power will be turned over to private utility interests. Few supporters of either side of the question will admit this frankly; some are not yet aware of the implications of the struggle. But basically this is what the contest is all about, as was well illustrated by some further revealing testimony which came to light during the irrigation committee's deliberations on MVA. Senator Murray was elaborating upon the reasons for opposition to the measure in his own state of Montana:

SENATOR MURRAY: All important papers with few exceptions in the state of Montana are owned and published by the Montana Power Company and the Anaconda Copper Company. In Butte, the city where I live, the morning paper is a Democratic paper, and the evening paper is a Republican paper, both owned and published by the Anaconda and Montana Power interests, and both printed on the same press, oppose this bill. The same is true with reference to Billings, Montana. The same is true with reference to Missoula, and in many other

330

important cities. Miles City has the Miles City *Star,* which bitterly opposes this program, but several other independent papers support it. Of course you find that in every state in the Union. When my predecessor, Senator Walsh, was here he made a thorough study of this power propaganda. He showed that they were even going into the schools and preparing the textbooks for our children so as to educate them favorably toward the power-crowd interests. That obtains in every state in the Union. The power interests will be against this bill; I will admit that for the record right now. You can put that in the record.

SENATOR OVERTON: As a further indication of public opinion let us take the attitude of the governors of all the Missouri Basin states, the governors of all the Missouri Valley states.

SENATOR MURRAY: They are against the bill.

SENATOR OVERTON: They have met and resolved against it?

SENATOR MURRAY: Yes.

SENATOR OVERTON: Are they dominated by the power interests?

SENATOR MURRAY: That is true in my state. I know that. There is no doubt about that. We have to be realistic in these things. We cannot shut our eyes to the facts.

There is more truth than politics in Senator Murray's testimony. Senator Walsh, Montana's famed congressional inquisitor, did indeed show the almost incredible lengths to which the private power interests had gone in placing propaganda in children's textbooks. And Senator Norris of Nebraska charged that the power trust had not hesitated to invade and attempt to influence the courts, the legislatures, and the pulpit.

The Montana Power Company, a branch of American Power & Light, which is a subsidiary of Electric Bond & Share of New York, seems to have been eminently successful in protecting its interests against encroachments—in Montana, at least. Indeed, the company may even be considered something of an authority on water—as it claims to be—for the federal government in 1945 ordered it to wring some $52,000,000 worth of that commodity out of its assets. This from total reported gross assets of $145,000,-000! In Montana, however, at the same time, the Montana Public Service Commission was able to find only $19,000,000 worth of water in these same assets—a difference which should indicate that perhaps Senator Murray knew what he was talking about.

LAND OF THE DACOTAHS

It is in the Missouri Valley that the battle lines are being drawn, and the power companies know it well. If an MVA were to be created, other valley authorities would be sure to follow; the federal government, which already produces a fifth of all the power in America, would soon monopolize the industry and nationalization would follow as a matter of course. MVA believers who clearly foresee this ultimate result are not inclined to be upset by it; instead they point to the shabby record of the private companies in giving service to the people of the upper river valley.

In North Dakota, for example, 85 per cent of all rural farm dwellings are without electric lights. In South Dakota the figure is 83 per cent, in Montana 72 per cent. In North Dakota, again, only 2.3 per cent of rural farm homes have mechanical refrigeration, only 6 per cent have running water, only 5 per cent have an installed bathtub or shower. In Montana and South Dakota the figures are but slightly higher. It is not that upper valley farmers do not want electric lights and modern conveniences; it is only because the power companies do not make electricity available to them that they are forced to go without. By contrast, the farms of Germany and Sweden in prewar times were almost completely electrified. If it is left to the private companies, say MVA supporters, the rural dwellers of the upper river valley will never get this elementary service.

The private companies, on the other hand, assert that they are quite willing to pass on to the consumers all savings made from the use of public power and that they are well equipped to carry power to rural areas whenever the time arrives. By this, of course, they mean when the time arrives that it is profitable for them to do so. There is little doubt that northwest farms will in time be electrified under whatever plan is adopted.

MVA supporters, however, point to numerous other fundamental needs in the valley aside from the need for cheap power. The Murray Bill would provide not only for the four basic purposes of a valley authority—flood control, irrigation, reclamation, and navigation—but would cover a multitude of other functions as well, which are not provided for in any of the government's present plans. In an article in the *Saturday Evening Post,* Associate Editor Wesley Price pointed out that the Murray Bill would: "Encourage agriculture based on family-type farming; sell water to farmers; limit irrigated holdings to 160 acres; provide low-cost fertilizer; conserve water, soil, mineral and forest resources; protect wild game; generate hydroelectric power; buy or build steam-electric plants and transmission lines. And develop recreational facilities; plan for the disposal of war and defense factories to encourage industrial and business expansion; foster interstate commerce; strengthen the national defense and restore the declining water table. Finally, the proposed Missouri Valley Authority would give due regard in its planning to 'such economic, social and cultural values' as might be affected by its own activities. That isn't the lot. But it's enough to show how a simple idea— fitting a flood-drought-control agency to an afflicted valley—can evolve into an intricate plan to raise the standard of living in a whole region."

It is the vastness and complexity of these proposed functions that causes MVA opponents to cry "Superstate!" and "Dictatorship!" and moan that Americans will lose their cherished liberty if an MVA is established. The *Saturday Evening Post* has never been considered a radical magazine, yet here is Mr. Price's conclusion as to the validity of these charges against an MVA: "It adds up to something tremendous. But it doesn't add up to a superstate, 'Russian communistic,' as it has been called, 'relentlessly authoritarian . . . sinister . . . Fascist . . . despotic.' Superstates can defy peoples and legislatures. TVA can't, nor could an MVA. If an authority goes bad, Congress can dig it out of its valley much quicker than that big mistake, prohibition, was dug out of the Constitution."

The argument of Senator Overton, who is frankly biased against "all these authorities," that the governors of the Missouri Valley states and the legislatures have for the most part opposed MVA, is not such a strong one as it appears. The governors, like the legislatures, have not accurately reflected the opinion of the people they profess to represent. The Gallup Poll has repeatedly indicated that the people of the United States favor an MVA by a strong majority; in the Missouri Valley proper the ratio is three to one for an authority, according to Dr. Gallup's figures. But the Congress of the United States, like the governors and the legislatures of many of those states, has seen fit to disregard these findings and to flout the will of the people.

Many senators and representatives, however, have fought hard for a valley authority. Both Senator Young and Senator Langer of North Dakota favor an MVA; Senator Murray of Montana, author of the bill, is quite naturally for it; and in the same state Senator Wheeler was defeated in 1946 for the Democratic nomination by an MVA candidate, Leif Erickson. Both of South Dakota's senators, on the other hand, are opposed to the measure. But this still leaves a majority of upper river senators in favor of the legislation.

There is not, and has not been, an MVA in existence; hence it would appear that the opposition of the valley states' governors is based on purely theoretical grounds. On the other hand, where such an authority is, and has been, in operation—in the Tennessee Valley—all seven governors are lavish in their praise of its work and unanimous in declaring that their states have lost no "rights" of any kind.

THE Missouri Valley constitutes a pressing national and regional problem. Its economy is unbalanced; it has steadily lost population to other more industrialized states for years; it is sorely in need of all the things the Murray Bill proposes to do. And under the Pick-Sloan compromise many of the things the Murray Bill deems essential to the full development of the region will not be carried out. The Army and the Bureau of Reclamation are purely functional in nature; they operate only in certain restricted fields and are not equipped by training, law, or desire to deal with the problems of the region as a whole.

The problem of soil conservation, for example, which is the basic and fundamental need of the upper valley, is within the province of the Department of Agriculture, yet this department has nothing but an advisory voice under the Pick-Sloan setup. The Northwest is losing its precious and irreplaceable topsoil at an alarming rate; without adequate conservation measures such as the Department of Agriculture is carrying out to the best of its ability, the whole territory could become a desert wasteland within half a century. Yet the Pick-Sloan Plan ignores completely this elemental need.

Under an MVA the historic functions of many of the old-line government agencies would fall to the new authority, and such groups as the soil conservation service, the reclamation people, and the forestry service might be stripped of a part of their present duties. This is not necessarily true, however. They could continue to perform their same functions under the MVA directors or they might transfer to the new agency and go on much as before. At least one high official of the Department of Agriculture has testified that the functions of the old-line agencies would actually be strengthened under an MVA. The cooperation in the Tennessee Valley in that respect has been excellent. But other agency members, probably a majority of them, fear that their life work would be jeopardized if an MVA should come about.

MVA supporters recognize the excellent and selfless work which these men, most of them greatly underpaid, have carried on in the valley over a period of many years, and agree that they should certainly have a place under MVA. There would be some hardship, of course, say supporters of the bill; but, they add, which is the greater hardship, that hundreds of thousands of people of the valley should suffer periodic depressions for want of a comprehensive over-all plan, or that a few hundred federal employees should have to remake their lives to some degree?

But while the talk goes on, the work does also. Construction is already under way on the Fort Randall dam in lower South Dakota, on the Angostura dam in the same state, and on the great dam at Garrison, North Dakota, a structure that will be when completed the largest earth-fill dam in the world. Countless lesser dams and reservoirs, as well as three more huge structures, are either in process of construction or well along in the planning stage and ready to be put into the building category whenever Congress gives the word and releases the funds.

Whether or not the valley is ever to have a Missouri Valley Authority, the agitation in its behalf has had a salutary effect.

335

The Army and the Reclamation Bureau have been forced to reconcile at least some of their differences—and the fear of an MVA if they should fall out will probably keep them in a more or less conciliatory mood and in closer touch with the wishes of the people of the area.

Not that MVA supporters have given up the fight. Far from it. MVA is slowly gaining support in the Northwest as the propaganda for and against it is gradually educating the people to its complex issues. "I am confident we will have an MVA," says Glenn Talbott, president of the North Dakota Farmers' Union. "It may take ten years, but I am sure it will come about." MVA bills will continue to be introduced in Congress year after year, and perhaps as George Norris won his fight for TVA by sheer persistence, so MVA enthusiasts will at length bring home to Congress the fact that a valley authority is what the people really want. The minority that opposes an MVA is wealthy, powerful, and vocal—but it may be that they will lose the fight in the end.

EVEN if the Pick-Sloan Plan is imperfect, as its opponents declare, the tremendous changes it will work on the face of the upper river valley are thrilling to consider and will be marvelous to witness. In the years to come, whether under that plan or another, the people of the valley will see great modern dams rising in this young land where the rutted grooves of Custer's wagon trains are visible still in the virgin earth.

The gigantic Souris River Valley diversion project will bring into being the greatest irrigation system ever known to mankind. New farms and homes for thousands of people—farms that will be free of the terrors of drought and periodic crop failure—will serve to check the exodus that has robbed the northern plains states of their richest resource: their young people. Vast amounts of power and electricity will turn the wheels of new industries and bring hitherto unknown conveniences to tens of thousands of people. The great floods that have devastated the land will be checked, and river traffic will once again make its way upstream to Sioux City from St. Louis, Omaha, and Kansas City.

After seventy-five years the optimistic boast of the settler of the 60's will at last come true: The whole valley of the Upper Missouri will "ring with the clatter of invincible enterprise," as clanking bulldozers and the shouts of toiling men mark the completion of the mighty structures that will transform the valley and give to the Big Muddy such a rude check as it has not had since the Wisconsin Glacier thrust it out of its course into Hudson Bay and flung it southward tens of thousands of years ago.

The harnessing of the great Missouri is an undertaking such as would have appealed to the pioneer men and women who first settled along its shifting banks. It is a challenge worthy of America's frontier spirit, the taming of this river, with its singing names and its rude friendly names: the Smoky Water and the Big Muddy and the Wild Mizoo. In the pageant of its past, old as time, are the dark shapes of prehistoric monsters that floundered in its murky waters, the shadowy figures of the first men to look on its vast reaches, the bold outlines of the bands of the Teton Sioux: the fierce Hunkpapas, the End-of-the-Circle band, who won their title from their stern hereditary right to camp where attack was likeliest to occur; the Itazipchos, the Bowless Ones, whom the French called Sans Arcs; the Miniconjous, they Who-Plant-by-the-Stream; the Sichanghus, the Burned Thighs; the Oohenonpas, the Two Kettles; the Sihasapas, the Blackfeet; and the Oglalas, Red Cloud's people.

In the yellow waters of this river you can read the story of the ghostly fleets of a bygone day: the canoemen, the brawling crews of the keelboats, and the stacks of the river steamers at the wharfsides. And there are names here, too, to be remembered: the names of Marquette and Jolliet, of Mike Fink and John Colter and Hugh Glass, of Meriwether Lewis and Sacajawea and Grant Marsh.

In the long panorama of its history appear the wild mountain men, the bearded miners, the lean, whip-hard figures of the cowhands; and in the voice of the prairie wind you can hear the drumming hoofs of mounted troops, the rattle of arrows in willow thickets, the screams of murdered settlers, and the lonely, prophetic whistle of the iron horse. Imprinted on this river and this land of

337

the Dacotahs are the names of mighty chieftains: of Gall and Black Moon and Crazy Horse, and the tragic name of Custer . . .

But now these are all dust and shadow, part of a dead and vanished time. Where the river once rolled its shining tide along, tawny in the sun, there will be placid lakes, blue as the flax and cornflowers in the fields that fringe their banks. Great dams, like battlemented towers, will leash the giant's brawn; levees and dikes will chain and bind him; his pent strength will turn great turbines for the pygmies who have enslaved him. And the mighty, the majestic, the tyrannical Missouri no longer will roll, immense and untrammeled, toward the sea.

ACKNOWLEDGMENTS AND BIBLIOGRAPHY

This book does not purport to be a history of the Upper Missouri Valley or of the land of the Dacotahs, for such a history would embrace many volumes—to say nothing of requiring historical talents which I do not possess. Indeed, in some respects this book is not strictly a history at all. The chapter called "Giants in the Earth" is of necessity partly fiction, although the details are faithful to truth and were gathered from personal conversations with old settlers and from letters of immigrants preserved in the manuscript collections of various state historical societies. Tragic news items like the one which appears in that chapter are common in all the territorial newspapers of the 60's and 70's, and although I have in this case altered the names and the locality, the accuracy of the quotation is otherwise unimpeachable.

In the chapter called "The Revenge of Crow King" I have likewise cast the story in fictional form. But it is a true tale, and as Indian Agent James McLaughlin has written, "The old men at Standing Rock still speak with awe of the time when Crow King defied the ghosts." Those same old men still tell the tale much as I have told it here—although it happened more than three quarters of a century ago—and not very differently is it told in McLaughlin's book, *My Friend the Indian.*

I wish to express my appreciation to Russell Reid, superintendent of the North Dakota State Historical Society, and to the members of his staff, as well as to Erana Stadler and the staff of the Bismarck Public Library, for innumerable courtesies in helping me find material for this book.

For invaluable aid in securing suitable illustrations for this work I owe thanks to Will Robinson of the South Dakota State Historical Society; K. F. Olsen, secretary of the Black Hills and Badlands Association; Nell Perrigoue, secretary of the Deadwood Chamber of Commerce; George Starring of the Greater South Dakota Association; A. H. Pankow, publicity director of the South Dakota

Highway Commission; Frank Fiske of Fort Yates, N.D., for his excellent Indian photographs; LeRoy Pease, secretary of the Greater North Dakota Association; Adrian C. Fox, Irvine T. Dietrich, and A. D. McKinnon of the Soil Conservation Service of the U.S. Department of Agriculture; S. A. Binek of Bismarck; and R. C. Henry, publicity director of Montanans, Inc. To the Risem Studios of Bismarck I owe a special debt of gratitude, and to Mr. Risem in particular for his efforts in unearthing for me old and rare photographs of pioneer days.

To the University of Minnesota, which awarded me a Regional Writing Fellowship, I am indebted for the opportunity and time thus given me to write this book.

Most of all, I wish to pay my respects to my mother, Mrs. Lillie B. Nelson, without whose patient aid and sage counsel this book would, quite literally, never have been written.

For permission to quote from "Mr. Lemke Stops to Think" by Walter Davenport (*Collier's*, October 17, 1936), I am indebted to the editors of *Collier's*; and acknowledgment is hereby made to the editors of the *Saturday Evening Post* for permission to reprint excerpts from "What You Can Believe about MVA" by Wesley Price (*Saturday Evening Post*, January 19, 1946).

I am indebted, further, to the editors of *Adventure Magazine* and *Frontier Stories* for permission to reprint portions of this volume which first appeared in the pages of those magazines in article or story form.

I wish also to acknowledge the courtesy of the several authors and publishers who have granted me permission to use excerpts from their books. The pages on which these quoted passages appear and the books from which they come are these:

page 17. MARK TWAIN, *Following the Equator* (Hillcrest edition, vol. 1. New York: Harper & Brothers, 1906). Quoted by permission of the publisher.

pages 42, 49–51, 76. MARK TWAIN, *Life on the Mississippi* (Hillcrest edition. New York: Harper & Brothers, 1906). Quoted by permission of the publisher.

pages 55, 75. HIRAM CHITTENDEN, *History of the American Fur Trade of the Far West,* vols. 1 and 2 (New York: Francis P. Harper, 1902). Quoted by permission of Harper & Brothers.

ACKNOWLEDGMENTS AND BIBLIOGRAPHY

pages 77, 295. Lewis Crawford, *History of North Dakota* (New York: American Historical Society, 1931). Quoted by permission of the American Historical Company, Inc.

page 111. Hiram Chittenden, *History of Early Steamboat Navigation on the Missouri River,* vol. 2 (New York: Francis P. Harper, 1903). Quoted by permission of Harper & Brothers.

pages 178–79, 180. Frank Fiske, *The Taming of the Sioux* (Bismarck, N.D.: Bismarck *Tribune,* 1917). Quoted by permission of the author.

page 204. Hermann Hagedorn, *Roosevelt in the Badlands* (Chicago: Houghton Mifflin Company, 1930). Quoted by permission of the publisher.

page 219. Archer Gilfillan, *Sheep* (Boston: Little, Brown, and Company, 1930). Quoted by permission of the publisher and the Atlantic Monthly Press.

pages 222–23. James McLaughlin, *My Friend the Indian* (Chicago: Houghton Mifflin Company, 1910). Quoted by permission of the publisher.

pages 246, 251. Rudyard Kipling, *From Sea to Sea* (New York: Doubleday & McClure Company, copyright 1899, 1907). Quoted by permission of Mrs. G. Bambridge and Doubleday & Company, Inc.

page 262. Herbert Gaston, *The Nonpartisan League* (New York: Harcourt, Brace and Howe, 1920). Quoted by permission of the author.

A partial bibliography of other books quoted or consulted follows:

Abbott, Teddy Blue, and Helena Huntington Smith. *We Pointed Them North.* New York: Farrar & Rinehart, 1939.

Armstrong, Moses K. *The Early Empire Builders of the Great West.* St. Paul: E. W. Porter, 1901.

Audubon, Maria R. *Audubon and His Journals.* Edited by Elliott Coues. New York, 1901.

Beach, Rex. *The Spoilers.* New York: A. M. Burt Co., 1930.

Blegen, Theodore. *Norwegian Immigration to America 1825–1860.* Northfield, Minn.: Norwegian-American Historical Ass'n., 1931.

Briggs, Harold E. *Frontiers of the Northwest.* New York: D. Appleton-Century Co., 1940.

Brinton, J. W. *Wheat and Politics.* Minneapolis: Rand Tower, 1931.

Bruce, Andrew J. *Non-Partisan League.* New York: Macmillan Co., 1921.

BURDICK, USHER L. *History of the Farmers' Political Action in North Dakota.* Baltimore: Wirth Bros., 1944.

BURT, STRUTHERS. *Powder River, Let 'er Buck.* New York: Farrar & Rinehart, 1938.

BRYCE, JAMES. *The American Commonwealth.* New York: Commonwealth Publishing Co., 1908.

BYRNE, PATRICK E. *Soldiers of the Plains.* New York: Minton, Balch & Co., 1928.

CATLIN, GEORGE. *North American Indians.* Edinburgh: John Grant, 1926.

CUSTER, ELIZABETH B. *Boots and Saddles.* New York, 1885.

DICK, EVERETT. *The Sod-House Frontier.* New York: D. Appleton-Century Co., 1937.

DIMSDALE, THOMAS J. *The Vigilantes of Montana.* Virginia City, 1921.

FAST, HOWARD. *The Last Frontier.* New York: Duell, Sloan & Pearce, 1941.

FEDERAL WRITERS' PROJECT, WPA. *A South Dakota Guide.* Pierre, S.D.: State Publishing Co., 1938.

———. *Montana: A State Guide Book.* New York: Viking Press, 1939.

———. *North Dakota: A Guide to the Northern Prairie State.* Fargo, N.D.: Knight Printing Co., 1938.

GARLAND, HAMLIN. *A Son of the Middle Border.* New York, 1917.

GILLETTE, JOHN M. *Rural Sociology.* New York: Macmillan Co., 1936.

HANSON, JOSEPH M. *The Conquest of the Missouri.* Chicago: A. C. McClurg Co., 1909.

HAVIGHURST, WALTER. *Upper Mississippi.* New York: Farrar & Rinehart, 1938.

HEBARD, GRACE RAYMOND. *Sacajawea.* Glendale, Calif.: A. H. Clark Co., 1933.

HILL, JAMES J. *Highways of Progress.* New York: Doubleday, Page & Co., 1910.

HOWARD, JOSEPH K. *Montana: High, Wide, and Handsome.* New Haven: Yale University Press, 1943.

KINGSBURY, GEORGE. *History of Dakota Territory.* Chicago, 1915.

LANG, LINCOLN. *Ranching with Roosevelt.* Philadelphia: J. B. Lippincott Co., 1926.

LARPENTEUR, CHARLES. *Forty Years a Fur Trader on the Upper Missouri.* New York, 1898.

LAUT, AGNES. *Pathfinders of the West.* Chicago: Macmillan Co., 1923.

LEWIS, MERIWETHER, and WILLIAM CLARK. *Original Journals of the Lewis and Clark Expedition, 1804–1806.* New York: Dodd, Mead & Co., 1904.

342

ACKNOWLEDGMENTS AND BIBLIOGRAPHY

LOUNSBERRY, CLEMENT. *North Dakota*. Chicago: S. J. Clarke Co., 1917.

NEAL, BIGELOW. *The Last of the Thundering Herd*. New York: Sears Publishing Co., Inc., 1933.

ORDWAY, JOHN. *The Journals of Captain Meriwether Lewis and Sergeant John Ordway*. Madison, Wis.: State Historical Society, 1916.

RÖLVAAG, O. E. *Giants in the Earth*. New York: Harper's, 1924.

ROOSEVELT, THEODORE. *Hunting Trips of a Ranchman*. New York, 1885.

———. *Theodore Roosevelt: An Autobiography*. New York: Charles Scribner's Sons, 1929.

STANDING BEAR. *My People, the Sioux*. New York: Houghton Mifflin Co., 1928.

TWAIN, MARK. *Roughing It*. New York: Harper's, 1906.

VAN DE WATER, F. *The Glory-Hunter*. New York: Bobbs-Merrill Co., 1934.

VESTAL, STANLEY. *Sitting Bull*. New York: Houghton Mifflin Co., 1932.

———. *The Missouri*. New York: Farrar & Rinehart, 1945.

———. *Warpath*. New York: Houghton Mifflin Co., 1932.

WEBB, WALTER. *The Great Plains*. Boston, 1931.

INDEX

344

LAND OF THE DACOTAHS

LAND OF THE DACOTAHS

Rustlers, 197, 207; trial described, 210–12; and vigilantes, 214–15

Sacajawea, 64, 66, 68, 69, 337
St. Charles (Mo.), 58
St. Cyr, 190
St. John, steamboat, 111
St. Louis, 3, 44, 65, 78, 81, 89, 103, 319, 321, 322; fur trade, 55, 82, 83, 87; steamboats, 104, 105, 111
St. Louis, steamboat, 111
St. Louis *Enquirer,* quoted, 97
St. Louis *Post-Dispatch,* 199; quoted, 326
St. Paul, 146, 183, 245, 248, 249, 253, 275
St. Paul *Pioneer Press,* 199
St. Peters, steamboat, 108
Salt Lake City, 163
Sargent County (N.D.), 310
Saskatchewan River, 40, 41
Saturday Evening Post, 332, 333
Scalping, 31, 35, 106, 168, 186, 237
Scandinavian-American Bank of Fargo, 285–86
Schurz, Carl, 135
Seattle, 193, 253
Seattle Exposition, 248
Seven Council Fires, 5, 9–10. *See also* Sioux Indians
Seventh Cavalry Regiment, 157, 164, 171, 179, 186, 188, 230. *See also* Battle of the Little Big Horn
Shafer, George F., 306
Shave Head, 226, 227
Shaw, Thomas, quoted, 247
Sheep (Archer Gilfillan), quoted, 219
Sheep-raising, 202
Sheridan, General Philip H., 107, 171, 183, 184, 185
Sherman, General William Tecumseh, 167
Shining Mountains, 3, 33, 34, 36, 64; La Vérendrye's quest, 35, 39, 40; Lewis and Clark expedition, 69–70
Short Bull, 226
Shortridge, Eli C., 255
Shoshone River, 77
Shoshoni Indians, 64, 68–69
Sibley, General Henry Hastings, 121
Sichanghu Indians, 337
Sihasapa Indians, 337
Sioux City (Iowa), 117, 122, 126, 131, 322
Sioux City *Register,* 102
Sioux Falls (S.D.), 117, 255
Sioux Indians, 21, 35, 36, 39, 40, 48, 109, 114, 171, 183, 241, 337; homeland, 5, 10–12; tribal origins, 9; meaning of names, 10; description of culture, 13–33; Lewis and Clark council, 59–60; and steamboats, 102, 105–6; uprising of *1862,* 121; confiscation of lands, 158, 167–68; Battle of the Little Big Horn, 169–89; name for

Badlands, 204; unrest, 219, 221, 223–24; ghost dancing, 220–25, 228; Messiah War, 225–32; since *1889,* 232–33; Crow King and medicine men, 234–43. *See also* Indians
Sioux River, 126
Sisseton Indians, 9
Sitting Bull, 136, 158, 187, 227, 228; as warrior, 179–80; in Messiah War, 221, 224, 225–27
Slade, Joseph, 113, 114
Sloan, W. G., 322
Sloan Plan, 322, 323–25, 326. *See also* Pick-Sloan Plan
Smallpox, 74, 108–9, 165
Smith, Jedediah, 91
Smith, Preacher, 159
Smoky Water, 3, 234. *See also* Missouri River
Snake River, 70
Socialism, charge against Nonpartisan League, 265, 267, 270, 280, 286
Socialists, 205, 261, 263
Soil conservation, 316–17, 318, 319, 328, 334–35. *See also* Powell, John Wesley
Somers, Jim, 118, 125
Sorlie, Arthur G., 298
Souris River, 36
Souris River Valley diversion project, 324, 327, 336
South Dakota, 10, 41, 84, 118, 219, 255, 311, 326, 335; Lewis and Clark expedition, 62; settlement, 117, 245–50; Nonpartisan League, 275, 278; farming conditions, 300; depopulation, 302; bank failures of *20's,* 303; dust storms of *30's,* 306; rural electrification, 332. *See also* Badlands; Black Hills; Dakota Territory; Upper Missouri Valley
Spain, 34, 88
Spoilers, The (Rex Beach), 127
Springfield (Ill.), 119
Standard Oil Company, 138, 271
Standing Rock agency, 179, 221, 223, 225, 243
State Mill & Elevator of North Dakota, 312–13, 314, 315
Steamboats on Missouri River, 97–107, 109–11, 114; *Western Engineer,* 97–98; *Far West,* 169, 180–83
Stevens, James, 156
Stinson, Buck, 113
Stone Age, migrations from Asia, 8
Story, Nelson, 207, 218
Stranglers, 215
Strip cropping, 317
Stuart, Granville, 214
Sturgis (S.D.), 164
Sublette and Campbell Company, 86
Sully, General Alfred, 204

Wheeler, Burton K., 275–76, 283, 334
Wherry, Jesse, 120
Whiskey Ring, 170
White, John, 110
Whiteside, Frederick, 137
Wibaux, Pierre, 195
Wibaux (Mont.), 195
Williston (N.D.), 248
Winchester, Judge ———, 211
Wind River Mountains, 77, 95
Winlock (Wash.), 278
Winnipeg, 36, 193, 245
Winter Count, 20
Wisconsin, 5, 10, 143, 275
Wisconsin Glacier, 337
W. J. Lewis, steamboat, 111
Women, role among Sioux, 17, 32, 33
Wood, Fred B., 262, 266
Wood, Howard, 266
Woodhawks, 101, 106–8
World's Work, 283
World War I, 252, 265, 276, 280

Worst, J. H., 257
Wounded Knee Creek, massacre, 228–31
Wovoka, 220–24
Wyoming, 10, 40, 41, 216, 218, 322

Yankton (S.D.), 118, 120, 125, 159; capital removal, 130–32; Thor Ericsson story, 144–53
Yankton Indians, 9, 42, 60
Yeager, Red, 113
Yellow Bird, 229
Yellow Hair, *see* Custer, General George Armstrong
Yellowstone, steamboat, 98, 99
Yellowstone Lake, 77
Yellowstone Park, 77, 251
Yellowstone River, 10, 44, 45, 55, 171, 182, 322; explorations, 40, 54, 65, 77; Fort Union, 84
York, 57, 61, 62, 63, 67, 69. *See also* Lewis and Clark expedition
Young, Milton R., 334

40046 FINES 5¢ PER DAY

**5 CENT FINE FOR EACH DAY BEYOND DATE
APPEARING ON CARD.**
